A SINGULAR EXMOOR MAN
HECTOR HEYWOOD

By Bruce Heywood

ryelands

First published in Great Britain in 2012

British Library Cataloguing-in-Publication Data
A CIP record for this title is available from the British Library

ISBN 978 1 906551 32 2

RYELANDS
Halsgrove House,
Ryelands Business Park,
Bagley Road, Wellington, Somerset TA21 9PZ
Tel: 01823 653777   Fax: 01823 216796
email: sales@halsgrove.com

Part of the Halsgrove group of companies
Information on all Halsgrove titles is available at: www.halsgrove.com

Printed in China by Everbest Printing Co Ltd

CONTENTS

FOREWORD
BY SIR ROBIN DUNN

THIS BOOK IS MUCH more than a biography of Hector Heywood, though it admirably fufills its avowed title.

The book gives a wonderful account of life in the hill farms of Exmoor in the late nineteenth and early part of the twentieth centuries. It was a hard and lonely life, especially for the women, which is why so many of the hill farmers' wives were themselves born and brought up on Exmoor hill farms. The true aristocracy of Exmoor to this day are the hill farming families. At least the men had the numerous stock auctions and sales where they met their peers and discussed topics of the day. But the women had no social life except for hunting, especially stag hunting which was unique to Exmoor, apart from the odd shopping visit to Barnstaple, Minehead or Dulverton. It was not until the advent of the railway that visitors started pouring into Exmoor from up-country, mainly attracted by the stag hunting and the beauty of the Moor. During the nineteenth century there were three large landowning families who owned land on the Moor: the Fortescues at Castle Hill, the Aclands at Holnicote and the Luttrells at Dunster. Then visitors with money came for the hunting, such as the Lloyds at Pitsworthy, and my first wife's family the Hughes and Pilchers of Lynch, and the Waley-Cohens of Honeymead and the Herberts at Pixton who all played prominent parts in the community and especially the local Hunts.

Hector Heywood had an impeccable Exmoor pedigree on his father's side. His grand-father was known as 'Whisky' John. For many years the family farmed at Nurcott Farm near Winsford, and the tradition must have continued because the farm was sold to the Hayes family. The Devon and Somerset branch of the Pony Club held their hunter trials there every year with Mrs Hayes as a welcoming and gracious hostess, We always used to take our children to compete there and one year we arrived at the farmhouse to be offered a drink by Mrs. Hayes. My mother-in-law asked for tea, to which Mrs Hayes replied "I'm sorry Lady Pilcher we've no tea, but there's plenty of whisky!" But she got her tea in the end. Hector was related to many of the hill farming families: His mother was a Bawden, sister of Ernest who was a legendary huntsman of the Devon and Somerset Staghounds and showed wonderful sport during the mastership of Colonel Wiggin between the two Great Wars in the twenties and thirties. At that time Hector was farming at Hinham in the Barle valley near Hawkridge where Hector married Joan Nicholson. As Bruce says "As chalk is to cheese, so Joan and her background was to Hector and his background." Her father was one of six sons, all of whom went to public schools, three of them holding posts in the family brewery. They lived in some style in an old Vicarage in Shiplake in Berkshire with a large staff of twelve, spending holidays on the continent and hunting on Exmoor where Joan met Hector. This difference in background made for difficulties in the marriage; Hector was a well educated and intelligent man but was also strong-minded as was Joan; and both sometimes resorted to violence. The marriage deteriorated while Hector was farming at Cloutsham where I first met him in 1940. He was an outstanding harbourer and naturalist. He must have been able to smell a deer and this book contains many fascinating accounts of hunts with Ernest Bawden and the Devon and Somerset (D&S).

He loved going to Scotland to view the deer and was much in demand as a companion as he could be excellent company. He was an expert at slotting or tracking the deer and from the slot mark could tell the age and sex of the animal. However, during the nineteen sixties Hector became increasingly frail and was more or less living on pain killers to ward off the pain of arthritis.

He was a truly remarkable man and I was honoured to know him and see him working in his prime.

INTRODUCTION

THIS IS THE STORY of my father Hector; however, I have started it with the first mention that I could find of a Heywood in 1745.

In the early 1980s when we had Dad to stay at Moor Farm, our farm in East Yorkshire, I asked him to tell me something of his Grandfather (his father's father).

"What was his name Dad?"

"John Heywood"

"Yes, and?"

"He was a bugger for the whisky."

"Yes what else?"

"I don't know of anything else."

I was flabbergasted. What an indictment, what sort of legacy was that, I thought to myself? There must be something more about the man. I was determined one day to find out.

In the fullness of time (2007) our son Oliver asked me for a photo of my father Hector as they had none, "And also Pop could you write a few notes about him." Ollie's maternal grandfather Dr. Richard Ashwin of Londesborough Park, York, had written several sides of foolscap of autobiographic notes for each of his grandchildren. This was fine but raised more questions without providing the answers, and sadly too late- Dr. Ashwin passed on in 2003 aged 90.

I was also inspired by my mother's first cousin Michael Nicholson MBE, of Bucknell near Bicester who had written an interesting and fine record of his life for his grandchildren, entitled "The Long Straw". I felt Hector too deserved his life recording.

I have begun with 'John Heywood, a bugger for the whisky' and all events down from him until my father's death in 1988. I also dwell a little on the interesting people whom he met and impinged upon his life. My task has not been easy as there is so little in the way of letters and diaries before 1938. Much is based on recollections by Hector's sister Jean Campbell and brother, John Heywood. Fortunately there were, and are, people still alive who remembered him, and these I approached for their reminiscences. For this I am especially grateful. I am very pleased that I interviewed Hector's first cousin Percy Bawden, aged well over 90, at length on a tape recorder in 2001 before so much information was lost forever.

On a stay at Moor Farm in early 2008 I saw that our two eldest grandsons, aged eight and ten, were practising handwriting with their Christmas present fountain pens. When I discovered George the eldest, was writing a primitive family tree, starting with himself at the bottom of the page and asking for names upwards I felt that my efforts of writing about Hector might not be wasted, indeed possibly in years to come, appreciated.

'WHISKY' JOHN

I WAS FOLLOWING a reference to there having been Heywoods at the village of Oakford, near Bampton, so on a visit to the churchyard there and whilst peering at gravestones, a chance meeting with a kindly churchwarden, 'Bunny' Burrows, led me to the house of E.W.Bentley from whom I purchased a copy of his recently (1982) published book, *Oakford the History of a Devon Parish*. From this well researched and documented book I gleaned that the Heywoods farmed at various farms in Oakford parish for 100 years.

In 1845 'Whisky' John's grandfather William moved from Oakford to farm 270 acres at Great Nurcott Farm, Winsford. Winsford lies on the eastern side of Exmoor, not far from both Dulverton and Minehead, in the County of Somerset.

'Whisky' John's father also, confusingly, called William went to farm at Harewood Farm (part of this farm now lies under Wimbleball reservoir), Brompton Regis, in a nearly adjacent parish. This was always called King's Brompton by the past generations, with a photograph of signposts thrown into a pit at the outbreak of war (WW2) clearly showing the latter use of the name until people thought better to change it. This William married an Elizabeth Ridler from Lower Kemps Farm, Winsford. Her lineage goes back via the village of Horner in West Somerset to Porlock.

Perhaps the fact that the Porlock Charity which owned 50 acres of Lower Kemps had a bearing on a Ridler from Horner going in as tenant. The late, greatly respected Jan Ridler MBE, local historian, district councillor and farmer at Blackford Farm in the Porlock Vale substantiated all this by writing out for me the descendants of David Ridler from Porlock.

There is some confusion surrounding the name of Kemps and Lower Kemps. Originally the farm was called Lower Staddon, as the now Staddon Farm was, prior to 1902 known as Great Staddon. Apparently Lower Staddon had the alternative name of Lower Kemps which in the course of time became just Kemps, as used today.

'Whisky' John was William's second child, born 2nd July 1848. The 1871 census shows 'Whisky' John, aged 23, had married and produced a son George William aged one year, and farming on his own account 220 acres of Lower Kemps Farm, Winsford. The fact that his mother was from here must have had a bearing on him farming this farm.

He was employing two men and two boys. This is surely the mark of a man who possessed drive and initiative. This farm, Lower Kemps abuts onto Great Nurcott. Lo and behold at the 1881 census at the age of 33 'Whisky' John is farming 580 acres of Great Nurcott employing six men on the farm and four people indoors and has now expanded his family to six, four yet to be born.

The three photographs of him would suggest a short but well dressed man, in contrast to his wife who appears much taller. Her name was Mary Norman, born 9th August 1847 at Staddon Farm, Winsford. This farm is adjacent to Kemps on the western side.

Interestingly Mary Norman's mother, Hector's great-grandmother, was Betsy Williams. One of her younger brothers was George, later Sir George Williams founder of the YMCA movement in 1845 and is buried in St. Paul's Cathedral. Sir George Williams was the great, great grandfather of Stanley Johnson of Nethercott, Winsford who is the father of the colourful Boris Johnson, Mayor of London.

A young 'Whisky' John.

A young Mary Norman
Heywood.

'Whisky' John and Mary had ten children:

George William born 1870 married Anna Loosemoor. They farmed at Chapel Farm, Bury, Nr Dulverton.

Frederick John born 1871 married Lucy Jane Derby. He emigrated to Kansas and farmed there.

Herbert Henry born 1873 married Mary Windsor. They farmed at Withycombe Farm, Chipstaple.

Harris Edwin born 1874 married Anna Pring. They farmed at Ruggs Farm, Brompton Regis.

Sidney Thomas born 1876 married Mary Elizabeth Bawden. They farmed at Hinham Farm, Dulverton.

Elizabeth Anne born 1878 married Ernest Bawden. They lived at Exford where he was firstly whipper-in, then huntsman to the Devon and Somerset Staghounds.

Laurence Edward born 1880 married to Anne Stephens emigrated to Canada, then to Kansas.

Maurice Eugene born 1882 married Emma Leah Turner. They farmed at Oldrey Farm, Winsford.

Frances Jane born 1885 married Richard Stephens. They farmed at Luckyard Farm, Wheddon Cross, Minehead.

Mary Norman born 1890 married Joe Bawden. They lived in Minehead.

Having ten children in twenty years seems par for the course in those days but having all survive to adulthood must be testament to Mary Norman and 'Whisky' John and robust constitutions all round.

From the above list it can be seen that a Heywood brother and sister married a Bawden brother and sister, with a third Heywood sister marrying a Bawden cousin.

It is not easy to be wholly accurate in painting the picture of 'Whisky' John and his farming at Great Nurcott. He was a man of small stature. He was a good shot and friend of the Head Gamekeeper for Sir Thomas Acland. He was very enthusiastic about cricket not only playing for and captain of the Winsford team, but he fielded a team made up of him and his children to play against Winsford. He rode as all farmers did in those days, either a pony or horse.

He was keen on following the Devon and Somerset Staghounds and was out on the day in August 1879 when the Prince of Wales attended the meet of the staghounds on Hawkcombe Head, way above Porlock. Just imagine the excitement of the whole of Exmoor; no prince had visited since Prince Charles (later Charles II) escaped from the Roundheads going from Dunster Castle to Barnstaple and the last royal person to hunt the deer was Edward, Duke of York in 1396.

Well-judged estimates put the crowd of people out at 15,000 or over. Of these 1,200 or 1,500 were mounted. The two highlights of the day would seem to be the Prince plunging into a bog out on Badgworthy Deer Park; fortunately he retained his seat even if he was grasping the horse's neck. A farmer on the spot remarked to the Prince, "Dirty going here about, Mr. Purnce." To this day it is called Prince's Bog. The second highlight was that the Prince, at Arthur Heal's invitation, administered the *coup de grace* to the by now captive stag using the huntsman's formidable clasp hunting-knife. Perhaps 'Whisky' John might have been there, in at the death, still with enough horsepower to ride back to Great Nurcott. Vast distances were covered on horseback in those days; it was about ten miles just from Nurcott to Hawkcombe Head before any hunting took place. They probably did the equivalent to the Golden Horseshoe Ride, which takes place every year on Exmoor today over 100 miles, every week they were out.

A cutting from *The West Somerset Free Press* dated January 28th 1939 reports of the proposed Point-to-Point Steeplechase meeting of the Devon and Somerset Staghounds after a lapse of thirty years. Included in the article are the results of the first ever such meeting held at Larkbarrow on September 20th 1897. There were three races. The first race, The Farmers Plate shows that 'Whisky' John had a horse running; quite clearly here was another sporting interest that he was involved in.

The Farmers Plate
Fifteen sovereigns, being ten sovereigns to the winner, three sovereigns to the second, and two sovereigns to the third, for horses that have been since August 15th, the property of bona-fide tenant farmers, or their sons, residing within 20 miles of Exford, and that have never won a steeplechase, hurdle race or flat race. To be ridden by tenant farmers, or their sons, over about three miles of fair hunting country.

There were nine starters, and the winners were: -
1, Mr. J. Bawden's b.g. Reago (E. Bawden)
2, Mr. J. Heywood's g. Don (S.T. Heywood)
3, Mr. J. Bawden's c.g. Pretender (J. Bawden)

The riders of all three horses were soon to become brothers in law as Sidney Heywood married Ernest Bawden's sister Mary Elizabeth in 1901 and Ernest married Sidney's sister Elizabeth Anne Heywood in 1904. This sort of thing often happened in large families. John, Ernest's elder brother, was on the third horse.

'Whisky' John's efforts at farming can be seen in context of the fortunes of agriculture in the last half of the nineteenth century. At the time of the Great Exhibition of 1851 held in the Crystal Palace built in Hyde Park, agriculture was on a roll. It provided **20.3%** of the national income. It was the largest single industry aided by exciting developments in transport via the new railways and canals, and the iron, steel and manufacturing industries. These made new complicated machinery such as reapers and threshing machines that could increase output on the farms at the expense of labour. There was confidence in farming resulting in capital expenditure in fertilizers, land drainage, buildings, roads and new machinery. Competence and output rose in the 1850s and 1860s, giving rise in 1868 to a figure of **80%** of food being home produced. Indeed it was a period of High Farming. However the 1851 census revealed that for the first time more people in mainland UK lived in towns than in the countryside, a dramatic contrast to the past. This growth in the towns and cities, especially the industrial ones, meant that labourers began the great drift away from the land resulting in a loss of over 40% of the male labourers by the time of 1901. Lows always follow highs, and so it was that a series of wet and bad harvests in the early 1870s coupled with a revolt in the fields stoked up by Joseph Arch's National Agricultural Labourers Union resulted in farmers and magistrates calling in troops to harvest the crops. This, alongside the opening up of the North American prairies, which grew huge quantities of high quality bread making grain which was then brought across the oceans by faster and cheaper shipping, together with wool from overseas gave rise to 'the Great Depression', not of course to be confused with that starting in 1929 with the Wall Street Crash.

The pastoral west of England was less severely affected with its milk, hay and straw not open to harsh foreign competition. Compared with 1851, the situation in 1901 was that agriculture now accounted for a lowly **6.4%** of national income. The majority of food and agricultural raw materials such as wool were imported.

Anybody reading Thomas Hardy's novels might be aware that the span of publication (1872-96) covered almost exactly the years of the agricultural depression. Although, as recorded in *A Devon Family, The story of the Aclands* the situation was still dire in 1900, please bear in mind that although 'Whisky' John was a tenant of the Earl of Carnarvon, the Acland Estate was neighbouring to it in Winsford parish and I quote from Anne Acland's book: -*These were bad times for farming, even on the rich Killerton land, and on the hill-farms in north Devon and Somerset the situation was almost desperate. In 1900 all the tenants at Holnicote and Winsford complained of low wool prices and scarcity of labour, and asked for reductions in rent.* I am sure that the situation would be exactly the same for Carnarvon tenants.

For at least 42 years 'Whisky' John Heywood was a good farmer and highly respected agriculturist as his obituary and farm sale results show later on in the story. Piecing things together it would seem that his sons Sidney Thomas, Hector's father, and Herbert Henry, were perhaps the only sons to stay to work on the farm with their father, until they married and went farming on their own account. From the 1901 census although no labourers are listed there are two male servants aged 20 and 14, so perhaps 'Whisky' John really was short of labour. This could explain why Sidney Thomas was living there, although his new wife is listed on the census day as being back at her old home, East Hollowcombe Farm, Hawkridge, with her parents and with her first-born, a daughter, Ernestine Mary.

It was fortuitous that my mother Joan had the foresight and presence of mind to make notes of a conversation she had with Sidney Thomas in 1956 then aged 80, when he talked of his days at Great Nurcott. This gives some authentic and interesting detail to a period of which would otherwise have had nothing. He was born 14th May 1876 at Lower Kemps Farm, Winsford.

As indicated earlier in the chapter 'Whisky' John started farming at Lower Kemps, this was possibly around 1868 when he was aged 20. I know from the Sale of Livestock announcement that he had established his flock of Exmoor Horn sheep in 1870 which would tie in with starting farming just prior to then. He left Lower Kemps in 1876/7 to farm at Staddon Farm, his wife's childhood home. He was here for a relatively short time and left sometime between 1878 and 1880 to go to Great Nurcott. This meant that Sidney had a walk of only one and a half miles to school at Winsford when he started aged four years and eight months, compared with his elder brothers who would have had nearly four miles to walk when they lived at Staddon. He was at Winsford for all his schooling and left aged 15 in 1891. He must have had academic abilities, as whilst there he won two scholarships, firstly for two pounds and ten shillings (£2.50) – today's worth about £850 – and secondly another for £5, worth today about £1675. In wintertime he combined going to school with feeding six bullocks in the village and 12 elsewhere, morning and evening. He used to carry his dinner tied up in a red handkerchief.

It is clear from Joan's notes that Nurcott was a thriving farm and completely self-sufficient. A word at this point about the farm. The house and old buildings lie facing south, on the side of a valley at about 800feet above sea level. The free draining land goes from around 600 feet down beside the Larcombe Brook up to over 1000ft at the top of the farm. One could describe it as an upland livestock-rearing farm. There were about 300 breeding ewes, mostly the indigenous breed of Exmoor Horn. They milked ten cows which were probably Devons as in those days that breed was dual purpose, i.e. they would produce enough milk to hand milk for cream and butter making and produce a calf that would grow into a good beef animal. The Devon is such a docile breed of cow that they were used back in time as a draught animal as well. 'Whisky' John produced beef cattle and kept pigs. To help feed these animals, wheat, oats and various root crops were grown. The wheat straw may well have been used for thatching the hay and corn ricks. On Exmoor rushes were sometimes used instead of straw, in this case the rick would first have been covered in dried bracken.

I am keeping with the order in which the notes were taken and slightly rewriting them to flow better, Sidney had several tasks that he had to perform regularly whilst growing up; one of these was to heat the bread oven. This was adjacent to the open fire, built of brick with a cast iron door. A fire was lit in the oven using specially collected and prepared small faggot wood with the smoke coming out and up the main chimney; when the heat of the oven was judged to be correct all the hot coals and ashes were raked out onto the open fire below. The bread was put into the oven on long wooden handled breadboards. After one and a half hours the bread would be baked and removed with the breadboards. All the cooking was done on the open fire or in the bread oven; an old favourite was Figgie Duff pudding wrapped in a cloth and boiled in an open crock over the fire.

Every week a quantity of wheat was taken to the miller at West Mill, Luckwell Bridge about three miles away, to be ground into flour. This mill had become disused by 1928. In the process of making the bread, the barm from beer making was added to the flour as the active yeast to make the bread rise. I don't know how the barm, the froth on top of fermenting beer, was kept for use, whether like a ginger beer plant or dried to a powder. Sidney used to help his father with the brewing when he was about 15 years old. They would brew a hogshead (54 gallons) for shearing and another hogshead for the tail end of harvest. This meant Sidney had to go to Wheddon Cross with a horse and cart, or perhaps pony and trap, to get the important ingredients – four bushels (eight gallons) of malt and 14lbs of hops per brew. It gave me much pleasure to learn recently from the late 92-year-old Arthur Webber at Cutcombe that it was his father William Henry Webber, a tailor from 'Dunkery View' at nearby Wheddon Cross, who performed the useful service of buying malt and hops from a chemist in Porlock to sell to all the local farmers including the Heywoods at Nurcott, for brewing on their farms.

Self-sufficiency or in other words growing as much food as possible on the farm for home consumption meant that four or five pigs were killed on the farm every year, four or five sheep and occasionally a bullock. Some of the meat was eaten fresh whilst the bulk was salted down. With 13 or 14 around the meal table a good supply of food was paramount. There were copious quantities of milk, cream and butter from the ten cows; Sidney used to go to Luckwell Bridge every Saturday with 40lbs of butter for sale, carried in a basket on his pony Nipper. The pony was very quiet and every gate on the farm could be opened and closed from off his back. Nipper was ridden to the age of 38 and died a year later.

Cider was also made on the farm in quite some quantity every year, about five or six hogsheads i.e. between 270 gallons and 330 gallons. A knowledgeable man who came down from Kent said it was the best in the country and fit for any show. I wonder how much he drank to make those flattering comments. Cider was always drunk at lunchtime and at any other time come to that. It was freely available for anyone to help themselves. The workmen used to fill a three-pint firkin and hitch it up to their horse's hames to carry it to where they were working. For those who don't know, the hames are the two curved pieces of iron or brass covered wood attached to the collar of the draught horse and stick up in the air.

There were eight working horses on the farm, which meant that there were four teams each pulling a single furrow plough. When Sidney first started he was third in line with the last team behind him. When an acre had been ploughed the men would stop to go about the chores of the farm. At hay time in the days before Sidney did man's work there used to be 13 men with scythes starting at 4.00 in the morning to cut grass. Later with the advent of a mowing machine Sidney would get up at 2.30 am then have the task of trying to find the horses in the dark and get going. Breakfast was always brought out to the meadow, hot teddies (fried potatoes) and bacon on a plate, with a bottle of tea. As I understand it a whole field was not mown but only enough that could be worked on in stages. When the sun got up and the dew had been burnt off the grass, or as it became hay, it was turned until just before teatime. After this, hay that was dry and fit to carry was brought in to the rick. This went on until it became dimpsey (West Country word for the time when the light goes).

Sheep shearing was another big event in the year when all the neighbouring farms helped each other. It usually lasted for about two weeks. At Nurcott there would have been about 1000 head to shear as this included last year's lambs; there was no such thing as a suck lamb, one that was still suckling its mother when it went to market, as is the case for much of the national lamb crop today. In those days, it was all mutton with much bigger cuts and joints to feed the large families. Sidney would get to a neighbours farm, go in to breakfast and have a plate of ham, then shear all day until 9 o'clock in the evening. Shearing with hand shears he would average 40 to 45 a day, compared with today's output with electric clippers of well in excess of 150 or even nearer 200 for the professional shearer with easy sheep i.e. with no belly wool. Beer would be the drink of choice rather than cider during the day's work. When the last of all the sheep was shorn on that farm, and the day's work done, everybody would go into whichever farmhouse it was and sit down to supper; this included cold beef and ham followed by trifle and cream. With supper finished the room was cleared and there was dancing and merriment until morning to music from Old Walter Darby's violin. Walter Darby was a local shoemaker who travelled around the farms and villages and made music. The more he had to drink the better he played. Sidney must have had a musical ear as Old Darby taught him to play the violin; Sidney in his turn in later years would be the music maker at shearing parties. I can hear him now, singing the first verse of 'John Barleycorn' when I was in my early teens.

Two little anecdotes Sidney told me that I found rather interesting of happenings at Nurcott. One day he and others decided to try to do some fishing on the River Exe near the bottom of Nurcott Lane. They went armed not with rods, bait or flies, but with a bag of burnt lime and a colander. Finding a large pool the lime was tipped into the river upstream; by the time it arrived at the pool the lime was well distributed and beginning to have the desired effect. The fish were asphyxiated and floated to the surface to be scooped out with the colander and thrown to the bank, the haul if my memory is correct was about 20 to 30 fish of all sizes, many of them trout. The second story is when curiosity got the better of Sidney. He wondered what would happen if he took out the lead from a 12 bore cartridge and inserted in its place one of the tallow candles hung up in the kitchen. These were made on the farm from rendered mutton fat or perhaps beef if there was plenty, although dripping would have been part of the diet whereas it is doubtful whether mutton fat would have been as it is not so palatable. So he cut one down from the bundle, eased it into the cartridge and then into the gun. Going out side he went over to the barn, walked ten paces away from the barn door turned to face it, upped and bang. The candle drilled a neat hole right through the wood. His curiosity satisfied and a bit shaken he did not repeat the act! The hole was in evidence for decades afterwards.

Continuing in the vein of shooting which must have been a regular pastime, the photograph (left) which came over from America shows Sidney in the middle, his younger brother Maurice sat upon the ground, the man on the right is called Flatman, a local gamekeeper. Talk about Butch Cassidy and the Sundance Kid!

In spite of the apparent shortage of labour things cannot have been too bad on the farm as there was still time to take the horse to the first point to point at Larkbarrow in 1897, and I feel sure that this would not have been an isolated case. 'Whisky' John cannot have been short of money as he was able to send his three daughters away to the then girls boarding school Edgehill College at Bideford. Why the preferential treatment for the girls as all the boys had to make do with Winsford School? There is no information about 'Whisky' John until we learn that his health has started to decline at the age of 59. Did he start to consume the whisky at around this time to mask the pain from some medical complaint or depression or even a strong-minded wife? Cousin Doris Mayfield from Tulsa, Oklahoma, when on a visit to the UK in 1983 stayed at the Royal Oak at Winsford and spoke to a very old man who remembered 'Whisky'

A smart middle aged John Heywood.

Maurice, Sidney and Flatman, the gamekeeper.

John. This man told her that John Heywood used to come to the pub on his horse, or horse and buggy, and when ready for home would just climb aboard and the horse would take him home. I suspect that this sort of thing was quite commonplace in those days. At any rate he decided in July 1910 that he could not go on and would have to retire. He would have given his landlord notice to quit. W.H.Vellacott had bought Nurcott from the Earl of Canarvon in or around 1897 and at some stage left it to his son Col. John Vellacott who lived at Wicken in Northamptonshire. It was then sold to the Hayes family in 1911. They very generously allowed 'Whisky' John and Mary to continue living in the farmhouse until his death on March 2nd 1911.The livestock sale was fixed for 23rd August 1910. His son Fred came back from the USA to help him get everything ready for the sale and returned leaving Liverpool on September 6th. Hector, as a five-year-old boy, told me of seeing him off at Dulverton Station; Uncle Fred took with him a bundle of ash sticks to make into walking sticks, (probably thumb sticks) back in Kansas. The poster advertising the sale is reproduced here. I have seen an original copy hung on the kitchen wall of my second cousin Virginia Jones at Wiggins in northeast Colorado.

Nurcott Farm sale poster.

Nurcott Farm sale report from
West Somerset Free Press

WINSFORD.

SALE OF LIVE STOCK.—Messrs. James Phillips and Sons conducted a very successful sale of live stock at Nurcott on Tuesday last for Mr. John Heywood, who is giving up the farm on account of ill-health. There was a very large company present. Luncheon was provided at 12.30, and the sale of sheep commenced at 2 o'clock. Mr. Phillips, sen., in his opening remarks, said that he had that day one of the best flocks of sheep he had ever had the pleasure of offering; the Exmoor horn ewes were very matching with splendid constitution; the lambs were very healthy and as even as possible, and the cross-breds were excellent quality. Mr. Heywood had always been most careful in the selection of rams to obtain the very best and most suitable for the country. The whole would be sold to the best bidder, as Mr. Heywood had now made arrangements to give up the farm at Michaelmas next, so that the stock was no good at all to him. The sale was then proceeded with and the following prices realised:—Six-teeth and full-mouth horn ewes, 37s. 6d.; four-teeth ditto, 40s. 6d.; two-teeth ditto, 37s.; cross-bred ewes, 40s.; ditto wethers, 36s.; horn ditto, 34s.; cross-bred lambs, 31s.; horn wether ditto, 24s. 6d.; horn ewe ditto, 27s.; ditto rams, £3 7s. 6d. Mr. W. G. Phillips sold the beasts, and before offering lot 1 remarked that he had an excellent lot to offer; the young heifers were splendid quality and matching, and the young steers were an improving lot and of the rent-paying sort. The following prices were realised:—Barreners, £15 15s.; maiden heifers, £31 15s. per pair; two-years-old steers, £30 2s. 6d. per pair; steer yearlings, £18 12s. 6d. per pair; calves, £10 15s. per pair; 2 cart horses were sold and made respectively 31¼ guineas and 31½ guineas. Among the purchasers were:—Messrs. Young (Salisbury), W. Shepherd (Bridgwater), Captain Mildmay (Dulverton), R. Williams (Gutcombe), Vellacott Bros. (Withiel), J. Kingsbury (Williton), J. Gregory (Dulverton), R. Knight (Tivington), W. Holly, J. Reed, H. Reed (Wootton Courtenay), E. Rawle (Minehead), T. Williams (Kingsbrompton), J. Thomas (Brendon Hill), W. Steer (Winsford), J. Tout (Morebath), R. Moorman (Williton), J. Blackwill (Cannington), T. Rawle (Porlock), S. Stenner (Timberscombe), T. Hill (Upton), T. G. Maunder (Withiel), W. Dascombe (Withypool), C. Milton (Withypool), H. Bishop (Treborough), J. Greenslade (Withiel), T. Howe (Kingsbrompton), W. Taylor (Quarme), W. Westcott (Hawkridge), W. Crick (Liscombe), Mrs. Stephens (Luckyard), R. Fulford (Kingsbrompton), H. Howe (Luxborough), F. Heal (Exford), and others. The grass of the farm to September 29th next will be sold on Wednesday next, and a sale of implements and surplus furniture will be held on or about Michaelmas-day.

On Monday the King and Queen of S...

Mills, Minehead, September 6th, 1910.

SALE NEXT THURSDAY,

CLEARANCE SALE.

NURCOTT FARM, IN THE PARISH OF WINSFORD, SOMERSET.

JAMES PHILLIPS and SONS have received instructions to SELL by AUCTION, on THURSDAY, SEPTEMBER 29th, commencing at 2.30, the whole of the undermentioned

IMPLEMENTS,

And a portion of the HOUSEHOLD FURNITURE, the property of Mr. John Heywood, who is retiring from business, comprising:—

Implements.—Waggon, large putt cart, 2 harvest carts, with ladies, small putt cart, 2 harvest single plough, Oliver digging ditto, Hornsby drags, 3 pair chain harrows, 2 pair iron drill, 2 grass seed machines, cultivator, turnip hay collect r, 2 turnip cutters, horse eddish rake, galvanised sheep troughs, 4 sheep racks, 6 winnowing machine, cake mill nearly-new d g-cart, with cushions; mowing machine, by Harrison McGregor; 2 hay machines, set breeching, complete; set cripping, complete; odd harness, hand sheep-shearing machine, 100 hurdles, Nicholson corn mill, horse hoe, grinding stone, manure sifter, 4 pig troughs, bullock chains, malt mill, cheese press and vats, rick cover, tools, about 1 ton old iron.

Furniture, &c.—3 iron bedsteads, 1 wood ditto, massive old-oak kitchen table, well fitted with drawers, 11ft. 3in. by 3ft.; walnut oval centre table, writing-desk, hand sewing-machine matting, quantity dinner ware, 2 antique brass milk pans, antique brass bowl, double-barrel gun, rook and rabbit rifle, gent's bicycle, brass kettle, to hold 18 gallons; 6 enamelled milk pans, butter pots, 2 frying pans, meat safe, zinc buckets, &c.

The auctioneers ask for a punctual attendance at the above sale, as the lots are very numerous, and as Mr. Heywood is giving up the farm, the whole is intended for absolute sale.

Sale SEPTEMBER 29th, at 2.30 sharp.

Dated, Bridgtown Mills, Dulverton, and Town Mills, Minehead, 14th September, 1910.

Commencing at TEN o'clock until further notice.

DULVERTON STATION NEW AUCTION MART.

JAMES PHILLIPS and SONS beg to solicit

Nurcott Farm clearance sale details.

After the sale of livestock there came that of the implements and surplus household furniture on 29th September 1910. One or two interesting items that indicate that 'Whisky' John was a man well up with the times are a hand sheep-shearing machine, a gent's bicycle, a rook and rabbit rifle, 100 sheep hurdles and a nearly new dogcart. Clearly he had not realised at the onset of his illness that he was going to have to retire so soon, otherwise he would not have bought a new dogcart.

I think it is wonderful to see from the list of purchasers that there are today, 2011, a hundred years on, still Stephens farming at Luckyard, Reeds at Wootton Courtenay, Miltons at Withypool, and Bishops at Treborough. They are the real strands of rural fabric that give so much cohesion and continuity.

Retirement photograph of John and Mary Heywood.

The above photograph was probably taken to mark their retirement, with Mary Norman Heywood sitting upon a chair, and rug brought from the house, in her finery with a very elderly and gaunt looking 'Whisky' John now aged 62 standing beside her. It is not hard to see the differences in stature between them.

A certified copy of his death certificate reveals he died of cirrhosis of the liver and general dropsy. In other words he had become an alcoholic for whatever reason; this is a sad reflection on a man who had achieved so much with, as his obituary tells us, a bright and cheery disposition, a good friend and a fine captain. Hector was right; he really was a "bugger for the whisky".

The final words on 'Whisky' John come after his death on 2nd March 1911 at Nurcott from the *West Somerset Free Press*. Underneath his obituary there is a report of a trap accident, clearly the reporter was unable to connect the people involved with their father. Mrs. Stephens was his daughter Frances and Mrs. E. Bawden was Elizabeth her sister. Hopefully their wounds did not make it difficult to attend to their father's funeral at Winsford Church.

John Heywood's obituary in the *West Somerset Free Press*.

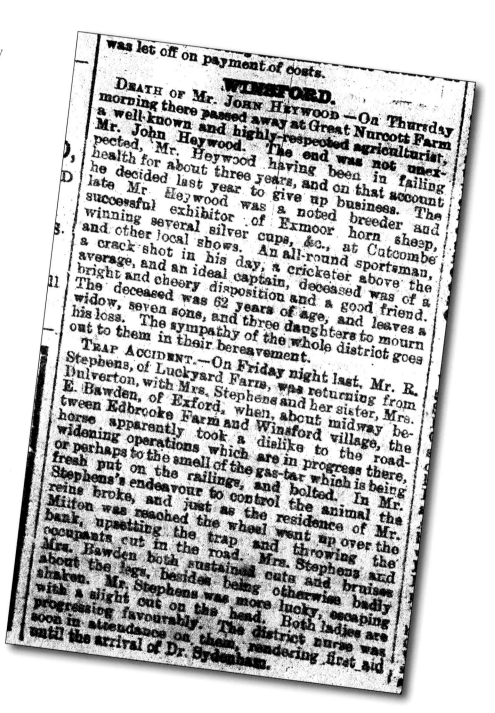

- 2 -
THE BAWDENS

SIDNEY THOMAS HEYWOOD, my grandfather had at sometime in the late 1890s met with Mary Elizabeth Bawden. Whether it was at a meet of the Devon and Somerset Staghounds, at pony races, or even at a local sheep fair, is all conjecture but Great Nurcott to Hawkridge is only a matter of five miles apart as the crow flies. The Bawdens are said originally to have come over from Brittany, true Celtic stock. There is a Bawdens Rock on the north coast of Cornwall off St. Agnes where they are supposed to have landed. One branch of the family had been tin miners for many generations near Bodmin when in about 1750 they decided to move and start farming. They settled on the southern slopes of Exmoor near the village of Hawkridge. They, being a Mr John Bawden and his family. In 1832 their son also called John married Mary Milton a local girl from the neighbouring village of Withypool. John and Mary took the tenancy of Cloggs Farm, 250 acres in the parish of Hawkridge. It is a livestock-rearing farm somewhat similar to Great Nurcott and they raised a family of five. Both Johns had earned a reputation in the community as true Exmoor farmers and were well respected. Of John and Mary's five children, the eldest was a son James, or Jim as he was called. In today's parlance Jim would have been called an alpha male, always looking for a female conquest, a wild, hard riding and daredevil horseman, hard drinking, and a bit of a gambler; in other words he was a 'Hell Raiser'. He was, according to Percy Bawden his grandson, "possessed of the 'Hawkridge Wild Streak' and he would do whatever he wanted with no consideration for others." In spite of what some would say were his failings and being weak in so many ways, he was a loveable man and well liked. He was passionate about stag hunting. Fred Goss the famous harbourer recalled an incident in his book *Memories of a Stag Harbourer* when Jim, then a young man, was ploughing his father's land at Cloggs when he heard the hunting horn. Unharnessing the plough horse, he jumped aboard and rode it bare back to the kill near Brushford, in the company of the six other surviving riders. The hunt from start to finish passed through thirteen parishes, namely, Upton, King's Brompton, Withiel, Treborough, Luxborough, Exton, Winsford, Exford, Withypool, Hawkridge, East Anstey, Dulverton and Brushford. Jim rode in nothing more than the clothes he had on whilst ploughing and with nothing more than a hemp halter on the horse.

It is said that opposites attract one another and none more so than Jim and Harriet Comer. The Comers were originally from East Grinstead in Sussex before coming to Exmoor to work for Frederick Knight on his Exmoor estate possibly as stonemasons, hence Comer's Gate onto Winsford Hill. Harriet's father became a wealthy lime merchant and farmer from Simonsbath. Harriet was a strong willed and well-educated woman; autocratic, redoubtable and formidable as her strong eyes and wide square cut jaw show gazing out from the photograph in front of Pixie Cottage, Exford, all those years ago. Theirs was one of the earliest marriages in Simonsbath Church on the 27th December 1865. There was not enough room at Cloggs for three generations so Jim and Harriet left and set up to farm on their own at East Hollowcombe Farm in the middle of the small village of Hawkridge. They had 250 acres and a share of moorland grazing; both Cloggs and East Hollowcombe belonged to the then Earl of Carnarvon.

Harriet Bawden dressed in black on the left, old Mr. and Mrs. Lock and a young Lorna Slocombe.

As with 'Whisky' John and his wife Mary, so it was with James and Harriet: they produced ten children in twenty years all reaching adulthood. This would certainly be a testament to Harriet, as she would have had little or no help from James who was farming, hunting or pursuing his other interests. Writing about the Bawdens gives the reader some idea of the background to my father's mother as she had a profound influence on his upbringing and character.

Harriet had only two daughters, one either side of her fifth child Ernest, in the line of ten children. Harriet or Jessie as she was known by, was the elder and Mary, Hector's mother, the younger. Above Jessie were three sons, John the first born being the favourite with his parents yet something of a bully as he was often deputised to keep order with his younger brothers and sisters. Within such a large family there were always cliques; Jessie lent towards her elder brothers and the exciting things they got up to, appearing hard and unfeeling towards Ernest in particular. Jessie might well have been in the group that smoked out several of the inhabitants of the neighbouring village of Withypool. As retaliation for being lured onto upturned chain harrows laid across the road in the dark (chain harrows are a chain linked spiked implement for improving grassland) by the young men of Withypool, the Hawkridge clan visited Withypool in the dark of night. They soaked hessian sacks in the river, which were then placed on top of the chimneys by the smaller and lighter members, with the likes of John Bawden ready with his fists to catch the troublemakers: as they fled the smoke filled cottages. We do know that Jessie married Harry Baker the landlord of the Royal Oak, Withypool at the age of 17 and he being 30. Perhaps he caught her red handed in the raid and one thing led to another!

Ernest got on well with his brother James, who was a kindly soul and taught him about nature and the wildlife. James taught him how to shoot by swinging through the quarry as he pulled the trigger; he taught him how to stalk the quarry and be unseen, how to tickle trout and gaff salmon in the rivers Barle and Danesbrook, needless to say poaching. Ernest's real companion was his sister Mary with whom he got on exceptionally well and who gave him in his younger years the affection that was missing in his life. I feel sure that he would have shown her all the things that he was discovering and learning about, especially the red deer which would have been all around them in the fields and woods and up on the moorland.

When Mary was aged three she started to go to school, less than 100 yards up the village street. Alas this did not last long as all the children were withdrawn from the school, never to go again; the two eldest were removed two years prior. There are one or two suppositions as to why this happened: firstly the teacher was a young and attractive Miss Park to whom Harriet's husband James undoubtedly took a shine and maybe she to him. The other possible reason for their removal was that Harriet Bawden was totally dissatisfied by the standard of teaching. Harriet was a strong-minded intelligent, well read woman who brooked no nonsense, so she deserves much praise and credit for establishing a routine of learning with children of divergent ages sitting around a beautiful William and Mary sectioned, mahogany dining table. The ink stains are visible to this day. Harriet would be doing this concurrent with running the household, nursing a child, probably pregnant with the next one and trying to keep a rein on husband James and keep him focused on the farm. Both the beautiful handwriting of Ernest and to a lesser extent that of Mary coupled with the construction and composition of their surviving letters and Ernest's hunting diaries are a lasting testament to Harriet's good work.

Mary would have grown up becoming acquainted with all household tasks such as sewing, knitting, and cooking as well as scalding milk to make clotted cream and using that to make butter. Clotted cream today is not the same in flavour or texture so it is worth explaining just what was involved in those days and still perhaps today in a few cases. The fresh milk (raw, unpasteurised) was put into a large glazed earthenware basin with a wide top (in later years an enamelled metal basin), it was left on a slate shelf in the north facing larder for twenty four hours for the cream to rise to the top of the milk. The basin was carefully moved to the place of heat where the milk was slowly heated to just below boiling so that the cream was gently cooked. At the right moment a ring of bubbles would begin to appear in the cream reflecting the base of the basin, this was the time to remove the basin back to the larder. Here it was left for another twenty-four hours to cool right through. The cream could then be scooped off the surface with a special perforated tool and placed into a dish or bowl as appropriate. Properly produced cream would have a soft crust and was delicious to eat neat, on bread with honey or golden syrup giving rise to the nickname 'thunder and lightening' or on cut rounds, scones, cake, even with fruit such as whortleberries, raspberries or strawberries. To make butter the cream would be put into a bowl and stirred with a wooden spoon until it turned to butter; the length of time of stirring depended on the air temperature and that of the cream. There were available special churns into which the cream was placed and a handle turned to cause the churn to rotate through 360 degrees, but I wouldn't know if one was used at West Hollowcombe. Mary might have learnt how to grow flowers and vegetables, certainly how to deal with rabbits, venison, and fish from the rivers, and perhaps game such as pheasant and poultry, involving plucking gutting and dressing.

Perhaps the most overwhelming interest during Mary's years at East Hollocombe, indeed for the whole family, was stag hunting, particularly with the Devon and Somerset Staghounds. It would have amounted to almost a religion. Whenever hounds were in the vicinity everything would have stopped and off on foot the young would go. James would have been mounted and maybe the elder two or three sons, but Mary never rode according to the memory of my father's sister Mrs. Jean Campbell now 91 years old. Mary was by all accounts always full of enthusiasm for life, quite excitable and passionate about hunting in particular.

Mary and Sydney were married on 26th March 1901 at Dulverton Registry Office, with Harold Bawden and Jessie Harriet Baker, her brother and sister as witnesses. Sidney's place of residence was Winsford and Mary's Hawkridge. The following month when the national census was taken, they are still listed as living apart. This would seem to indicate a variety of problems. There was the overriding problem of where they would live. We know from Jean Campbell that Mary Norman Heywood who came to live at Hinham following 'Whisky' John's death was a 'contry [contrary] old toad' and not at all affectionate, a complete contrast to Harriet Comer Bawden. It is possible that Mary would have preferred to stay at home in a happy environment than live under a cloud with her mother in law. How long they were apart is unknown, possibly until Sydney took the tenancy of Hinham on Lady Day (March 31st) 1902. It also raises the question as to why Sydney took the tenancy of a 92 acre farm rather than farm alongside his father who was established in a 580 acre farm, and then taken over when his father retired, as was common practice. Perhaps it was simply that they did not get on when working together, which is often the case for many father/son situations, when both want to do things differently and each is convinced that he is right and the other wrong. Perhaps 'Whisky' John was starting to hit the bottle at this time and became very unpleasant. At any rate Hinham became the salvation.

- 3 -
HINHAM THE EARLY YEARS

THIS PHOTOGRAPH was taken in 2008. If the tin shed on the left, the bungalow on the right of the group of buildings, and the machined trimmed hedge in the foreground were not there, it would be exactly as Hinham would have been when Sidney and Mary arrived there on Lady Day 1902 to take over from Mr. Harry Elworthy. You are looking at the most level fields on the farm, the remainder are sloping and north facing or 'backsunded' as they are described in local parlance; these start reasonably level before descending. The east wind comes funnelling up the Barle valley to have the effect of making grass slow to grow in the spring. These factors, combined with competition for the grass or in Sidney's day, oats, wheat, potatoes and other root crops as well as by the deer (shown in the field on the right of the photograph) made Hinham

Hinham Farm, note the deer in the right hand field.

a difficult farm. Nevertheless Sidney farmed it well and it was a wonderful place to raise a family; in later years long after the family had left, whenever Hinham was talked about it was in terms of reverence and endearment.

In 1897 the Trustees of the late J.A. Locke Esq., Mrs. A.C. Locke deceased and Arthur C.E. Locke Esq., sold the Northmoor Estate, which lay a mile upstream of Dulverton, in and around the Barle valley. The estate of 1025 acres, included the farm Haynham of 92 and a half acres let at an annual rent of £58, 10 shillings. The new owner of Northmoor was Sir Frederick Wills, Liberal Unionist MP for North Bristol and director of W.D. & H.O. Wills the tobacco dynasty. He was created 1st Baronet of Northmoor on 15th November 1897. He was credited as having the foresight in beating off the North American threat to the British tobacco industry by organising the Imperial Tobacco Company of Great Britain and Ireland Ltd.

Whether Sir Frederick purchased the estate to commemorate becoming a Baronet is not recorded but it is quite feasible, as the members of the extended Wills family were immensely wealthy. For example when Sir George Wills died in 1928 he left £10,000,000, with more than £4,000,000 going in death duties. It could very well be that Sir Frederick took a benevolent attitude to his farms and tried to help the farmers in the difficult times to which I alluded in Anne Acland's book earlier; at any rate in 1899 he had built at Haynham a new range of farm buildings to the east side of the farmhouse. These included a trap house with harness room adjacent and a granary above, stables, a cowshed having eight tie-up stalls, with an area for fodder or roots, a calf house and pig's house. All the buildings were of stone construction with brick quoins, window and door surrounds, and the floors were of segmented hard brick, or Candy brick as they are referred to. In the 1897 sale particulars the house and buildings were all thatched. I would conclude that all the outbuildings were replaced in 1899 by the new range and thatch replaced by tiles. Today 112 years on the buildings are still very much the same as they were then.

Sir Frederick died in 1909 and left the Northmoor Estate to his son Sir Gilbert Wills. Sir Gilbert was Conservative MP for Taunton 1912 to 1918 and MP for Weston-Super-Mare 1918 to 1922. He was a hunting man, being Master of the Dulverton Foxhounds for twelve seasons.

Haynham, Hynham, Hinham or Hinam as it is now, became their new home. Whilst on the subject of the name, Mary Heywood would always insist on the spelling that occurred on the 1897 estate sale particulars as the correct one, which was Haynham. The ending of a place name with ham means in Old English home or settlement of somebody, which in this case would be somebody or family called Hayne. Casualness or sloppiness has resulted in the bastardising down to Hinam, which is a great shame, so I always use Hinham as a compromise. The farmhouse and buildings lie about 600 feet above sea level on a ridge of land about 150 feet above the River Barle. It is three miles to Dulverton lower down the valley and about a mile to the nearest neighbours at Draydon Farm. It feels isolated and in a world all on its own, which in a way makes it very special.

Sidney Thomas was a man of great courage, patience, gentle and full of kindness as well as being a good farmer, having acquired all the skills from his father. He knew the value of liming the ground and would go to Minehead with a horse and butt cart and bring back between 12 cwt and 15cwt (three quarters of a ton) of burnt lime. This is known as quick lime (Calcium oxide) a dangerous highly caustic material. Minehead was about 16 miles away depending on what route he took, which was probably the shorter harder route empty and longer easier route back, loaded. It is doubtful that he could have brought more than one load a day. If it was a corn stubble field to be limed, the soil was dug back, the cart tipped up some lime raked out; and then the heap was covered with loose soil to be left for several weeks when the rain would slake the lime to a more benevolent material (Calcium hydroxide), soil scraped off and the lime spread. Imagine the process if he was liming a grass field, in which case the turf would first be removed to be carefully replaced after the slaked lime had been spread. Shoals of herrings used to arrive in the Bristol Channel periodically and if a catch had been landed at Minehead he would always come home with a dozen herrings that provided a rare treat for the family. I dare say that his cart trips to Minehead passed by Nurcott which would provide a stop off for food, drink or catch up on news with his parents, or even food and water for his horse.

In later years lime, fertilizer, basic slag, calves or cabbage plants were collected from the railway at Anstey Station, just three miles away. He, in conversation with me, would talk about white clover and Eaver Grass, how important this was to grow in the sward. It was only years later when I was at Seale-Hayne Agricultural College in a botany lecture that the name cropped up again as Devon Eaver, an indigenous native variety of Perennial Ryegrass, which was a very productive 'good' grass to be encouraged. He also used to talk of using Peruvian Guano. These were great deposits of birdlime on the seashore rocks in Peru that was mined, bagged up and exported as a nitrogenous fertiliser. He grew potatoes for home consumption, oats for the horses and sheep, wheat for the pigs and to provide straw for thatching ricks, turnips and swedes for the sheep, and possibly he used forage rape to act as a nurse crop for new grass seeds. Lambs would be fattened on this before moving on to turnips in the autumn. All the time a battle had to be waged against the deer that would try to come in and eat and sometimes spoil his crops. They might have been dogged out with the farm dogs encouraged to give chase and bark, sometimes cord soaked in 'Reynardine', a foul and strong smelling product, would be strung up to deter them. The deer would come in to fields over the hedge banks in one place, which they would use exclusively and thus form a rack, until they decide to create or use another one. It would have been across the racks that the Reyardine cord would be strung, or perhaps deer offal, tin cans on string, anything to keep them out. One of the finest devices that Sidney used was the trip wire that when caught by the deer would set off a blank twelve bore black powder cartridge in a simple contraption. Sometime in the early days, certainly before 1912 as he was setting up a fresh blank cartridge it went off and the blast caught his top lip, causing a split and his eyes to be filled with black powder. He was blinded and had to lie bandaged up in a darkened room for nearly two weeks. His sight gradually recovered with no lasting ill effects, but to hide his disfigured top lip he grew a moustache. He did not use the device again.

Sometime early in the first decade of the century Sidney rented land on the outskirts of Dulverton. He had an eight-acre meadow beside the River Barle known as Sealey's Ham opposite Battleton that he continued to rent until he retired in 1942. It lies just over the hedge from the cricket pavilion. It is surprising what a small boy's mind retains as I remember Sidney telling me of how the hayrick one year was commandeered by the War Department and baled by a stationary baler. These big wire tied bales were loaded onto carts, taken to Dulverton Station and bundled somehow onto railway trucks bound for France. I was a little sceptical about the size of the bales. However, during a visit to a new museum at Perronne on the Somme at around 1995, some cine film taken during the Great War revealed a stack of large bales beginning to catch fire and the men struggling to roll and manhandle these big bales out of the way. It was only a few years ago that a lovely sepia photograph of carrying hay in Sealey's came into my hands. On top of the rick is Sidney complete with straw hat, waistcoat undone and wearing a tie eating something, standing next to him a helper with a hay fork, behind him is a woman dressed in white also with a pitchfork, then a younger girl say about 13 years old with two boys lain down on the hay. There are five other men to help. It could be that the girl and two young boys are Dolly, Freddy, and Hector which would date the photograph about June or July 1911. It is so sad that there is nothing written down to be absolutely certain, but Sidney has been positively identified by his son John Heywood.

Sidney around the time of his marriage, and before being blasted by the black powder explosion that disfigured his top lip.

Ernestine Mary their first-born was so named in deference to Mary's brother Ernest whom she thought the world of, but she was always known as Dolly or Doll; she arrived 9th February 1901. There followed then a son Frederick Sidney, who as far as I can tell according to the Hawkridge School register was born on 27th March 1903. Two years later my father Hector was born, on 9th May 1905, at Hinham. In all the years I knew Dad he never once intimated as to why he was christened Hector. I cannot think that it had the classical connotations as was suggested to my young schoolboy mind when we had to sing:

'Some talk of Alexander and some of Hercules,
Of Hector and Lysander and such great names as these,
But of all the world's great heroes,
There's none that can compare,
With a tow row row row row,
To the British Grenadier.'

Haymaking,
Sealey's Ham.

Sidney and Mary were very good friends with Hector and Harriet Pearce of Draydon Farm just across the valley, so perhaps they had a happy association with the name Hector and chose it for their son. Indeed the Pearse's christened their own son Montague Hector, who was born in 1908 and became a good friend of Hector. Little did anybody know just how Hector would live up to the meaning of the verb to hector (talk to someone in a bullying way) later in his life. Another two years passed before the arrival of another daughter Marjorie who was born on 1st September 1907. Life was reasonably settled and the children grew up doing childish things as they would on such a farm in those days without potted entertainment, no motor car, no telephone, no wireless set. They would have roamed the woods and fields observing nature, built dens, climbed trees and even helped on the farm with tasks such as fetching the cows in for milking, or moving the sheep. Dolly started school in 1908 at Hawkridge village school; to begin with, someone may have walked partway along the two miles through the woods beside the River Barle, up to Hawkridge Ridge at Great Gate and then left her to walk the last three parts of a mile across the fields. Perhaps the reverse on the way home, to give confidence, before being left to fend for herself. From the school register I saw that all four children did not start school until they had reached the age of seven. This is a little unusual as the starting age was five, but with the memories of her own education from her mother perhaps Mary wanted to lay the foundations of their education at home. Maybe she felt that the journey to Hawkridge involving a drop of 150 ft down to the River Barle and then a 400 ft climb up to Hawkridge over the distance of three miles was too much for little legs and exerted her strong will to get her own way.

At some time in these early days, when Hector was about four or five years old he pushed a peach stone down between the wall of the house and surrounding lip of cement. To his infant mind it was responsible for the thatch on the house catching fire. The house did not burn to the ground, but how the fire was dealt with is still a mystery. I was told once, that the thatch was in the process of being replaced on the roof with new reed (wheat straw) and whilst burning up the old straw in the nearby field the wind changed direction and a spark landed on the new. I have in the deep recess of my mind Hector telling me that all of their possessions were saved. This could be quite feasible as there would have been several men working on the roof. No doubt neighbours on seeing the smoke, as it was daylight, would have come to help; somebody might have galloped off for the horse drawn fire engine. The family moved into the loft above the trap house to sleep, this perhaps giving ideas to Sidney and Mary in years to come when they started having paying guests. What a burden for the mind of a small boy to carry until old enough to rationalise that the peach stone was not the cause of the fire.

- 4 -

THE TRAGEDY

AS A SPECIAL TREAT the family used to visit the travelling circus that came once a year to Beasley Farm, Dulverton. History does not relate how they got there and back, but in all probability it would have been Shank's pony i.e. walking the five miles there and five miles back. As it was a treat they may well have gone by horse and cart, or even pony and trap, but people walked enormous distances in those days and thought nothing of it. When they were supposed to be going to bed that evening following their visit on Monday 3rd June 1912 the two boys started larking in their bedroom, trying to re-enact what they had seen in the circus ring. I have seen two of our grandchildren at the same age as Freddy and Hector doing similar things on the double bed in the spare room; I have no doubt all young boys still do such things. Why the china chamber pot was not under the bed no one knew. Tragically Frederick crashed down upon it, smashing it to pieces and cutting himself badly in the groin (as I seem to recollect my father telling me a long time ago). Imagine if you will the scene, Mary flying up into the room to see her son in pain and panic and bleeding profusely, with blood everywhere in the room; perhaps she was just packing Marjorie down for the night. Dolly might have been dispatched to find Sidney if he was not in the house. He quickly sums up the situation, tears outside to bring in his horse, and saddles it up, then gallops like hell the three miles down the track and stone road to Dulverton to locate Dr. Sydenham. The Doctor may well have kept a horse in the stall, always on hand for such eventualities. An equally quick saddling up, gathering his Gladstone bag if he was at home and not miles away on another case, then they both would have galloped back to Hinham. I cannot think that they would have just trotted or even cantered; they would have pushed their horses over the 15 to 20 minute journey to get back to deal with the emergency. People in the town would have seen and heard them and would have deduced that there was a crisis; news would have spread like wildfire. The good doctor managed to stop the bleeding and sew up the wound making Freddy comfortable for the night. Mary, helped perhaps by eleven-year-old Dolly, would have cleared up the mess, and normality gradually restored for all in the house to face the night, perhaps to sleep in spite of all sorts of thoughts going through their minds from the traumatic experience.

All was going well with Freddy and to all intents and purposes he was making a good recovery. I would like to think that he was out of bed, dressed and walking around the farm and everyone thankful that he was getting better. Then, fifteen days later on Tuesday 18th June, he complained of not feeling well so Dr. Sydenham was called again, and visited several times only to recommend that Freddy be sent to Taunton Hospital. Immediately hearts would have sunk, and a state of great anxiety would have come over everybody. How do you move a weak sick boy to Dulverton Station, which is six miles down the valley? Was it a soft and comfortable seat using hay, which would have been made up in the trap, or cart? There were few ambulances in those days, but there just might have been one come out from Taunton to collect him. Loving goodbyes and tearful kisses and he was gone, perhaps with his mother at his side. He was moved somehow to Taunton and Somerset Hospital, where it was found that he had lost a lot of blood, so to stop the bleeding he was operated on, only to die of heart failure and loss of blood on Wednesday 19th June. The culprit being a concealed haemorrhage, i.e. bleeding internally to the ignorance of everyone.

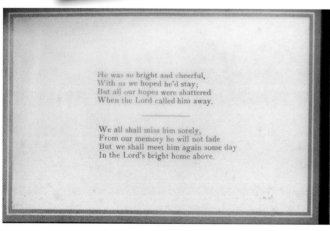

householders over 60 years of age resident in Dulverton; £500 to his brother, Petherick Bunt; £200 to Robert Williams; £50 to Elizabeth Cullen; and the residue of his estate he left to Johanna Mary Hicks, Elizabeth Parminter, and his niece, Rosa Mary Bunt.

DULVERTON BOY'S EXTRAORDINARY DEATH.

The extraordinary death of a Somerset farmer's son was investigated at Taunton Hospital on Thursday afternoon. The deceased was Frederick Sidney Heywood, the child of Mr. Sidney Thomas Heywood, of Haynham Farm, Dulverton, and he was only nine years of age. He and a younger brother, aged seven, were put to bed together on the 3rd inst., and in larking together in the bedroom deceased fell from the bed on to a ware vessel, which was smashed to pieces. The boy sustained a wound which bled a good deal. A doctor was immediately summoned, and the sufferer progressed favourably until Tuesday last, when he complained of feeling ill all over. The doctor frequently visited him, and on Wednesday he was removed to the Taunton and Somerset Hospital, where it was found that he had lost a good deal of blood. He was at once operated upon to stop the bleeding, but he died suddenly four hours afterwards from hemorrhage and heart failure. The hospital house surgeon stated that the wound was perfectly healed on the exterior, but bled extensively underneath. It was a most extraordinary thing, and was known as concealed hemorrhage. The jury returned a verdict in accordance with the medical evidence.

This event was to have an enormously profound psychological effect on Hector for the rest of his life. As the two brothers were the only parties involved, there is no evidence coming down over the years as to what went wrong or who if either was to blame. Did Hector push him? Tim Williams, a psychotherapist, has said that Hector would have had a feeling of guilt all his life. As a result of this he would have known no fear and when feats of great daring were accomplished he would have had an exhilarating lift that brought temporary relief from the feeling of guilt. He seemed also, to possess the utmost of confidence in his own abilities. Mary was mortified with Freddy's death and kept all his clothes, boots and shoes in a cupboard on the landing upstairs until the day she died. Dolly was equally affected, as she never ever mentioned it to her younger son, Pat Chanter, now in his mid seventies. He was in total ignorance of the existence of Freddy. This could have applied to Pat's elder brother and sister as well.

Life had to go on and slowly the mourning subsided.

He was so bright and cheerful,
With us we hoped he'd stay;
But all our hopes were shattered
When the Lord called him away.

We all shall miss him sorely,
From our memory he will not fade
But we shall meet him again some day
In the Lord's bright home above.

In Loving Memory

OF

Frederick Sidney Heywood,

Of Haynham, Dulverton,

WHO DIED JUNE 19TH, 1912,

AGED 9 YEARS.

HIS END WAS PEACE.

Interred at Hawkridge Churchyard, June 25th, 1912.

Top: Report of Fred's death from the *West Somerset Free Press.*

Above: Freddy's memorial card.

There are two photographs from that period of time, one showing Dolly with Marjorie sitting in the middle and Hector at the back on a horse called 'Cabinot' about to set out for school. There is a bag of food for it over the withers, for it to eat during the day whilst it was stabled at Rowe Farm, Hawkridge. At the end of school they would all jump up and ride home. They used 'Cabinot' very often when he was available. Note the open window in the building to the right, the granary. It was to here that the family would decamp to sleep when there were guests in the farmhouse, later in the 1920s and 30s.

Two things of note, firstly how smart Hector looks in his suit and Eton collar, secondly how relaxed Sidney is with his dog. He was often photographed with a dog, not knocking it away but kindly patting or scratching it which tells me how kind he was, as dogs always avoid people who are not kind; they seem to have an inbuilt sense to people's feelings. Hector has now moved to the role of only son and accordingly was doted upon by his mother. As he was sandwiched between two sisters he became

'Cabinot' with the three children Dolly, Marjory and Hector setting off to Hawkridge school, outside Hinham.

L-R: Dolly, Mary, Marjorie, Sidney and Hector outside the front of Hinham.

deeply attached to them both, no doubt they would contribute to spoiling him as well as his mother. By all accounts he had an uneventful time at Hawkridge School, starting at the same time as a cousin Ivor Baker. Mary's elder sister Harriet or Jessie as she was mostly referred to, having married Harry Baker, lived in Hawkridge with their family. In the words of Hector, Harry fulfilled the role of 'Quack Veterinary Surgeon'. Harry was a horseracing fanatic to the point of naming his sons, Mornington after Mornington Cannon, flat race jockey, Kempton after Kempton Park Racecourse, Ivor after the jockey Ivor Anthony, and Gordon after jockey Gordon Richards. Hector left school on 13th March 1918 two months short of his 14th Birthday, with the ability to write a good letter and straightforward prose, as extracts from his stag-harbouring diary will later reveal. He was literate, and an intelligent young man. Along with other children from the environs of Hawkridge he was brought up in the Christian faith and was confirmed by the Bishop of Bath and Wells. However he never went to church except to a funeral, or an occasional wedding.

Hector upon leaving school would become his father's main help on the farm, able to turn his hand to anything, putting the harness on a cart horse, ploughing ground, shearing sheep or using a scythe which in his later years when I saw him cutting weeds, nettles and long grass, made it look so easy and simple. Who needed a strimmer? He became skilled at laying hedges and took great pride in hanging gates and stone ditching i.e. building stone faces to the hedge banks and in particular at each end of a gateway. He was a good shot with a twelve-bore shotgun. As well as assimilating everything that was necessary to being a good farmer, Hector would have taken a keen interest in all things to do with nature that he would have come across every day at Hinham. He would study the habits and characteristics of the red deer until he could look at a hoof print or slot mark in the soil or grass and be able to tell at a glance the age, sex and approximate weight of the animal that made it and how fresh it was. He would have been able to look at a great mass of slot marks and read them like a book. He used to find antlers after the deer had shed them in the spring using his eagle eyes as he went about his daily tasks on the farm, or walks in the woods. His mother would have been most interested in what he had seen each day and their conversations would have quickly turned to hunting, particularly as her brother Ernest was making his mark on the Devon and Somerset Staghounds. Ernest started as whipper-in, in 1904, turning hounds to the legendary Sidney Tucker and then taking over as huntsman in 1917 of the often regarded 'premier pack of hounds in the country'. What an impact and influence on the mind of a twelve year old seeing his uncle in a scarlet coat hunting hounds and blowing the horn for the first time or on the countless other later occasions when hounds were in or around the Barle valley. To see the hunted deer pass nearby followed some time later by the wondrous music created by the pack in full cry enough to make the welkin ring, and to hear his uncle's magical blowing of the horn carried on the wind or echoing down the valley would have set his pulse racing.

In 1921, when Hector was aged 16, he carried out an act of derring-do, the sort of thing that would become fairly frequent in his active years. Hounds were hunting their stag down the Barle valley when it was killed on the opposite side of the river to Mrs Wiggin. She was the wife of Col. Walter Wiggin the Master, and couldn't face riding across a rather full river. She was most anxious to get to the other side and on the horns of a dilemma when young Hector who had been running down the valley after hounds volunteered to give her a piggyback. He hoisted her up and set across the river without losing his feet and kept her dry. History does not relate whether she had such a lift back across to her horse, but I would expect she did because she returned the act of bravery with the gift of a silver cigarette case inscribed "Hector 1921".

Ernest Bawden outside the huntsman's house at the kennels, Exford.

RABBITS AND SUMMER VISITORS

HECTOR PROBABLY never received a wage for his work on the farm, as times were hard when he left school. The country had been at war with Germany for four years resulting in great shortages all round. Britain's economy relied on trading with overseas countries, and this was handicapped by the loss of 40% of the merchant fleet to submarines, tariffs raised by other countries to protect their own economies, and our factories, mines and machines were outdated which hurt our industries. There was a moderate recession for most of the 1920s. Help, however, came to the Heywoods in the form of rabbits and summer visitors.

It is most likely that Hector was the greatest beneficiary of the rabbit at Hinham. Before 1953/4 when myxomatosis was introduced into this country from Australia, rabbits were the farmer's greatest pest, yet were eagerly consumed in the great cities as good meat. The greatest number of rabbits were caught or shot after the corn harvests, through winter until spring. The war was waged by four methods, trapping, snaring, shooting and ferreting. Gin traps with vicious sprung loaded serrated metal jaws were carefully installed in a rabbit's run from its burrow. After anchoring it with a small metal peg, the gin would be lowered into a scraped out area bringing it level with the ground, its jaws then set open as gently as possible with the catch. A little dried grass and a sprinkling of soil would help camouflage the gin from the rabbit, which unsuspectingly would tread on the plate to release the catch that meant either instant death or extremely painful capture. Gin traps were inspected on the rounds twice a day, the rabbits despatched if alive and put into a carrying bag across the shoulder, the gins reset and onwards. The horrendous gin trap was outlawed at about the time of the arrival of myxamotsis in 1953/4.

The setting of snares was a little more humane and less likely to mark the carcases so were used to harvest the 'crop', whereas the gin was used more to control the pest. The snare was made from thin multistrand wire with an eyelet at one end through which the wire was fed and then attached to a small length of cord. This in turn was attached to a peg that was used to anchor the whole. The loop of wire to form the noose was put over one's knee and the wire pulled to put it into the shape of a pear. On finding the run of the rabbits, usually seen by pressed patches of vegetation formed by them hopping along, the wire is positioned about four inches off the ground midway between patches and held in place by a small hazel stick with a slit in one end, the other pointed end pushed into the ground. Again when the wires are set, twice daily visits are made to take out the rabbits that are either dead from the wire around the neck, or held by one around a leg. It is then a question of dispatching it; reset the wire and carrying on. If the traps or wires were not inspected regularly the rabbit might more often than not, provide a convenient meal for a fox, buzzard, crow or raven.

The method to catch rabbits with a ferret and nets is more of a social occasion as it is always better to work with two or three people. A visit to an active burrow means that all the holes have to covered by nets which are about two feet by two feet anchored by a peg attached to some strong string; all work is carried out in silence or whispers so as not to alert the rabbits which might escape unscathed. When ready a net is lifted and the ferret introduced to the hole. With bated breath eyes scan the nets until suddenly a rabbit hits one to become entangled; quick as a flash it is caught despatched and the net reset. When all rabbits have been cleared the ferret will emerge blinkingly into view. On occasions if the burrows are deep or longer than first thought and the ferret will not appear it could mean that it has a rabbit trapped at a dead end or that it has killed one and is eating it. A line is attached to another ferret with a bell on its collar so that as it moves around underground it can be gauged where it comes to rest. Vigorous digging ensues taking care not to hurt the ferrets. Today there are electronic bleepers instead of a bell.

Finally there is shooting which would involve shooting the bolting rabbits from the burrows using a ferret but no nets. Hector was guilty on one occasion of shooting both ferret and rabbit dead. A quiet walk around the farm in the evening when they all are out feeding would provide the chance for a few shots, occasionally two or three could be killed with one shot. Cartridges would have cost money so during the hard times they were used sparingly. The dead rabbits would have been paunched whilst still warm and they would have been 'hucked'. This word is probably a corruption of hocked; basically one hind leg would have a slit cut between tendon and bone above the hock, the other leg would have been pulled through the slit. The rabbit could then be carried on a stick over the shoulder. If two rabbits were 'hucked' together they could be hung over a horizontal bar. It was not uncommon for a brace to be sent through the post with brown paper wrapped around the middles and a label tied around the necks with the address on it. Alan Bawden, Hector's first cousin, told me how the system worked. The local buyer of rabbits was an Arthur Court of Dulverton who would visit the farm at least once a week; he would set up his scales, weigh the rabbits and then pile them into his cart. This in later years was replaced by a big van. Two or three times a week a special rabbit train would stop at Dulverton Station with a destination of the big cities up country. The carcases were placed on three racks, free to hang down in large wicker rectangular baskets; there were no lids but two men would stack the baskets, as high as practicable.

On many farms at this time rabbit money would pay the annual rent, yielding as much or more than the lamb crop. Certainly for Hector, money came for firstly a Diana air rifle that is still in the family having been used by myself a lot whilst growing up; then it was Oliver's turn; today the grandsons have been introduced to it. This was followed by a dinner jacket that I in turn, wore in my late teens and early twenties, and still have. Then into his possession came the serious items, a model T Ford motorcar, replaced later by a Wolseley. After this was worn out, he bought an 'AJS' motorbike to be in turn replaced by a Morris Cowley motorcar. I can but speculate that all Hector's spending money was generated by rabbit money for trips to Bristol and Exeter, suits of clothes, and shotguns etc., for from where else was money forthcoming? He might have had a few sheep or a calf to call his own but that would not generate the sort of money to buy cars. There was never any talk by Hector that I can recall, of him going off the farm to work for others elsewhere, so rabbit money must have been his source of income.

When I had reached the age of nearly twelve Hector thought it was time for me to start catching rabbits for myself and initiated me into the making of snares. In January 1954 just before I went back to school I see from my diary that I caught five rabbits. Imagine my delight when a letter from home arrived with 15 shillings and seven pence in it, my first and only rabbit money. We were allowed to take back £1 pocket money to last the whole term, so 15 shillings and seven pence was good money. Sadly, soon after this event Myxomatosis arrived and nobody would even consider eating a rabbit after seeing the blind, swollen headed creatures pathetically hopping around.

The first ever summer visitors to Hinham came in 1922. They were an Indian Army officer, Major Sampson and his family who stayed the whole summer, occupying the house. The Heywoods moved into the granary above the trap house to sleep, and ate meals in the kitchen. Major Sampson drove a model T Ford and clearly made an immense impression on Hector, now aged 17. He was given driving lessons, having to reverse around the big water tank in the middle of a field called Great Green and drive between two sticks representing people. When Hector knocked a stick over the Major shouted, "You've killed that man." Hector realised that a motorcar would give untold freedom and excitement, so he acquired his first driving licence on 4th July 1923 when he was 18. No test was necessary in those days; it was not until 1935 that a test to drive was introduced. He got his licence when he probably bought his own model T Ford around that time. Much to Hector's chagrin, ill founded rumours were circulated that the Heywoods had bought their car with deer damage money. This was money given to farmers as compensation by Captain Wilton, upon his assessment of damage to crops by the deer. He must have been in charge of deer damage payments, and later became the Secretary of the staghounds. Hector, full of righteous indignation, claimed that the only money the Heywoods ever received was £5 for damage to a crop of mangolds. Henry Ford started his first assembly line in 1913 after William 'Pa' Klann came to him with the idea, having seen the disassembly line at the Chicago Union Stock Yards where the animal carcases were cut up, whilst moving along a conveyor. So successful was the work that it took only 93 minutes to build a complete car, coming off the line every three minutes. In fact the bottle neck was the drying time of paint; the only paint to dry fast enough was Japan Black, there being no fast drying colour paint until 1926. This led to Henry Ford's apocryphal remark "You can have any colour you like as long as it is black" The 'Tin Lizzies' as they came to be called were produced from 1908 till 1927. They would do 13-21 miles per gallon and cost £100. Percy Bawden verified that Hector had his new and cost him the £100.

When it came to the times of a General Election, Hector became an ardent Conservative supporter. He liked to bedeck his car with blue ribbons and fly the Union Jack when he drove around ferrying people in from the outlying countryside to vote in Dulverton Town Hall. This enthusiasm became evident to me when I voted for the very first time. He insisted that I wore a blue tie, as he did, when I accompanied him to the polling booth in Minehead. In my naivety I did not know about tellers in those days, to whom the blue tie was an indicator. I remember thinking at the time that it would not be a good idea to disagree with him back then whatever my political thoughts.

It is important to mention at this stage that Sidney and Mary had a daughter Marian Diana born on May 12th 1920, this was thirteen years after their last, Marjory, and fifteen after Hector. She was never called by those names but known always as Jean. Three years after Jean came the last, a boy Mervyn John born on 10th February 1923. The large age gap between them and Hector meant that he was always involved in other things to them and was often somewhat disparaging towards them and exploited them to the extent that they didn't like him much of the time. Certainly there was no love lost between them; but John and Jean have always been close.

Hector in the orchard with Jean; in the background Marjory and toddler John.

With Hector's apparent good looks his mother was always saying that he should go into films and become a film star. I think that she would have encouraged him to cultivate his speech modelled on the well to do summer guests, for although all his life he would converse with his peers in his native dialect, he could and did speak in his "five pound note" voice to his superiors and strangers he thought warranted it, not so much to impress them but to show he could be their equal.

One family of visitors that Jean can remember was a Captain Bovell, his wife, a young daughter named Dawn and her nanny. When Jean was aged eight, (about the same age as Dawn), and John aged six they used to go off and play with Dawn making a house with a little garden down by the river. Primroses and other flowers were planted, all marked out with stones. A sign was written and put up that said:

This house was built by childish hands,
Good luck to he who lets it stand.
Bad luck to he who pulls it down
And in the river may he drown.

They were very proud of their little house back on the Hinham side of Castle Bridge near the confluence of the rivers Danesbrook and Barle. The late Jack Hurley, editor of the *West Somerset Free Press* and compiler of "Notes by the Way" in that paper, wrote sometime in the 1970s in "Notes" of having back in the 1930s seen, and been most moved by the little 'fairy' house, and wondered who the children were and what might have become of them; he remembered and quoted the verse on the sign. In a letter to me he wrote, *"You have recalled that some years ago I wrote in my Notes of the little 'fairy' house children built on the Barle banks in the 1930s. I was astonished and delighted when they identified themselves to me in their adult state, and I do not think anything I have written in Notes since I started in 1963 ever gave me greater pleasure than the outcome to the fairy house paragraphs."*

It also gave great pleasure to Jean and John.

An interesting visitor in the 1920s was a man called G.L. Hawkins who came to stay frequently with his caravan and made camp in the field Great Green where Hector had had driving lessons. Leslie Hawkins was eight years older than Hector having been born in 1897 in Sidcup (or Sevenoaks), Kent. He was educated privately in Kent and on leaving school was sent to Paris to study art. When the First World War started he came home to join up as an officer in the Marines; he fought at Gallipoli in 1915 and on the Western Front. He was wounded and his left arm was badly damaged, resulting in numerous stays in hospital, leaving him with a very weak arm. He was awarded the Military Cross. This did not deter him from racing the car his parents gave him for his 21st birthday present in 1918, at hill climbs and around Brooklands, and for many years racing against the likes of A.G. Frazer-Nash, R. Mays and H.F.S. Morgan. It is very apparent that he took a huge interest in photography and was an avid student in chemistry; he became a noted pioneer in the Bromaloid process of printing, which he introduced commercially in 1951. A brief summary of its implications is quoted: *Oil and bromoil afforded many opportunities for control, manipulation and personal expression. It gave a painterly appearance that allowed photographers work to be expressive rather than explicit.* In other words it was an art form in black and white photography. His work has become quite valuable as collectors' items.

He married in 1921 and his parents bought him a farm near Thame in Bucks, this did not fire him up and after two years moved to Oxford where his parents bought him all the photographic shops in the city. A well-meaning gesture but they did not allow for his free spirit to take control; he put managers in all the shops so that he was free to wander wherever his fancy took him with his cameras. This included Hinham on many occasions. Did Hector regard him with admiration and awe? I can well believe that they walked the woods and countryside together with Hector showing him the deer, birds and wildflowers etcetera. Hector never made a disparaging remark about Leslie

Hawkins, but in general if he thought the occasion or person warranted it, would soon speak his mind.

Leslie Hawkins had three children by his first wife whom he divorced in the mid 1930s. It is through his daughter Pauline Balder, now in her late eighties living in New Zealand that I have had details of their holidays at Hinham. In 1933 and 1934 they stayed for the whole of the month of August. The children had great fun playing with Jean and John Heywood down by the River Barle making tree houses. In spite of being brought up in the era when children were seen and not heard and therefore not having much contact with adults, she remembers Hector explaining about hunting and harbouring the deer to her, and also the buzzards that Hector had a special regard for, including a tame one that used to sit on his arm. He also had a tame barn owl that he would call down from its roost in the big fir near the house. He would feed both birds with pieces of rabbit. 'Toby' the barn owl tragically died in the rainwater butt. It was suggested by Hector to me that the owl was challenging its reflection in the water. He was buried in the orchard with a headstone and 'Toby' carved in it.

Hector with the pet buzzard.

Leslie Hawkins married again and lived in three adjoining thatched cottages in Culmstock, where he had two more daughters. Towards the end of the Second World War there was a fire that burnt the cottages to the ground. He lost his life's work in the fire; this initiated the onset of his depression that was with him for the rest of his life. After this they moved to Ford Cottage, Wootton Courtenay near Minehead, from here they moved to North Hill in Minehead. My mother took us one Christmas time to see them and I have hazy memories of Betty Hawkins, who soon after died up in London in strange circumstances. I got to know their daughters Judith and Diana as we went to St.Theresa's Convent in Minehead and my mother had become good friends with Virginia, Leslie's third wife. We still have several Christmas cards featuring his photos on them. I remember visits to the Old Coach House at Alcombe tarnished by being told, "Hush, no noise please, Poppy is having a bad time" and brief appearances of a quiet and somewhat grumpy old man. He died a horrible death, taking three days to go, after drinking some of his photographic chemicals and some mercury in November 1958 but left behind a legacy of films and photographic work, which included: The Slave Road to the Congo 35mm 1924, Motor Cycle and Motor Car Races 1925, Slate Quarrying of North Wales 16mm 1935 and an African Tour for Kodak. He published an authoritive work, *Pigment Printing* in 1933,

Sidney Heywood ploughing by G.L. Hawkins M.C., F.R.P.S., F.I.B.P., F.R.S.A.

'The bromoil process from negative to the transfer.'

In 1922 a family came to stay at Hinham for holidays that were enormously wealthy. They were the Johnsons, who had a pottery at Queensborough on the Isle of Sheppey in Kent. If today you look underneath a plate you may see Johnson Bros., as they are still in production. They brought with them their chauffeur, Ottham Bunstead, and ladies maid, Lily Wilson. The chauffeur drove the Rolls Royce down with the luggage and family whilst Mr. Johnson drove the Bentley. The Bentley was a lovely three-litre sports car, the cream of the day, one of which won the 1927 Le Mans 24-hour race. To make sure of fish to catch on the Barle they had Exe Valley Fisheries release 400 trout below Hinham. They generously gave a Spitfire fighter plane to the war effort in the last war. Lily Wilson and Hector must have hit it off with one another as she wanted to elope with him; Dad never told me of where she was thinking of going, but he felt at aged 17 he couldn't take it seriously enough. Besides he had a girl friend on the go, Audrey Uppington, she was the only child of Tom Uppington, butcher in Dulverton. He, somehow, took Audrey to the Exford Horse Show and to the pantomime in Exeter and romantic walks to Brewer's Castle in the Barle valley. The Johnsons must have come for several years to Hinham as mention is made of giving Hector a £5 note for his 21st birthday in 1926, with which he bought some gold cuff links.

Finally Steve Ritchie first came to stay with his mother and father at Hinham in 1927 when he was 13 years of age. Ever since the tragedy of losing his brother Freddy, Hector has always related well to boys from aged nine to their early teens; whether deep in his psyche they struck a chord with Fred who knows? At any rate there was never any devious ulterior motives in befriending young boys; today any such relationship would immediately be questioned. Rear Admiral Steve Ritchie now aged 97 very kindly spoke on the telephone and sent me a letter by e-mail with difficulty, as he is partially blind. In 1927 his parent's two horses were sent from Barnet to Dulverton by rail, then ridden up to Hinham, where they were stabled together with two hirelings, along with an Exmoor pony called Heather. Apart from hacking in the Barle valley, they would all go hunting with the Devon and Somerset Staghounds. He relates as to how *"Hector would go hunting in his ancient motor car* [Model T] *from which the folding hood had been removed to form an open vehicle with an all-round view and it was always an exciting experience to go out with Hector as he scaled or descended the steepest and roughest tracks"*.

He went on, *"I thought your father was a great man and impressed me greatly when I was a small boy of 13 as I was interested in nature and he taught me many things. I remember going with him to see kingfishers' nests at Hele Bridge and buzzards' nets in high trees near Molland Moor Gate among many other adventures. Mind you he had quite a bit of a temper. I was helping with haymaking, leading in the horse and loaded cart to the rick in the rickyard. The trick was, as we got close to the rick to turn before stopping to unload, in readiness to leave when empty. I turned too quickly and the horse nearly went down between the shafts, he gave me a really good cussing then sensibly said that I had better go on leading the horse to get my nerve back."* He also said, *"Your grandmother was always full of enthusiasm especially for hunting, a very nice woman and she cooked well. Her husband was very quiet."*

When Steve Ritchie entered the Royal Naval College at Dartmouth at the end of that wonderful holiday in 1927, his boyhood hunting days on his Exmoor pony, Heather, were over and the pony loaned to Hector's sister Jean. She used it as transport to go to Dulverton School for several terms; whilst she was at school it was stabled at the blacksmith's shop, currently a beauty salon. When she no longer had use of Heather, the pony was taken back to Hertford where the Ritchies lived, to see out her days in a paddock there. Steve Ritchie had a long and successful career in the Royal Naval Hydrographic Service rising to the rank of Rear Admiral. During this time he was a keen member of the Royal Naval Bird Watching Society, no doubt Hector must have had an influence in that direction.

Jean also remembers an authoress who stayed at Hinham and wrote a book about the place and the Heywoods, but gave them different names. Was this published and what was its title?

- 6 -
WORK AND PLEASURE

SIDNEY HEYWOOD was a quiet almost shy man; he had the patience of Job and could endure privation. He worked hard, enjoying simple pleasures yet was a most knowledgeable, gentle, and loving man. Two incidents stand out that typify him. His sister Elizabeth who was married to Ernest Bawden came with their son Percy, still a small boy, to visit Hinham one winter's day. As the time came to leave, to walk home to Exford, it had started to snow, as they watched and waited the snow got heavier and worse. There was nothing for it but to stay the night. By the next morning it had stopped snowing but the snow lay very deeply on the ground, there was no alternative but to get the bridle on the carthorse; with his sister and her small son astride the cart horse, Sidney walked or struggled sometimes waist deep through the snow leading the way. After several hours they managed to cross Winsford Hill and arrive at Comer's Gate. "You will be alright now to get back to Exford all you have to do is follow the line of the road". With that he bids them goodbye and rides away home.

The other incident relayed to me by Percy was of the time when he had appendicitis.

"Uncle Sid, being like he was, he would never give up; he kept taking the tablets he got from Dr. Collyns to make the pain go away. He got in such a bloody state and nearly let it go too far, he nearly came to peritonitis. Just in time, and being such a modest man as that you'd have thought there wouldn't be anything the matter".

In the end he was sent to Minehead hospital and successfully operated upon. When his sister Elizabeth came in from Exford to visit him the hospital sister asked her, "Is that your brother?"

"Yes." she replied.

"What's he like normally?"

"Very placid, you know."

"Well," replied the sister, "If you had been here to record what was happening under the anaesthetic you'd change your mind! We've never heard such a string of language under that anaesthetic. The patient swore at anybody."

Percy then went on to say, "Course they asked him about it afterwards and he was quite shocked."

Sometime in the early 1920s, possibly after Hector had acquired his Model T Ford, he would now have been aware of the advantages of the new technological developments in the world. He would have been, as all young men are, keen to embrace new ideas. Was it Hector who persuaded his father to make an approach to their landlord for a Blackstone oil engine, all the equipment to run from it and a barn to house it? Their landlord, Sir Gilbert Wills, must have agreed for there appeared at Hinham the requested barn and its attendant machinery.

The Blackstone engine had to be started with a blowlamp to heat a hot bulb inside the engine, and then a massive flywheel was turned by hand until it fired up. It drove, when needed, many items of machinery by belts and shafting, namely a root slicer, cake crusher (a by-product of commercial milling were slabs of dried linseed that needed to be crushed up to be mixed with grain for the animals), corn mill, chaff cutter, two shearing sets, circular saw for providing all the logs for cooking and heating the house, grindstone and a small barn threshing machine. It was an enormous labour saving outfit enabling the farm to be run by the family.

Hector became a very proficient shearer of sheep and took great pride in not cutting or damaging them. I still have the family letter H marking iron with which to mark the shorn sheep using special coloured paint. These would have been either the native Exmoor Horns or Devon Closewools; the Closewool was Hector's favourite breed of sheep. Sidney always made cider to drink on any occasion, especially when working hard, as had been the custom at Nurcott and from where he acquired the skills. Apples were fed into the root slicer and mashed up, and from the receptacle under the slicer the pulp was conveyed to the cider press at the end of the cowshed; when the cheese, having been made of alternate layers of pulp, and clean straw, was complete, the press wheel was turned until no more juice flowed out. The apple juice was transferred to barrels in the harness room where it was left to ferment to a finish. Jean told me of how, when she and John were children, they would find a long piece of barley straw and surreptitiously suck up mouthfuls from the barrels. I don't think they ever got drunk!

One of the annual tasks that became quite a ritual was the castrating of the male lambs. This involved a visit from Harry Baker the quack veterinarian from Hawkridge; Harry was Mary's brother in law. Hector once described the 'performance' to me. Harry would arrive by horse with two irons hanging down in front of his saddle, and then a fire started using wood, never coal, to heat the irons. A form was brought out from the house, someone would sit astride the form and hold the lamb; its legs would be tied with rope to allow the wool to be shorn from the scrotum. Two holes were then cut and the testicles squeezed out to be cut off with scissors, the hot iron was applied to sear the wound. A handful of bacon fat mixed with verdigris was put into the pit of the back legs to act as a mild antibacterial salve. The verdigris is basically copper carbonate; today copper sulphate is in widespread use in aerosols for foot rot or wound dressing, a cheap antiseptic astringent. The lambs were then carried back to the cowshed and when all were done they were let back out into the field with the ewes. During the afternoon and evening they were gently moved around to avoid stiffness. Barbaric as this method would seem today, they never lost a lamb. It was just not possible to leave male lambs entire in those days, as they would be a hazard to getting ewe lambs or older ewes in lamb and the meat would be unpleasantly strong to smell and taste, especially if they were not slaughtered until their second year. One year Hector lost his 21st birthday present tie pin. When getting ready for the work ahead, off would come coat, tie, and sleeves rolled up. He felt sure Harry Baker had stolen it, and I think said as much, "Jessie wrote a snotty letter back to return it, she wrote *found stuck to his bag."*

Harry Baker used to supply horse drenches, wormers etc and deal with minor ailments to the farm animals. Another speciality of his was the docking of carthorse and cobs' tails, the method of which, for the sake of history, is worth recounting. The horse to be docked was tied up in its stall with a gate tied across the back of the stall hard against the horse so that its tail hung over or through the gate. The requisite amount of hair to be left was tied up and the rest removed from the site of the cut. Using an instrument like a large pair of secateurs the tail was severed with a sudden sickening crunch, no doubt accompanied by a groan and snort from the horse. Following this, there would have been flying back feet crashing against the gate; because the animals would have been docked when young and unshod, the extra hazard of iron shoes did not apply. As with the wound on the castrated lamb, so the wound of the tail stump would have the hot iron applied to sear it and then the tried and tested bacon fat and verdigris applied. If there was a real emergency then Erskine the veterinary surgeon from Dulverton would have to be sent for; this necessitated riding to Dulverton to alert him if he was at home, and he would ride out to deal with the problem.

Another task that Sidney was involved with, and Hector too, although strictly speaking not farm work, was the butchering of any deer carcases that the Devon and Somerset or Tiverton Staghounds killed when hunting in the area. The custom was, and still holds today, that the farmers and landowners were given joints of venison as a gesture and thank you, for having the deer feed on their land or the hunt to have been across it. Two treasured possessions, one akin to an exercise book and the other a hard backed ledger contain information appertaining to who had what and when. Although the Heywoods first started venison distribution in 1919 the first entry appearing in the first book was *"March 3rd 1925 one small hind found White Rocks killed Batsam"*. Of all the names to appear in the book in 1925 there are today three families still in residence in their farms, the Bawdens at Cloggs, Daveys at Lyshwell (listed in 1925 as Buckingham whose daughter married a Davey), and a Clatworthy at Westwater, although the late daughter who was in residence, married a Branfield. The last entry was December 9th 1941 written in beautiful handwriting by Jean. On average ten to twelve deer a year were dealt with and the joints taken round, in all probability by Hector in his motorcar of the day. The first time Hector ventured forth was a call at Zeal Farm, Hawkridge to give some venison to Mrs. Sydney Westcott. It was from a stag in the rutting season, a bit dark coloured and with a strong staggy smell. He was met with, "I'll take it, but it looks as though Colonel Wiggin's hounds could do with it." His next port of call was at Shircombe Farm; Hector was greeted with the words bawled out from the cowshed, "Twont roar in the crock I spose?" from Martin Westcott lying comfortably drunk in the manger. During the rut stags roar, bell or belve as they issue a strong vocal challenge to stags of the neighbourhood to keep away from their hinds, or the opposite message "I am a fit young stag come mate with me."

Work, of course, was always there to be done, each task or job according to the farming year. Unfailingly Sidney would be present to see that things were accomplished on time and in the proper manner. In contrast, Hector and Percy frequently left the farm.

The 1920s are sometimes referred to as the Roaring Twenties, with Hector and his cousin Percy Bawden doing their best to comply. There is no doubt whatsoever that Hector had inherited the genes of his grandfather James Bawden and possessed 'The Hawkridge Wild Streak'. This together with the continual need to seek relief from the feeling of guilt over Freddie's death led him to do extraordinary feats of bravery in normal people's eyes, as they were oblivious to his absence of fear.

His and Percy's trips to Bristol and elsewhere were always full of adventure. As Percy said "We'd never be home you see. If you didn't get home, you stopped somewhere else. It's hard to explain, it's a mad period. We both used to go to Bristol for a bit. Suddenly he'd say 'what about it then? Let's go'; we had to, but it left Uncle Sid holding the baby again, him having to do all the farm work."

Hector and Percy (left) in Exford with the Holly Tree behind them.

They would go to stay with Dolly after she had married Alec Chanter from Dulverton; Alec was chauffeur to Miss Abbot who at the time lived on the Downs at Clifton, Bristol. Dolly and Alec lived at 65 Alma Vale Road, Clifton. Only once did they go on Percy's motorbike, a racing Norton, as Hector preferred the comfort of his motorcar and he didn't always trust Percy's lust for speed. Percy after all, when he was working for his father's friend Harry Prideaux in his garage at Barnstaple, used to cover the 18 miles from Exford to Barnstaple in 26 minutes on the stone roads of those days. Another stretch of road Percy used to like was that from South Molton to Aller Cross where there was about a mile straight. He would wind up the Norton to about 90 mph. On one of the trips to Bristol, Hector wanted to take advantage of the flights being offered from Filton airfield it might have been part of Cobham's Flying Circus as Sir Alan Cobham in 1929 in a six month period visited over a hundred towns and cities promoting aviation in his deHavilland DH61, an eight seater single engine bi-plane. When airborne and in the vicinity of the Clifton Suspension Bridge, Hector did his best to try to get the pilot to fly under the bridge, alas no, just over it, he could never say "I've flown under the Bristol Suspension Bridge".

He had a fascination for the bridge and as it was but a short walk from Dolly's house, he and Percy went down one day for a closer look. When they had reached the middle Hector quick as a flash, was up onto the wooden handrail, wrapping his legs around it and dropping his body vertically down over the outside. It is 245 feet to the water at high tide and in the words of Percy, "If he'd fallen down there, he'd be a gonner, he wouldn't have survived that. They go up there now and commit suicide, see? Same place. When the man came out of the kiosk where they collect money and things at the Clifton end, cor he was shouting and waving his arms and all the rest of it."

"Now what are you doing? You want to come away from there! Why, what did you go out there for?" said the man.

"Oh I only wanted to see whether it was all bolted together or riveted,' said Hector

The man said, "You mustn't do that! People commit suicide up here jumping out over the top."

Sometimes their trips up to Bristol included going to see a football match, either Bristol City or Bristol Rovers. On the subject of football matches Hector also went on occasions with Vivian, son of Farmer Gregory from Draydon (neighbours across the valley, following the Pearses), who had a Brough Superior motorbike with a Swan sidecar, with Hector sitting in the sidecar enjoying the relative warmth and comfort it provided.

Funnily enough, I have never heard mention of alcohol on these trips but girls yes and here I quote Percy again: "He used to have some goes with the ladies mind. My gosh he was a smart chap when he was dressed up. Oh yeah 'cos Aunt Mary always used to say he aught to have gone in the film business with his profile and good looks, he would've done the trick, and he had – he got it from his father, that crafty little smile. Oh he used to go in the town hall in Dulverton, have a bit of a do; you know get the band going!"

A more peaceful caper came with the purchase, by Mary at a sale, of a small flat-bottomed boat, somewhat like a punt, in 1928 or '29. It was tried out on a small pond but that proved to be too tame, as it couldn't go far enough. There was nothing for it but to carry it down to the River Barle where great fun was had, being taken down the river by the force of the flow, and avoiding the multitude of rocks, just as the plethora of canoeists do today, during the winter months when the river is full of water. What's new? Unfortunately the effort of dragging the boat back up stream or carrying it back took the fun out of it and it was soon abandoned.

One of the highlights of the year was to visit Bampton Fair, which he did many times over the years, until about 1952. He frequently came out with the remark of "going to Bampton Fair with a shilling". He would, as he confessed to me, put the finishing touches of making himself smart by applying engine oil to his hair to slick it down and comb it in the reflection of the stable window. A shilling would give him all the amusement and entertainment from the sideshows and allow him to come home with a paper bag of brandy snaps. I remember, on perhaps his last visit, being given one as a treat, which indeed it was.

There was a mineshaft in one of the fields at Hinham, according to G.L.Hawkins's daughter Pauline Balder from New Zealand, *"Dad used to take his caravan and make camp in a field on the left not far from the house. I remember there was an old tin mine shaft in the field covered by corrugated sheets which we were warned to keep away from."* Hector could not resist the temptation of investigating it, his ingenuity resulted in a sixty foot rope ladder; this he attached to two stakes driven well into the ground and down he went the forty or sixty feet into the vertical shaft. Sadly there were no gold nuggets, lumps of silver ore or any interesting artefacts, only the rusty remains of a lantern.

Hunting, as I have said already, was never far from his thoughts and would have become an ongoing subject, particularly as every year a couple of hound pups would be sent to Hinham to be at walk. Spending the time from when they are weaned from the bitch, to when they become a mature hound ready to enter the pack makes or breaks a hound. They have to learn in a farm environment how to behave and relate to other animals, horses, humans etcetera. It is here that they are loved and encouraged to use their noses to acquire a repertory of scents, yet they will be chastised heavily if they do wrong, such as dig up the garden, enter the kitchen and steal food or heaven forbid chase and kill a cat. Hector being no cat lover would not have minded, indeed perhaps encouraged it, which would be of no use later in the hound's life when moving through a village or small town where cats were about.

At the end of the Great War replacement hounds for the pack became scarce and expensive. Fortunately Mr. H. Gosling, Master of the Garth, happened to visit Exford early in 1919, and at the request of the new huntsman, Ernest Bawden, presented a favourite old bitch, 'Harmless,' to the pack. Mating her with 'Comus' from the Heythrop produced a litter of seven pups that were reared successfully, one of them a bitch 'Harmony,' walked by the Heywoods at Hinham and immortalised in paint by Lionel Edwards. These were to become the foundation stones of a wholly homebred pack. The annual Puppy Show at the Kennels at Exford would have been a regular highlight for the puppy walkers such as the Heywoods. Hinham was a paradise for a hound pup and as they grew up were allowed, even encouraged to hunt the line of the deer as a portent of things to come.

On September 11th 1928 Mrs. Stone, who used to clean for Mary at Hinham, took Jean and John; together with her own two children, Clifford and Joyce, down the lane towards the River Barle in anticipation of seeing some action as hounds were about. Jean recalls that the stag had been brought to bay by the hounds in the river at the bottom of Hinham Lane. There was a lot of water going down, when in waded Hector and Tom Bawden from Cloggs, they each grabbed an antler and were all submerged on several occasions with the fighting stag before they brought it to the bank and it was dispatched. Jean was mortified at the sight of and thought of her brother getting drowned, consequently the words 'Found in Yamson, taken under Hinham September 11th 1928' are forever etched in her memory. The head was stuffed by a taxidermist for Col. Wiggin. When the Colonel retired he had a sale of surplus possessions including many good heads; Sidney bought this one which is still in Jean's family today.

Hector's two sisters Dolly and Marjory both rode hunting and Marjory rode in the pony races at Stoke Pero and Withypool. A Mr. Jack Hill from Henspark, Waddicombe near Dulverton gave Sidney a thoroughbred mare called 'Stella' from whom they had a foal 'Beeswing'; it was Beeswing that Marjory rode in the races. I have no recollections of Hector saying that he rode ponies or horses in his early life at Hinham, but he certainly did late in the 1930s. Instead his hunting was carried out in his car, indeed in the words of Percy Bawden it would seem that Hector was the first car follower: *"You see Aunt Mary was different, she was, in other words she preferred to mix with the elite; she was the first one to start this hunting lark with the vehicle or car you see. Following immediately*

after were the Misses Abbots, then there was a colonel from Porlock he was the next one on".
This is substantiated by Richard Stapledon in his book *Elegance and Rhythm.*

> *Soon after the First War ended cars began to appear at meets. And it was not long before a terrific sporting rivalry developed between three "chariots". Mrs. Abbot, Mr. and Mrs. Collingwood and Mrs. Heywood – Alec, Charlie and Hector were their respective "Jehus". In their eagerness to outwit each other and so to be first on the scene, they developed such craft and cunning which was as intense as it was times spectacular. They would stop at nothing and their finesse was a joy to watch compared with the rather ignorant tactics of some present-day enthusiasts. At that time cars were open, and I have seen Mrs. Abbot bounced quite a foot out of the back seat, also Mrs. Heywood in the redoubtable "Tin Lizzie" almost thrown out of the back of the car with most of the family! But it was all clean stuff, so different from today.*

This book was printed in about 1967, what, I wonder, would Richard Stapleton say today 2012?

On non-car hunting days when the meet was a local one, Mary Heywood would take herself to her seat on a tree stump on Brewer's Castle the site of the Iron Age hill fort opposite to Mounsey Castle in the Barle valley. Hector had at some time removed trees and bushes in a swathe down to the river, so it was an easy task to keep it clear of growth. This enabled his mother to have a good view straight down to the river, she could also see down to the Danesbrook if she turned her head. I again quote Richard Stapleton:

> *I can recollect no woman – except Mrs Slader of Hacche – who was blessed with such keen sight or who possessed such a deep knowledge of wild life and deer in particular. She used to regard hinds as her special prerogative. On hunting days she would leave the farm for her "throne" on Brewer's Castle in the Barle valley; and there she would sit, apparently engrossed with the sock she was knitting. But no hind coming down or up the water could escape her eagle eye. When Ernest was casting the water and on coming to the "Castle" he would pause momentarily to await her signal; if there was no response, he would immediately take hounds back again – so great was his trust in his sister!*

Is it any wonder that Hector was to develop into such a knowledgeable man in the realms of nature, birds and hunting?

There is no family record of Sidney riding hunting whilst at Hinham as I am sure his time was taken up with the farm, being the diligent person he was. There is however an article from *Country Life* that reveals that he was riding Ernest Bawden's famous and favourite mare 'Gina' on 16th August 1927. This was the time when his brother in law was reaching his peak as huntsman, and the beginning of the golden years of the Devon and Somerset Staghounds.

I take these words from Paddy King-Fretts:

> *There are many points of note about this remarkable hunt. First the sheer distance, although the point was thirteen and a half miles that is more or less as the crow flies. A study of the map and measuring between the points mentioned makes the distance just over twenty-five and would have been further still had the measurements followed the actual routes taken. Secondly the climb, Dulverton stands at 500ft above sea level but Exe Head is over 1,500ft and they ran straight over it. However one must add to that the numerous combes and valleys between which all but trebled the total height climbed. In short it was the equivalent to a run from the Exe at Tiverton to Barnstaple but with a three thousand foot climb in between.*
>
> *How much more Bawden would have ridden it is impossible to say but the hack to the meet was six miles and the ride home at the end of the very long day was a further eight. And what of the Huntsman himself? The report says he took to his feet and ran across the Exe valley. That would have been the best part of a mile, flat out through bog and sedge, the runner in hunting boots, cord breeches, heavy hunting coat with waistcoat underneath, plus hat, whip and horn – and the man was fifty!*

All I can add is that it was a seventeen mile hack home to Hinham for Sidney, now aged fifty-one, this together with the twenty-five miles mentioned above, measured

A GREAT DAY ON EXMOOR.

Dulverton, that sporting little town on the River Barle, in the south-eastern corner of Exmoor, has recently rebuilt its Town Hall, and the honour of opening it was offered to and accepted by the Master of the Devon and Somerset Staghounds, who on the 16th inst. attended in his official capacity to declare the building open. He was supported by his wife and a large number of local sportsmen and sportswomen. The ceremony over, a great meet was held in the Fore Street, which little thoroughfare was choked to overflowing with riders and motors and a dense and enthusiastic crowd of footpeople and cyclists. It did one's heart good to see such keenness. Bawden, supported by Lenthall and Slocombe, had the bitch pack out, and it was a very notable occasion, for the whole pack comprised bitches only to the number of 20½ couple, including 6 couple of young hounds. Never before, it is considered, has a pack of bitches only been used from the Devon and Somerset kennels, and the good sportsmen of Dulverton and district were appreciative of the honour thus extended by the Master.

The morning, remarkable to relate, was fine with clouded skies, and after all the recent downpours one longed for a non-mackintosh day. In any case a grand gallop was in store for the large field, and it will be seen that out of the large numbers who followed the pack out of Dulverton to Hinam Farm to kennel very few indeed ever reached far-distant Badgworthy and the end. Ned Lang had a good stag harboured in Buckminster Wood, near Castle Bridge, in the Barle Valley, and tufters roused him at once. He broke away through Lower Durham Wood, crossed the Danesbrook to Hawkridge, and so into Three Waters Cleeve, where he joined some hinds, but tufters stuck to him and forced him over Hawkridge again to Church Wood, and to the Danesbrook below. Then came a downstream course and up right-handed to White Rocks and Five Cross Ways, where the cars and footers blanched him, so he turned back over the Hinam enclosures to the plantation of that name and gained Shircombe Slade and Wind Ball, where tufters were stopped and the pack sent for and laid on. Hounds went away to Burridge Wood, overhanging Dulvertown town, and here the stag joined another, and both had to hop it to such purpose that they soon got separated, and the rightful deer broke back up valley to Draydon Ford, where he crossed the Barle. The water was coming down in spate after the previous night's heavy rains, and hounds were encouraged over by Lenthall, who had been sent round by Marsh Bridge. No horse could ford the stream, so there was a rush for Thornton's Bridge higher up, and Bawden was given way and quickly got in touch again with hounds in Ashwick Woods and Mounsey Castle. A hind now got in the way and led part of the pack astray, but the main force held to their stag and hunted him across the Barle to Buckminster Wood, White Rocks Down, and on towards Drucombe Gate, where occurred a check and evidently a change on to another stag.

At this point the pack was reinforced by the hounds that had gone astray for hinds, and a fresh lay-on took place, when hounds raced away at a great pace over Anstey Common, Molland Common, and Moorhouse Ridge, to sink to Lower Willingford Bridge, where the deer had roused two hinds. Bawden stopped hounds off these and cast forward to Sloleys Allotment and hit the stag's line off to a nicety, hounds streaming away to New Plantation in Lords, left-handed on to Worth Hill, and across Withypool Common to the Barle above Lanacre Bridge. Hounds took an up-stream course and soon hit the line from the left bank up the hillside to Bradimoor and across it to the top of Shutscombe Bottom and the fields of Ashett Farm. Then on very fast up Ashett Bottom to Gipsy Lane and Honeymead and the road between Exford and Simonsbath, which the deer had crossed for the Prayway Wall, which he had followed for a mile ere turning down to the Exe River below Warren Meads. Owing to the steep and boggy ground Bawden had to foot it across the Exe Valley while his horse was sent round by Black Pits Gate to Trout Hill on the north side, where hounds carried on into Buscombe to receive a short check. Bawden held downstream, and at a sheep clammer hounds picked up the scent again and carried on to the upper reaches of the Badgworthy. The heavy waters had done the stag good service so far, but hounds hit off his line up into Oare Deer Park, and in the long heather at the top of Woodcock Combe worked right up to him and roused him out of it. A wild dash down to the Badgworthy Water near the famous waterslide, where the rhododendrons grow, was the last movement of this long and arduous chase, and at 4.15 the mort echoed in the wild haunts of the legendary Doones.

The stag was a light galloping one, and carried a nice even head, with brow, trey, and upright both sides. Except for 2 couple of hounds that went astray at Willingford Bridge, all were up at the finish. The day's hunting made a point of thirteen and a half miles straight across the map, but as hounds ran it cannot be short of twenty, and over a beautiful line of country, particularly after Drucombe Gate. The moor was riding very wet, and horses had a severe gruelling, many saddles emptying after reaching the open moor north of Honeymead. Not many were up at the finish, but among the gallant band of die-hards, in addition to the Master and Bawden, were four stout-hearted south-country farmers who had galloped from the rouse to the kill. They were Sydney Westcott (Hawkridge), Maurice Westcott (Anstey), Sydney T. Heywood (Hinam), on Bawden's famous mare Gina, and Tom Bawden (Cloggs).

"A Great day on Exmoor".
Hunting report from *Country Life*.

on a flat map that cannot take into account the extra distance covered going up and down hills would make the forty-two miles nearer to fifty that Sidney and Gina would have covered. Having been lent such a prize asset for the day I feel sure that Sidney would have looked after her, giving her a rest where possible by jumping off, and taking the best route maybe cutting corners via short cuts, making the best use of his local knowledge, perhaps having shouted suggestions by Ernest, mindful of Gina, galloping past. All in all a day for the history books especially this one!

I see from notes by Admiral Steve Ritchie in *Harbourer* the official hunt newsletter July 2007 making reference to this day 'We were to see the body of the stag when it was brought to Hinham in Hector's car where he showed us how to skin and butcher the carcass before distributing portions of venison to farmers in the district'.

It is worth recording the way Christmas was celebrated at Hinham, which is so different from today's goings on. The important feature was the burning of the ashen faggot on Christmas Eve. This was a large faggot made of ash sticks and bound tightly with hazel or withy bands. In the evening when the time was right, drinks were poured, the ashen faggot put on the open fire and as each band went snack a toast was drunk. The only people to receive presents were John and Jean who had a stocking at the end of their beds. They also tied up hay on a gate for the reindeer.

- 7 -

A DECADE OF SADNESS

SIR GEORGE WILLS, president of Imperial Tobacco died in 1928. Sir Gilbert Wills his nephew then became president and in the following year was raised to the peerage by being created 1st Lord of Dulverton. As a result, Sir Gilbert decided to sell his Northmoor Estate and offered all sitting tenants the chance to buy their farms. Sidney must have felt it the right thing to do and accordingly took out either a mortgage or a loan from the bank. Indeed, it was only having sight of a letter written by Mary to her brother Harold and making reference to it that confirmed the vague idea in the family that Sidney did buy Hinham. It was so unfortunate that the next year, 1929, saw the Wall Street Crash and the beginning of the Great Depression. The buying of Hinham, and probably a further 77 acres, and a pair of cottages at the top of Hinham Lane became a millstone around his neck. Hinham was 92 acres when Sidney first went in as tenant, and was 169 acres when sold in 1943. It is only guesswork as to when the extra land was added but the sale of the estate would seem a good opportunity, especially as life, apart from Freddy's death, had been fairly plain sailing up until then, with no portent of things to come.

With good fortune, Alan Bawden produced two letters that his father Harold received from Mary. They reveal the extent of the financial difficulties that the family were experiencing.

Haynham
Dulverton   Jan 7th 1930

Dear Harold,
You will wonder why I am writing but this morning Master has heard from the Bank and he has overdrawn his account; and I am wondering whether you could let me have £50 until April. Master has kept 5 bullocks and has them in Dulverton to eat the hay that we were unlucky enough to spoil (for sale), and he finds now that by paying up his bills that he is short, and he does not want to sell the bullocks now, as he has started the rick of hay and it is the wrong time to sell the bullocks now to make the best of them. I am writing this to you as I feel sure if it is possible you would help us just now. I will see you are paid as soon as ever we sell the bullocks and the interest too, that is if you really can lend it to me. I am ever so sorry to worry you and I hope you will not think that we are getting in a poor way. Of course I blame Master really as I'd much rather he sold them longer ago and made sure of having his accounts at the bank more in order. But as you know he is no man for business it's all very well as long as things go on all right, but as soon as things are otherwise he does not worry to put them right. I've had a time of it and I find that I have to see to things more than ever, he is getting very dull. Perhaps you would kindly write to me as soon as you can. The banks are far different to deal with than what they were in years gone by.

I get worried dreadfully somehow having had such trouble over the buying and losing money on this place and Master's Mother's affairs. I get such a bad head at times, I feel wretched, and it's nothing more than worry that has caused it.

We've all had the colds dreadfully they are all now just on the mend thank goodness. I hope Nell and the children + yourself are keeping fit. I should like to come up but must leave it till the summer, it's terribly cold and such a white frost we can hardly put up with it.

Good bye with love to all from Mary

Please Harold don't let Ernest know as he is so fussy and narrow-minded.

Again the next year, there is another request to her brother for help:

Haynham,
Dulverton   10.1.31

Dear Harold,

We are in receipt of registered packet with bank notes value of value £40 and Marjorie have this forenoon paid it into the Bank. I am extremely obliged to you for your kindness, and it shall be paid back to you in April with interest. I hate to write to you but thought it best to try to put matters more in order than be worried.

I can assure you it was much against my principle to ask you to loan us the money and I hope it will be the last time I'll have to do such an unpleasant bit of business, enclosed please find receipt with best thanks.

I am awfully sorry to hear you have the Flu. I do hope you will soon get over it. The weather has changed thank goodness. I always think frosty weather brings illness. We have been jolly rotten lately, all of us but we are on the mend now.

There has been no hunting lately I'll send you a bit of venison the next we have.

Hope the baby is growing and all improving.

With love

from Mary

Accompanying this letter there is a receipt signed by S.T.Heywood over a tuppenny stamp.

Harold Bawden was five years younger than Mary and had gone to Wiltshire on leaving Hawkridge to be with his elder brother Jim, working on a threshing and baling gang. This followed time in the army during the First World War, and during one period of leave he came to the kennels at Exford, where he met his wife Nell, a nurse; they were married in 1920, and went back to manage a farm in Wiltshire. It is interesting that Harold was in a position to help his sister and brother in law not once but twice during very difficult times. His wages were a mere £3 per week but they did have a cow, poultry and rabbits were plentiful. This meant that there was milk, butter and eggs for sale to supplement his income. They were the last people to live in the farmhouse at Eddington near Westbury as it was destroyed in the last war as a target for artillery and tanks. He was very close to Mary and every year he and his family would visit Hinham for their fortnightly holiday during autumn stag hunting. Harold would hire a horse from 'Farmer Fry', that is Edgar Fry from Old Shute, to ride hunting. Old Shute had been, until sold to the sitting tenant, a farm on the Wills's Northmoor Estate adjacent to Hinham. Hector became great friends with Harold's son Ken and would later work with him in farm contracting work.

One incident of excitement came on August 8th 1931. From the 'Fifty Years Ago' column in the *West Somerset Free Press* August 7th 1981, it read, "*Anti-staghunters demonstrated at the opening meet of the Devon and Somerset Staghounds at Cloutsham. In struggles with hunt supporters banners and umbrellas were ripped up. Cheers were given for the police 'who handled the situation tactfully'*". Dense fog prevented any hunting.

Hector recounted the incident to me:

"*A lot of hunt supporters turned up in anticipation of some kind of struggle between the rival parties. I well remember seeing my Mother race at Mrs. Walker-King and rip the umbrella out of her hand. We had it as a souvenir at Hinham for many years. Hemingway, the leading member of the opposition was there with his camera to take pictures. We surrounded him, including myself and forced him back down towards Webber's Post. During the scuffle he dropped his camera in the ford at Cloutsham. But he was very quick to retrieve it. We met the police coming in the road towards Cloutsham and they led Mr. Hemingway back to his car at Webber's Post. As far as I can remember he never again appeared at a meet of the Staghounds. Two years after this Mother died April 1st 1933."*

Did Mary become a sufferer of the depression that Hector was to experience later in life? Was there a clue when she wrote, "I get such a bad head at times, I feel wretched, it's nothing more than worry"? In years to come Hector would also say, "my head's bad" when his depression was in the black dog stage. Did carrying the woes and cares of not only the family but the farm as well and all the worry and unhappiness help the onset of cancer? According to her funeral report in the *West Somerset Free Press*, Mary was in ill health for twelve months, and spent a spell in Minehead and West Somerset Hospital, coming home two months before she died on April 1st 1933, aged 53. Hector recalled to me the fearful anguish of having to hear his mother screaming with pain and begging for morphine. To lose his mother so agonisingly must have been a dreadful blow to Hector, as he had occupied a special place in her heart after Freddie had gone, but then again all the family would have felt the loss and been affected in different ways. Her coffin was brought up from Hinham by horse and Kerry-cart led by Bill Stone from Hinham Cottages past Castle Bridge and up the long pull over some very rocky ground, through Great Gate and over Hawkridge Ridge, and the bearers were four cousins, one of who was 'Uncle Jack' – J.F. Clatworthy from Westwater. She was buried in Hawkridge churchyard. Fred Clatworthy, son of Jack, was fittingly much later to be a bearer of Hector's coffin.

Mary's passing left Marjory, now aged 25, in charge of the household at Hinham, she did all the cooking of meals, housework, and all the chores. She was also in charge of the summer visitors, welcoming them and seeing to their needs. Dolly had married and was living in Bristol; Jean was aged 13, John 10 and both going to school. It would have been a bonus that Hector and Marjory were very fond of one another, as she would have helped control his volatile, ready temper. He even permitted her to drive his car!

At the back of the venison distribution book is written a poem, in unidentified handwriting possibly that of Marjory. I reproduce it here with its slight mistakes, as I feel it reflects the sentiment of this sad time.

Isle of Beauty

Shades of evening close not o'er us
Leave our lonely bark awhile
Morn alas! Will not restore us
Yonder dim and distant Isle
Still my fancy can discover
Sunny spots where friends may dwell
Darker shadows round us hover
Isle of beauty fare the well

2
Tis the hour when happy faces
Smile around the taper's light
Who will fill our vacant places?
Who will sing our songs tonight?
Through the mist that floats above us
Faintly sounds the vesper bell
Like a voice from those who love us
Breathing fondly, fare thee well

3
When the waves are round us breaking
As I pace the deck alone
And my eye in vain is seeking
Some green leaf to rest upon
What would I not give to wonder?
Where my old companions dwell
Absence makes the heart grow fonder
Isle of beauty fare thee well

The End

Was this a valediction to Mary? It might well have been. Was it an antidote to the loss of his mother that Hector began his other lifelong passion around this time, of bird nesting and collecting eggs? As a man so at one with nature, bird life would always have been an everyday observation, so that he became familiar with song, food, nests and eggs as a matter of course. Amongst his few personal possessions is a hard backed notebook, with one page at the back listing nests found and birds seen, five of these in the month of May following his mother's death. This list illustrates the diversity of species on Exmoor at that time, and the extent of his travels: -

Dolly; Hector, Marjory with Jean in front, about 1923.

Twite	Nest found Racecourse	
	Anstey Common	May 1933
Pied Flycatcher	Nest found Three Waters (Barle valley)	May 1933
Kingfisher	Nest found Winsford	May 1933
Sandpiper	Nest found Landacre Bridge	May 1933
Grasshopper Warbler	Nest found Rackenford Moor	May 1933
Siskin	Seen Hinham	Feb 25th 1934
Brambling	Seen Hinham	Feb 1934
Red Backed Shrike	Nest found Bossington	May 1934
Peregrine Falcon	Seen Molland Moor	Dec 21st 1934
Raven	Nest found Deer Park	March 10th 1935
Hen Harrier	Seen Braunton Burrows	May 5th 1935
Peregrine Falcon	Nest found Treborough Quarries	May 12th 1935
Oystercatcher	Nest found Hartland Quay	May 29th 1935
Woodlark	Nest found Hinham	March 10th 1936
Crow	Nest found Old Barrow	April 27th 1936
Ring Ouzel	Nest found Weir Water	May 1936
Redshank	Nest found Porlock	May 8th 1936
Merlin	Nest found Poulthouse Combe	June 5th 1936
Chiff Chaff	Seen Hinham	March 21st 1937
Wheatear	Seen Hinham	March 9th 1938
Lesser Spotted Woodpecker	Nest found Three Waters	May 23rd 1938
Chiff Chaff	Seen Bodmin Cornwall	March 24th 1939
Lesser Spotted Woodpecker	Nest found Three Waters	June 13th 1939

Hector, enlisting or perhaps as they would see it, press-ganging Jean aged 13 and John aged 10, found the Grasshopper warbler's nest on Rackenford Moor. They walked several yards apart and in line back and forth across the moor until the bird flipped off the nest. This was to be one of the few times they ever went out with their brother.

In 2009 I spoke with 98-year-old Henry Horseman, who told me that he had taught Jean at Dulverton School and had met Hector. Henry, a Yorkshireman, was also a keen ornithologist and had first taught at Porlock School, before moving to Dulverton. When

Hector told him that he was trying to locate a Redshank's nest and thought that they nested in reed beds, Henry was able to put him straight by saying go to look on the pebble ridge in Porlock Bay. From the above list he had obviously found it, and was heard to say "That's the one I have been looking for, for ages," Henry was amazed at Hector's ability to recognise birds at a distance.

By 1930 Hector had changed his motorcar to a Wolseley 12/16 Open Tourer. This model first came out in 1912 so one can quite understand Percy Bawden saying that "The Wolseley was rather vintage, it had a four speed box, not a bad old vehicle but it was a bit of a shift down from the T model Ford". Hector christened it 'Belinda', it was coloured brown and had a dicky seat (that is a fold out seat at the rear of the car). Most important of all it had plenty of room for a deer carcase, probably tied onto the dicky seat.

'Belinda'

Mary's brother Harold decided that he wanted to come back to Exmoor, and had accumulated enough money to consider buying a farm. When West Liscombe Farm, East Anstey came onto the market he asked Sidney to act on his behalf at the auction. The 80-acre farm was knocked down at £1700 on the first of November 1934. Early in 1935 they moved down from Wiltshire, Marjory met them at Dulverton Station in Belinda. On arrival and walking into the farmhouse, Harold and his wife Nell were shocked to find that conditions were very primitive, a complete open fire in the kitchen with nothing else to cook on, and the walls just whitewashed. Marjory in her good-natured way said "Don't worry I'll come in and paper it for you with wallpaper". Good as her word she did just that. Marjory was never talked about much by Hector when he was alive, so my picture of her is sketchy. She was a quiet, kindly soul just like her father Sidney, very similar to her sister Dolly, and a hard worker. She was a very good horsewoman, loved riding and had success at Exford Show winning the local mare and foal class; Marjory hunted with the staghounds and competed in the many pony-racing meetings around Exmoor with great success, on 'Beeswing'.

Imagine the shock, the worry, and the awful anticipation when Marjory was finally diagnosed with tuberculosis or consumption as it used to be called. This is a disease as old as man, way back in 460BC Hippocrates identified phthisis (the Greek term for TB) as the most widespread disease of the times, involving coughing up blood and fever which was almost always fatal. It was not until 1946 with the development of streptomycin that effective treatment and cure became possible. She went up to Winsley Sanatorium near Bath through the kindness and generosity of the Robinsons who lived

Harold Bawden and Sidney Heywood with a fine stag's head at Hinham.

at Marsh Hill House, lower down the Barle valley. Hector used to visit her, taking Jean in his car with him. Eventually Marjory came back to Hinham to end her days. The role of running the home now passed to Jean aged fifteen; she also did sterling work nursing her sister through those dark days. Help came in the evenings when Jessie Baker would walk from near Dulverton, or Nell Bawden would walk in from West Liscombe bringing flowers or something nice to eat, to sit with Marjory through the night. This enabled the others to get some sleep. She died at the end of February 1938, aged 31.

The grey carthorse Diamond seen here at Hinham with the Hawkins children astride, four years before in 1934, towed a long flat cart with Marjory's coffin on it up to Hawkridge church. Perhaps it was the same outfit that took her Mother's coffin five years previously.

I too had a ride on Diamond when I was aged three, at Cloutsham, and once had a ride in the cart she was pulling, before she disappeared.

Diamond produced a colt foal, appropriately named 'Jubilee' in 1935, being the Silver Jubilee of George V. When Sidney went to mow a field of grass for hay in the meadow just above Marsh Bridge, a mile or so down the river from Hinham, the foal went too. It was shut in a small linhay whilst Diamond pulled the mowing machine, then let out at intervals to have a suck. At the end of the day it trotted along behind Diamond to go home. Very sadly when Jubilee was about a year old he trod on a rusty nail, got tetanus and died. There were no antibiotics or vaccines in those days to help such cases. Diamond never had another foal.

The loss of Marjory, although a merciful release for her, was a bitter blow to the family coming so soon after the death of Mary. Hector by now aged thirty had lost his elder brother Freddy, his mother Mary whom he adored, and now a favoured sister of whom he was especially fond. It is possible that it enhanced or caused the insomnia

'Diamond'

that became apparent around about this time. Having gone to bed early, as was his habit, so akin to the natural world, if there was any noise, or light to interrupt sleep, look out! Jean and John readily recall trying to listen to the wireless or just talking when they would be greeted by bumping on the floor or an irate Hector's head round the door telling them loudly to be quiet. The very same would occur during my teenage years when I would be at home talking to my sister or mother, "Can't you buggers be quiet, I want to get to sleep" or if we were hunched over the wireless listening to Radio Luxemburg, with the volume turned right down low, it would be worse "Turn that bloody litter off, it's time you went to bed."

His other medical problem of indigestion could also have been a direct result of the stress of their deaths. By the end of the war when he stayed at West Liscombe in 1946, whilst he was harborouring, he was heard to say "Cor don't I feel bad Auntie". Also during my life with him "My guts are bad" was quite a common occurrence. It was not until the National Health Service came into being in 1948 that he was able to get free, positive help in the form of barbiturate sleeping tablets; and he was opened up by Dr. Tatlow in Minehead Hospital in a fruitless search for ulcers. Thereafter an important ingredient in his daily life were a variety of antacids, and a regular supply of peppermints, the consumption of each rose or fell according to the stress he faced. Today's drugs Zantac or Lansoprazole would have given untold relief, as he was no doubt producing excess gastric juices; the drug in effect tells the brain to tell the stomach to cut back on production.

As a man who took great pride in the things he did, or achieved, he was well rewarded in the construction of a bonfire on Court Down, a piece of high ground above Dulverton, to mark the 1935 Silver Jubilee. This was to be lit as part of the national chain of beacons. Faggots of wood were prepared at Hinham and on neighbouring farms, and then carried to the site were Hector and chums built the fire. What an impressive achievement.

Below left: Building the 1935 Silver Jubilee bonfire. Hector is second from the left, Sidney on his right, and his pal Monty Pearse on his left.

Below right: On top of the finished work, Hector is planting the Union Jack.

A cutting from the *West Somerset Free Press* found in Hector's small suitcase of treasured items, reveals that he was actively involved in the 'Farmers' Ball' held in the Dulverton Town Hall in1935, to raise money for the Dulverton Foxhounds (before they were split into two packs, East and West in 1940). He was Hon. Secretary to the organising committee and had the responsibility of decorating the hall; he was chief gatherer of greenery. The article tells of 250 people being present, quite some party for the Town Hall, which is modest in size. A group photo shows Hector in his dinner jacket, wing collar and black tie sitting on the floor, in the middle of the front row, looking life and soul of the party. His sister Jean, third on his right has her mouth open laughing with John on her right.

About this time Hector started to take an active interest in harbouring deer for the D&S Staghounds. The official harbourer was Ned Lang whose job it was to locate the right deer for hunting, be it a bunch of hinds, some spring stags or the individual older autumn stag. The autumn stags were the most difficult as they were the most cunning, and able to avoid detection in the full foliage before the leaf fall. It was important to remove the dominant older stags to avoid father on daughter mating, with its attendant problems of inbreeding. The harbourer had to use all his powers of tracking i.e. reading the slots to find a warrantable stag, with endless hours of looking through binoculars seeing but not being seen, as the deer have an acute sense of smell, the slightest whiff of danger such as a human, and they are off. He does his work in the evening before a meet; having spoken to local farmers for a few clues he will walk, ride or drive, until he sees signs of a stag or stags. He would hope to get a sight of a suitable one as it makes its way out of the woods or deep bracken beds in twighlight to its feeding ground, in order to identify how many points it has on its antlers. In the morning he has to be up before daylight, in order to be on site, to observe the stag or stags going back from their feeding ground to their beds. The big autumn stag prefers to be on his own, quietly putting on condition before the rut when there are more important things on his mind, and to be done, than eating food! The harbourer has to be absolutely certain of where his stag is lying, and then he leaves him at the last possible minute to

The Farmers' Ball, Dulverton Town Hall 1935.

go to the meet to report to the Master followed by the huntsman. He will then lead the huntsman and the tufters (older, more dependable and more biddable hounds) to rouse the stag from his bed, to begin a perhaps glorious hunt. It is easy to overlook the fact that the weather is not always clement, but can be bitterly cold or driving rain that finds every gap in clothing to wet or freeze, or both. The minute that eyes come off the quarry is the moment he will choose to evaporate; however the rewards for hard endeavour and enduring hardship are very satisfying.

Hector told me that as Ned Lang began to fail Ernest would often turn to his nephew and say, " Do you know of anything?" Ned Lang became jealous and would never call at Hinham to see if Hector knew of the whereabouts of any stags, but would go straight to Hawkridge to look for one himself.

September 5th 1935 there was a special meet at Molland Moor Gate, a short memorial service was conducted by the Suffragan Bishop of Taunton for Phillip Froude Hancock who had died in 1933. He then unveiled a large memorial stone to his memory, which is sited upon part of Anstey Common, purchased by public subscription. This lump of rock was hewn from G.B. Fisher's quarry in Northmoor Road, Dulverton and created quite a problem as it broke the first vehicle it was placed on. It was brought up onto the moor by a steam lorry, not by Windball Hill or Andrews Hill, but by Cottage Lane out of Dulverton. Froude Hancock 1865-1933 was one of ten brothers, five of whom played rugby for Somerset, and brother Frank was a Welsh international. Froude played for Blackheath and was an original member of the Barbarians; he played for the British Isles XV against South Africa on the tours of 1891 and 1896. He was a giant of a man and played in the scrum as a forward. He was a member of the family business, the Arnold and Hancock Brewery at Wiveliscombe. His other great passion was hunting on Exmoor, with the Dulverton Hunt and the D&S Staghounds, having been Field Master back in 1907 with the latter pack. He was loved and respected by all who knew him, including Hector. When Hector was in his last years, he had a photo of him along with some other notable figures of the hunt to decorate his room. It is worth to record the entry in Ernest Bawden's private diary to illustrate two things, one the feelings towards Froude Hancock and secondly to show the prose from one who was educated at home, by his mother Harriet Bawden: -

"In my humble opinion he was the greatest authority on Staghunting ever, his great knowledge of the country enabling him invariably to get in at the end, no matter how long or difficult the day might be. He always took a great interest in the staff no matter whether on or off the hunting field and rarely, if ever, did he fail with a cheery word if the staff had had a hard and unsuccessful day.

Most people are loud enough in their praise when a great triumph has been scored but few ever remember that it is the cases of disappointment when hounds and servants need sympathy and encouragement most. His kindly manner and complete understanding of Westcountry people had endeared him to all…He will assuredly go down in history as the greatest Staghunter of them all."

Hector referred to this day as "Catching the stag twice in a day." Ned Lang had harboured a stag (an autumn stag) on this occasion in the Parish Quarry at the top of Hardway leading up from Penny Gate on the River Barle. "When Ernest Bawden and Ned Lang went to rouse the stag my car was positioned on the opposite side of the road. The stag was so confused it did not know which way to break, it tried to burst its way through the beech fence opposite, and the tufters had got him by his haunches. I grabbed his antlers as he tried to force his way through the beech fence; at that moment Ernest Bawden came out of the gate from the quarry and saw the stag and me on the ground. He shouted 'Let him go, let him go' the stag got to its feet and galloped off down Hardway. I later took the stag (shot it), after going through the streets of Dulverton, on the sawdust pile from the Lion Hotel stables. The procession down Lady Street was firstly Captain H.P. Hewitt's horse, and then the stag followed by me in my car. The stag gored the horse up the backside." As a sign of the times the site of the Lion Hotel stables is now a car park!

8

TOUGH TIMES OF CHANGE
AND THE END OF HINHAM

SIDNEY HEYWOOD, having purchased Hinham Cottages in 1926 from the Northmoor Estate with a mortgage from his brother in law Ernest, which may or may not have been the actual time of buying Hinham Farm as well, is down on a legal document as selling the two cottages to Ernest 7th January 1928. Ernest must have had an ulterior motive, maybe thinking of his ultimate retirement, perhaps a future home, or perhaps as an act of kindness to provide two cottages for any member of the family, or workman. When he did retire in May 1937 it was to a new bungalow that he had had built just beyond Hinham farmhouse. This must have been started in 1936 to be ready for May 1937. At some stage Ernest had taken the millstone from Sidney's neck, the mortgage on the farm, and discharged it to become the new owner of Hinham.

Judging by entries in the venison distribution book, that side of life went on. Hector was 33 years old when Marjory died and now his forceful personality dominated the household in spite of his father, as there would be no one left to rein him in. Sidney worked on in his quiet, kind, reliable way; he reminds me of "Boxer" the carthorse, in George Orwell's *Animal Farm* saying, "I will work harder". Hector was the bane of Jean's life, frequently raiding the larder if he was hungry with no regard to the forthcoming meals; he would attack the cream bowl with a vengeance, to have with the oddments of comb honey that he hadn't sold. He had been instructed in the art of bee keeping by Bill Stone at Hinham Cottage, and had acquired several hives that he kept in the orchard between the farmhouse and woods. Selling sections of comb honey was another modest source of income. Around this time he possessed a Cairn cross terrier, 'Fido' and a collie 'Rover'. For some reason he worshiped his dogs, and they him, as I was to see twenty years later. He took delight in setting Fido onto John saying "Bite him Fido, bite him". John somewhat frightened used to hate these episodes of the dog nipping him or his trousers. I can only guess that Hector was channelling his emotions into his dogs in place of others to love. The entry in his notebook was: -

Sunday Nov 20th.1938.
  Had my darling Fido put down today.
  HH.

This was followed by another, two days later: -
  Tuesday Nov 22nd 1938. The Park Deer Accounted for.

After an exciting chase from Summerhouse, Rover and I accounted for the park stag in Hinam Lane at 8.30 a.m. An old deer probably fifteen years old, brow, tray, and two, brow, tray and an upright.

It is hard to comprehend how Hector could be so soft with his dogs and yet be so hard in dealing with other animals, thinking nothing of dispatching them with gun or knife.

During the late 1930s Sir Alfred Munnings, the well known artist and Royal Academician, and his wife used to come down from London to their cottage in Wootton

Courtenay or, during the War, their house in Withypool. They sometimes had a day hunting with the Devon and Somerset on their own horses, and if the meet was in the Barle valley area they stabled them at Hinham. Their horses would be hacked to the farm the day before by one of their grooms, either Harry Bayfield or Tom Slocombe, and it was Jean's job as often as not, to look after them. The horses would have to be ready at such and such a time when the Munnings would arrive by motor car, leave it and Lady Munning's Pekinese dogs in Jean's charge and ride off. On their return Jean had to be ready with the Pekinese to pass them up to Lady Munnings to kiss and fuss over before she dismounted her horse. Sir Alfred told Jean one day that he wished he had brought his paints as she made such a picture doing whatever it was, and he would love to have painted her. Hector told me that Sir Alfred did paint Diamond the cart horse as he had a fascination and great love of greys. Where is it now? Sir Alfred was very friendly with Hector's cousin Froude Bawden and his wife Gladys from Newland Farm, Withypool and produced several paintings of their ponies, sheep and cattle. He produced a wonderful portrait of Gladys on her thoroughbred mare, Harmony, a granddaughter of the famous horse The Tetrarch. Gladys won many local horse races on the mare. Sir Alfred gave her the picture and it hung above the fireplace in the parlour. Where is that picture now?

Nobody is sure when Hector met Joan Nicholson; vague references to them seeing one another have been made as to about 1933/4 onwards. I will devote a chapter to her later, but will tell a couple of stories about Withypool, as told me by the late John Blackmore which are chronologically correct. A Mr. Bob Stewart, who lived at Mill Cleave at the time, was an avid moth collector. Hector used to go out looking for moths with him and helped him when they had a nighttime session, Joan would be in on it as well. At night a large sheet was hung up in front of the car with headlamps blazing and anything of significance was netted by Bob Stewart. When a change was needed, down with the sheet and move on to a fresh site. John Blackmore said it was all part of their courtship. Bob Stewart was a very good shot and organised a small clay pigeon shoot at Uppington, John Blackmore, Hector, Froude Bawden from Newlands Farm, Tom Barrow, Mr. Heale and one or two more took part. "I've only got an old hammer gun," said John, "Have one of mine," said Hector. John hits 14 out of 15 "this is easy" he said. John told me he went to another shoot with his own gun and never hit a thing. Hector had two hammerless guns. On the odd occasion when John had ridden with Hector out hunting he said that he was not wild on a horse, didn't go mad, he was a good rider. I think that at other times he might well have been very different, I will illustrate that later.

Ernest Bawden coming to live in his new bungalow at Hinham on May 1st 1937 cast a gloom over everything. For Hector it was a love hate relationship. Ernest had been an inspiration to Hector bordering upon hero worship; they were after all so very similar in all aspects, looks, behaviour and neither suffered fools gladly, yet they could be absolutely charming when they chose to be. They were, in the words of Percy Bawden, both hewn from the same tree and both possessed the dreaded Hawkridge wild streak. It was inevitable that there would be a clash of Titans at some point in time.

Ernest was now lord of all he surveyed, and without the pressing demands of being in charge at the hunt kennels, began in his sergeant major manner to assert himself in all spheres with boundless energy. Firstly it was to be tidying the bungalow surrounds and creating his garden; then it was the deer coming into the fields that he could not countenance. Whereas over the years a continual war of sorts had been waged against them, from now on Ernest felt it his bounden duty that no deer were to trespass on his land at all. This is a bit rich for a man whose life had depended upon the deer, and their survival, and getting on to farmer's land was an accepted happening. A massive fencing operation was undertaken. He would always be on the prowl questioning why things were done in such a way, or why they hadn't been done at all and when they would be done. This attitude upset the rhythm of daily work and sorely tried the patience of both Sidney and Hector. Ernest purchased in 1937 one of the first tractors in the area, a Standard Fordson, together with a new Ransomes trailer plough and Ransomes cultivator, and a new Bamford mower. These were to enable Hector to set up a contracting business. What the arrangements were, history does not tell, whether Hector leased the machinery or was lent it, is conjecture. A few invoice sheets survive, the telephone had arrived in 1937, and here is one that had been started: -

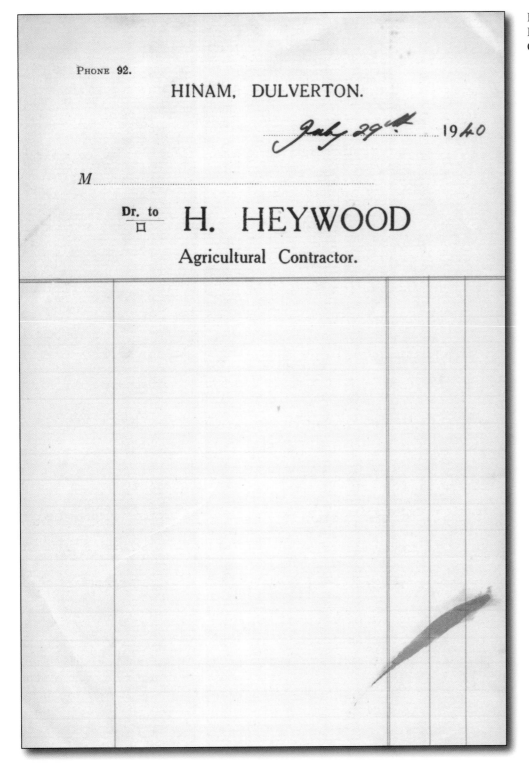

Invoice page: H. Heywood, Agricultural Contractor.

His work was within a few miles radius of Hinham; a lot of it was ploughing especially during 1939 and 1940. When WW2 began, the drive for home production got going on the back of the U-boat menace to the convoys bringing food and materials from North America. By the summer of 1940 it would appear that he had a binder, as there were several entries for cutting corn.

Ernest Bawden did not drive a motor car so would, when the need arose, hire one with a driver from Greenslades in Dulverton. There were times however when he could not resist being driven out hunting by Hector, in the vehicle of the day, which by now was a bull nosed Morris Cowley. This is something he swore he would never do, and to quote Paddy King-Fretts 'the mighty hunter of yesteryear had become *"one of they damned motor people."* He had always treated those who followed by car with contempt; in his eyes they were an inferior race. Now he was one of them – him of all people. To his credit, when they challenged him about it and pulled his leg, his face puckered into a mischievous grin *"Ah, but its different now. Things are different these days."'* When harmony reigned, who knows whether Ernest would have encouraged Hector in his thoughts about becoming the official Harbourer to the D&SSH? Hector applied for the job upon the retirement of Ned Lang and was appointed on May 1st 1938. Indirectly this would enable Ernest to keep in touch with the everyday goings on at the kennels.

With Ernest's wife Elizabeth living so close by, she called in to help or advise Jean on household matters nearly every day. This was a great boon for Jean, especially when she had to make butter, a frequent task, but made a little easier with a proper butter churn. By this time when making clotted cream, a separator was used on the fresh milk and the volume of cream to be scalded on top of the milk was greatly increased. As the butter was sent by post to various people including the Robinsons in Bristol, it was important to get the butter hard enough to withstand travelling. In summertime with no aids like refrigeration, there was only one thing to do, take the butter down to the hydraulic ram pump house, and leave it there in wooden tubs to bring the temperature down. Once hard enough it was packed into special cardboard boxes to hold four and a half pounds of butter rolls, and dispatched by post.

Miss Abbott, for whom Alec Chanter was chauffeur, had an elder sister Anne who married a Robinson of Robinsons Paper. This family came to stay in a house that they owned, Mounsey House above Mounsey Castle in the Barle Valley, locally referred to as 'Mounsey in the Wood'. The nationally known family firm manufactured these butter boxes, amongst a raft of other paper goods, and would send a regular supply to Hinham.

To overcome the problem of keeping up with his contracting work at the same time as undertaking his harbouring duties, Hector called in his cousin Ken Bawden, son of Harold and Nell at West Liscombe, to help when needed. Occasionally he had the help of young Clifford Stone from Hinham Bungalow, son of Bill Stone. One day Ernest chanced upon Clifford, by now about fifteen or sixteen driving the precious Standard Fordson and blew his top, saying, "I am not having anybody except Hector or Ken driving my tractor." Of course it was inevitable that a major row would break one day, and it happened thus: – Ernest was a stickler for tidiness and putting things away in their rightful place after use. When the new tractor came onto the scene he had a special shaped canvas cover made that had to be on at all times when not in use. Hector had been working with it, and parked it hot, at the field entrance. He thought that the common sense approach would be to come back after his tea, as it was a dry day, and put the cover on when it had cooled down. Alas, along comes Ernest to see his precious tractor without its cover on. He proceeded to go ballistic with rage and would not listen to anything Hector had to say. He summoned his son Percy from Exford to remove the tractor to West Liscombe, for his brother Harold. Harold is reputed to have said "I don't want anything to do with that" as he did not want to upset the good relationship he had with his sister and brother in law Sidney; but his wife Nell said "You have got to buy it for Ken", so they gave Ernest £150 for the whole outfit. Percy felt terrible about the whole affair. *"That's one of the incidents that I'd rather forget all about it. It put me in a terrible position. To have to go there and take the thing away. For my father to do that –was nothing, but for me to do that, he didn't think about my feelings at all you know. Just take the thing away, that's it. I wanted the earth to open and jump in the hole, out of the way. After we had been such buddies for all those years to come to grief just like that. I had to do what my father wanted obviously, much against my will. I'd done anything to let somebody else do it. We were never the same afterwards. There was always that, just that something any time I met your father."*

It was Hector's nature to take nearly everything to do with the Devon and Somerset Staghounds very seriously, and responsibly, so his appointment as the official Harbourer he considered a very great honour. He would do everything within his powers to make a success of it. He kept for the first two years a most interesting and informative diary, the pressures of wartime and a move to Cloutsham in 1940 brought it to a close. Most of the time he rode out from Hinham and would stay the night at a farm nearby to the next day's meet. Sometimes he rode to the kennels and stayed the night there, leaving very early on a hunt horse. Three names of those horses are mentioned, Minette, Swiss Navy and Rapture but little ever written about them. There are occasions when he used his car, but these are few and far between as petrol, becoming rationed, was a precious commodity. Great distances were ridden, which meant leaving Hinham before or after lunch the previous day. This would account for him having to get help with his young contracting business and making demands on Jean to getting his horse ready in good time. He carried a little leather saddle hamper in which he screwed up a pair of silk pyjamas, a shaving brush, soap and razor with a small piece of mirror. It was not unknown for him to have a shave beside a stream with the mirror stuck in a thorn bush, fifteen or twenty minutes before reporting to the Master at the meet. He took great pride in looking decent, and presentable. Here are fourteen entries from his diary to give some flavour and hope they will be of interest to the reader. There were numerous occasions when he would be joined by Joan in the evening or afternoon of the day before, of which he makes mention, so their courtship was very much ongoing in 1938.

Tuesday July 19th 1938. County Gate.
My First Meet.

I left here Monday 1.00pm for Yenworthy, went by way of Withypool to Larkbarrow and down the Badgworthy Water to Malmsmead and up Ashton to see George Lang.

I tried through Yenworthy Wood and along through Seven Thorns to Glenthorne Drive without seeing any signs of deer. I rode the cliff path through Wingate Wood and along Rodney then turned up on to the main road and back to the top of Glenthorne, in Seven Thorns Combe I saw two hinds and a four year old stag two atop and upright, it was now 9.30 pm and I gave it up for the time. Getting up at 4.30 am I first went to look for a stag reported in Broomball but failed to see him. I then rode out to Glenthorne Lodge where I met George Lang and failing to see a deer we tried the Drive down and saw slots of a couple stags that had gone into the rhododendrons. There was nothing further could be done so I rode back up to County Gate for my first meet. We kennelled at Yenworthy and drew out the rhododendrons first getting on to a calf and then a hind but eventually we found the four year old that I saw the previous evening and the Master decided to hunt him, he ran up through Magpie plantation and up over the Yenworthy fields on to Yenworthy Common where the pack was laid on at 12.noon. He ran over North Common into Beggars Knapp where hounds got onto fresh deer and nothing further was done.

***

From Hinham to Ashton is very roughly 20 miles on the OS map taking no account of rising or falling ground. Then he would have ridden a further six or seven miles before bed, more in the morning followed by a 20 miles ride home. A total of well over 50, probably nearer 60 miles in all. He was out again on Wednesday afternoon for Thursday's meet. The duties of the harbourer are finished when the pack is laid on. Before doing this he would have shown the huntsman or Master to where the deer is lying, helped rouse the deer with the tufters and got it away. The tufters are older steady and biddable hounds; once they have the deer well and truly going, they are stopped or held up to await the arrival of the pack to join them. The huntsman will, when ready, let them away on the line of the deer with a resounding cheer and doubling his horn.

Saturday August 20th 1938. Brendon Two Gates.

Left for Farley 11.00am Friday and went out to Larkbarrow, Tom's Hill and along Pinford to Buscombe where I got my first view of some Forest stags there being five of them standing on Trout Hill, three of them very fine deer. I arrived at Farley at 5.00pm. After tea Walter [*Lang*] and I rode out over Cheriton Ridge to Hoar Oak where we parted company, Walter going by the lower crossing to Shallowford while I tried up Long Chains Combe and along the head of Ruccombe Combe to Saddle Gate to look into Butter Hill Plantation but saw nothing. It was a bitter cold morning when we rode out from Farley at 6.00am. I went out over Cheriton Ridge to Hoar Oak and on to Shallowford but only saw two hinds and a calf in Butter Hill. I then rode up to Woodbarrow and looked right out over Longstone and around the Chains but saw no signs of a stag.

Returning to Hoar Oak I met Walter who had seen two stags in Gormers Lake above Hoar Oak, they were two six year old stags and after seeing the pack laid on to them at 11.45 am I turned for home after on of the most miserable and unhappy mornings of my life.

***

Saturday September 10th 1938. Sandyway.

It was a brilliantly fine day when I rode out to Stitchpool on Friday.

I tried down the whole length of Longwood to Heasley Mill and Home Park down to Brinsworthy without success but at Brinsworthy I had news that stags had been seen on Barcombe Heath recently. I met Bill [*Joan's brother*[in Heasley Mill and we both went up to Radworthy to look across the valley on to Barcombe Heath but up to 7.30pm and with light failing we had seen nothing. Having one final look back I saw the spread of a stag on the skyline on Barcombe Heath and was followed by four others the leader appeared to be a good stag.

Next morning we were only just in time to see them return to the gorse and again light was not good enough to say what points they had.

At 8.00am Bill produced a frying pan together with bacon and eggs and after breakfast in the open on Radworthy Down I wandered away up to Sandyway this being my easiest harbour up to date.

It was some little time before we roused the stags the two better stags were laying in a small patch of gorse away from the main brake.

Under Southwood they divided the one the tufters settled on ran up the valley under Tabor Hill and up left-handed over the Longstone Lane into Longwood where the pack was laid on at 1.15 pm. He was taken in the Westwater stream under North Barton and was a fair-bodied stag with a small forest head of brow, bay and trey and four one side brow, trey and three the other.

***

Thursday September 15th 1938. Alderman's Barrow.

I went out to Exford by car on Wednesday and rode Minette up to Pitsworthy where I had news of a big three and two atop stag in Wellshead Cleeve. I then rode on out by Larkbarrow and in the fern beds on Kittucks I saw two three atop stags. I dismounted and watched them for some time but at 4.30 fog descended and I had to return to Hill

Farm for the night.

I got up at 5.30.am and went out to the long field above Pitsworthy and at daybreak I saw the big stag beating down the stream under Wellshead Cleeve. I saw him leave the water and put Fred Westcott to watch him.

Joan had now arrived and we rode on out to Larkbarrow and again my luck was in for the two stags were again lying in the ferns on Kittucks.

We spent a very leisurely morning with them and then went back for the meet.

The Master decided to go for the Pitsworthy stag first on account of the damage to Fred Winzer, we roused him at once and after a fast hunt back to Horner he was accounted for at 12.40.pm

They then returned for the Kittucks stags and getting away on the smaller of the two they hunted him till 6.30.pm when he was taken at Burrow Farm, Wootton Courtenay.

***

Saturday October 15th 1938. Shallowford.

I started on the long ride out to Woolhanger on Friday at 10.30.am. Calling at Wester Close [*Joan's home in Withypool*] I went up Gypsy Lane to Prayway Head and down Long Chains Combe to Hoar Oak.

On Benjamy I saw a magnificent stag galloping after four hinds from the direction of Ruccombe Combe, he had a wonderful spread with brow, tray and two atop each side, he was a deer I had not previously seen this summer.

I rode on to Shallowford and over Butterhill to Woolhanger but here I only found slots of hinds and a young stag.

It being such a nice afternoon I decided to go further on and rode up over Lock's Allotment to Chapman's Barrows and over Longstone to look down into Swincombe. On Swincombe Allotment I saw a herd of eight hinds and a good stag with three and two atop.

I returned by Butterhill to Shallowford where I had tea and back to Farley after my longest ride this season.

I decided to leave the big stag at Hoar Oak and go farther out. In Butterhill Plantation I saw an old one-horn stag and decided on him, watching the Plantation until 9.15am. After which I went out to Woolhanger for another look at the root field there, deer had again fed there in the night and were lying in the laurels under the house.

We took the tufters out to disturb these deer and found four hinds and a calf, and a five year old stag with two atop and an upright, after which we returned to Butterhill and found the one horn stag, he turned up over Longstone in company with a three year old, the pack were laid on to both deer at 12.40pm.

Hector would have ridden about 23 miles to Woolhanger, then ridden a further 10 miles looking for deer and going back for the night with Walter Lang at Farley Farm; the next day perhaps he rode 8 to 10 miles before he turned for home with another long ride of 23 miles say 60+ miles in total. This is on top of harbouring for the previous Monday at Alderman's Barrow, then Cloutsham on Tuesday, and Bickingcott Cross on Thursday. The week before that he had harboured Monday Hawcombe Head, Tuesday at Hawkridge, Wednesday for the Tiverton Staghounds at Five Cross Ways, Thursday at Robin How and Saturday at Winsford. For all these meets he had ridden, not having used a motorcar. From a small photograph taken of him at what looks like Five Cross Ways, Dulverton, he really does look the proverbial rasher of wind. The little hamper attached to his saddle is clear to see, as is the binocular case over his shoulder. Note as it is wartime the signpost is absent, it should be between the man and other horse's rear end.

***

Hector at a wartime
meet at 5 Cross Ways,
Dulverton.

Friday March 24th 1939. Racecourse Farm, Bodmin.

Having had an invitation to take the pack down to Cornwall to hunt a stag reported near Bodmin a meet was arranged for March 24th. I left home on Thursday and arrived at the village of St. Breward at 1.30pm where I was taken on to Lydicott Farm where the stag was last reported to have been seen.

I tried up the valley first through Dewick Wood in the direction of Bodmin Moor without finding any sign of a deer; I then decided to try down the water, which I followed to Ladybrook Bridge but still no sign of a stag.

It looked an impossible task to try and harbour a single stag in such a hopeless place and it was 6.00pm. and the light fast failing when, trying up through Callywith Wood I saw the recent slots of two stags. This was a great stroke of luck and quickly I decided to put all I knew into it and try and harbour these deer. They were apparently feeding off the scrub oak and whortleberry bushes and lying in Callywith Wood.

I spent the night at St. Breward and getting away at 5.30am, on Friday morning I made off for a point where I could look into Callywith Wood and there at daybreak I had the great thrill of seeing two stags, the deer I thought it never possible to harbour.

One of them appeared to be a very old stag with a poor head of brow, tray and an upright and brow and upright, the other a well grown five year old with two atop each side.

They fed about on the open hillside till sunrise and then wandered into the young larch plantation. At 9.30 I tried round the covert but could find no sign of where they had moved out and at 10.30am. I made my way up to the meet thrilled with the great pleasure and satisfaction of having harboured red deer so many miles away from our native Exmoor.

The tufters roused them at once and, settling on the older deer they drove him away up the valley past Ladyvale Bridge into Dewick Wood where the pack was laid on at 12.45pm.

***

Monday April 10th 1939. Cloutsham

Sunday afternoon Joan and I walked out over Pool Plain to look into Nutscale.

On Great Hill there was a large herd of some forty hinds and with them two spring stags.

There was another herd of fourteen hinds out on Acmead. It had been a very pleasant afternoon for, besides seeing the large number of deer we saw a pair of Merlin and at least three male Ring Ouzel in Chetsford Combe.

It was a brilliantly fine morning when I got up at 7am, on Easter Monday. I rode out to Nutscale and again saw the large herd of hinds feeding on Great Hill and although I searched every combe out to Lucott Moor the two stags had entirely disappeared.

It was 9am when I turned back over Dunkery for Annicombe in search of the large herd of stags. There were at least another fifty hinds between Langcombe Head and the Dunkery Gate road, but on reaching the head of Annicombe I got among the stags, there was a herd of about twenty feeding in the side of the combe and through the heavy haze I could just distinguish three more in the fields by Annicombe House.

We laid the tufters on to the big herd and it was a thrilling ride I had in cutting out a three year old at the head of Bincombe and riding him out to the open moor.

He ran along by the Codsend fence to Luccombe Post where with the deer pointing for Chetsford the tufters were held up and the pack laid on at midday.

***

Wednesday July 19th 1939. Birchanger.

We had been having shocking bad weather lately and it was still raining in torrents when I drove out to Exford on Tuesday.

Riding Minette I went out across Lucott Moor and around the head of Bury Castle calling in at Bromham to see George Westcott and on by Park Corner to the Toll road which I tried down to Porlock without seeing the slot of a huntable stag.

Having had news of stags in Hawcombe I went round to see Sidney Tucker and we walked up the path under Ley where I spotted the top points of a stag's antler in the scrub oak under Peepout. He was a very good stag having three atop each side.

I then went back and tried through the Parks with Bill Pollard but we could not get on to a stag anywhere and it was still raining hard I gave it up for the night.

Getting up at 4.00 am I road through Porlock Village and up to where I had seen the stag the previous evening and as it was pouring with rain still it was some little time before I saw a deer but eventually spotted the same three atop stag sheltering under the tree opposite.

The rain eased off, he shook himself and laid down in a patch of gorse.

The tufters roused him immediately and he ran up through Holmbush Wood on to Whitstones where the pack was laid on.

A very successful start to another season.

***

Saturday August 12th 1939. Comers Gate.

There was a decided improvement in the weather and it was really warm when I rode out to Comers Gate on Friday.

Riding down over the rocks in Room Hill I saw the antlers of two stags that were lying in Nethercott Brakes opposite and after going up to Staddon and calling in to see Blakes I went back to tea with Joan.

We drove up to Room Hill and saw the same two stags and there was a bunch of hinds behind Lyncombe.

There was a frosty nip in the air when I got up at 4.30am Saturday and the whole of the Exe valley was covered in a thick blanket of fog and it was 8.30 before I could look across the valley.

By now all the deer were settled in their beds and the only hope of finding them was slotting them off their feeding ground.

I went down to Lyncombe and up to Peters Corner and tried a field of corn at Staddon without success and I then had a look at a cornfield at Nethercott, here I got on to three stags and by his slot one of them appeared to be a good stag. I found where they had left the corn and crossed a root field pointing for Nethercott Brakes but I had great difficulty in following them across the grass fields on account of the tough nature of the grass and there were sheep all over the place but I had made up my mind to find them and eventually succeed.

I slotted them into a rough field at the top of Lyncombe Cleeve and looking ahead I saw the tips of three pairs of antlers in a patch of bracken.

A very successful conclusion to a difficult morning's harbouring.

***

Tuesday Sept 5th 1939. Mounsey Hill Gate.

The outbreak of war had interfered with all the previous arrangements for this meet and it was only a few local sportsmen and farmers that assembled at Highercombe on Tuesday morning.

I looked through Ballneck Monday evening and found where at least five huntable stags were feeding in a piece of rape and grass opposite Highercombe.

I went up to the Lousel fields Tuesday morning to look into Ballneck and although I was there before day break they had left the rape and I could hear them beating their antlers in the withy bushes at the top of the covert, and some ten minutes later through an opening in the covert I saw four of the stags, they were pointing for the rhododendrons behind Higher Marsh.

Things did not start too well when we went to draw for them, the tufters got onto a small stag at first, the big stag with four and three atop had bolted out across Marsh Hill and although the tufters ran him very well to Draydon Ford nothing further was done with him. Returning to Ballneck we soon got on to another stag with all his rights and two which ran out by the same line across Bird Field where the pack was laid on.

He did a double in Draydon Wood and crossed the Barle at New Invention and ran on down into Burridge.

The day had turned out very close and warm but the pack soon had him back up the Barle valley again and after a very fine hunt he was taken at Shurdon Hutch.

A six year old stag and in splendid condition.

***

Thursday April 11th 1940. Alderman's Barrow.

He describes this with a note in the ledger as his best ride.

I had heard reports of deer in Redstone Plantation but could see no signs of them there Wednesday evening.

I stayed the night at Exford (*with Alfred Lenthall, the huntsman*) and left the hunt stables at 6.am on Thursday. Riding up past Western Mill I tried Redstone and the Exe Cleeves with the glasses and looked up Ramscombe and Orchard Combe but again I saw no sign of any stags.

I then rode on out past Larkbarrow looked over the Kittucks and manor Allotment and as I unfastened the gate to go in on the Deerpark I saw a herd of eight stags lying just inside the gate. Seven were big deer, one was huntable, a three year old with brow tray and upright. I left them and rode down to Badgworthy and they were still in the Deerpark when I went back to the meet.

They bolted across Badgworthy Water when we came to draw for them and Sydney (*Bazeley*) and I went off in pursuit. The whole herd ran up over Badgworthy to the head of Hoccombe where they joined eight other stags and the whole herd crossed the

Brendon road together. I had a terrific ride down over Farley Hill and parted out a three year old just as they reached the Farley Water, he crossed the water up onto Cheriton Ridge where the pack was laid on some fifteen minutes behind him.

Running up Long Chains he swung right handed down over Benjamy where hounds were in trouble with some of the fresh stags that had gone on from the Farley Water. The Master was collecting hounds when I saw a single hound running the hunted stag back into Baker's Cleeve. We got the remainder of the pack on to him and here commenced the greatest ride that I ever had with the Devon and Somerset Staghounds. *[The joint master Miss B.K.Abbot, as Dad recounted to me, had said to him, "Hector keep the deer in sight"].*

I kept the stag in sight right back over the Forest till he joined a herd of hinds on Pool Plain, parting him out I got going again and followed him as far as Sweetworthy Plantation when I went back to look for hounds.

I found them on Pool Plain and after lifting them to where I last saw the stag they hit the line off again and ran on across Allercombe and over Rexstile on to Robin How. Hounds hunted slowly on round the side of Dunkery into Annicombe and as hounds were hunting him down the Combe I saw the stag running up by the wire fence at Eastland's Corner. We got hounds close to him and they ran him back in to Luccombe Allers where he was taken against the deer fence after a great hunt.

Running a map measure over the country, Hector must have ridden approximately 45 miles, some of which would have been fast and furious, including riding straight down over Paddy's Dyke. We must remember that he had no fear, but he was not reckless and would not have put his horse in jeopardy. On returning to the hunt stables at Exford he would have had a further ride of some nine miles to get home to Hinham. The next day during the afternoon he would have ridden again to harbour for the meet at Exford on Saturday. The irregularity of eating and long times between his meals could not have helped his digestive problems. For instance on April 11th between his breakfast at 5.30am at the kennels and his meal at night, he might have had a couple of sandwiches.

S.L. Hancock, son of Ernest, one of the ten brothers from Wiveliscombe, took over the mastership of the Devon and Somerset Staghounds, upon the retirement of Col. W. Wiggin, in 1936. In contrast with his relationship with Ernest Bawden, which was not good, he got on very well with Hector; they shared good mutual respect for one another. S.L. or 'Tommy' Hancock as he was known lived at Rhyll Manor in the parish of East Anstey, about a mile and a half from Hinham. He had married a part American woman called 'Flo'and they had two children Rex and Tamsie. Rex recalled to me: "Hector had a lot of influence on people. You could say he had an influence on me. There was something about him that you sat up and took notice, I don't do it for everybody but for Hector I certainly sat up and took notice. He was a very fine naturalist of the first class order. He and my mother used to talk about birds, not just hunting; they both got very excited and enthusiastic if one or other had seen something out of the ordinary."

Hector and sometimes Ernest when he had come to live at Hinham, used to visit Rhyll and take Rex ferreting below the big house, in the valley, called The Grove. Here they taught him all about catching rabbits; it was another case of Hector relating so well to a boy of the age of his lost brother Fred.

When Ernest Bawden retired in 1937 his successor was Alfred Lenthall, a small light wiry man, an excellent horseman and good with hounds. Unfortunately he suffered bouts of ill health, which on one occasion lasted for all of the spring stag hunting in 1940. When he was poorly Tommy Hancock carried the horn and hunted hounds himself, during the time just mentioned, according to Capt. H.P. Hewitt's book "Mr. Hancock, who showed excellent sport, and accounted for fourteen stags."

Some mystery surrounds the fact that Hector on several occasions acted as the whipper-in to Tommy Hancock. I found an entry in a hard backed book for Monday 5th December 1938. Larcombe Foot. *'My first day as Whipper-in'*. I have lost the two or three sheets of foolscap in his handwriting of the days that he was whipping-in. Sidney Bazeley and Ralph Slocombe the official whips had joined up by 1940. Rex Hancock was able to tell me that his father, when hunting hounds, would more often than not, provide a horse for Hector, referring to him as "My extra special tufter."

Hector had been seeing quite a bit of Joan Nicholson and their relationship was moving towards marriage; he had purchased an engagement ring and proposed to her in Lord's Plantation, about a mile and a half south of Withypool and at the right moment produced the ring from his waistcoat pocket. Whilst her father was alive he disapproved of her seeing him and on the other front so did Ernest Bawden in particular. Now that he was in the driving seat at Hinham he felt all powerful and issued the edict that if Hector did marry Joan he would have to leave Hinham. They did marry, in September 1940, so he had to leave. Even the gentle, kindly Sidney was against it. After they were married his feelings were made known to Sidney Westcott, then a boy living at Wilmersham Farm, neighbouring to Cloutsham, whilst the two Sidneys were walking sheep up over Langcombe Head towards Exford Common. Sidney Heywood made the declaration "I would never have married a Nicholson even if her arse was encrusted in diamonds."

This left Sidney to work the farm as best he could. John had worked with him at weekends and school holidays, but when the time came to leave school he was virtually dragooned by his brother in law, Dolly's husband Alec Chanter into working for G.B. Fisher, builders in Dulverton as a junior clerk. John never wanted to be indoors and hated every minute, so as soon as he was able i.e. old enough, he joined up for the Navy in 1942. He started at H.M.S. *Collingwood* the new entrant training camp and was then posted to serve on a converted Hull trawler H.M.S. *Lord Essedon* listening for submarines with ASDIC out in the North Atlantic. They would have been very vulnerable to a submarine attack; this fear added to the somewhat soul-destroying existence, however thoughts of Exmoor and the wonderful Barle valley were never far from the forefront of his mind. After the war he married a Wren, Doris Mills, and came back to live in his beloved Barle valley, working at Zeal Farm Hawkridge.

Sidney decided that he could not carry on farming on his own so had a farm sale in early September 1941. From the livestock movement books that even to this day farmers are compelled to fill in, I have deduced that he sold 27 head of cattle, 110 head of sheep and two pigs. Six pigs and 25 sheep had been moved to Cloutsham for Hector some months before. These may have been Hector's own stock or a starting up gift from father to son, or even been bought by son.

The last entry in the venison distribution book is for December 9th 1941. In early 1942 Sidney moved out of the farm and into Hinham Cottage. Jean stayed with her sister Dolly, who by now was living at King's Corner, Dulverton, to begin nursing and administering to evacuee children in Dulverton. In 1943 she was then called up into the Navy to nurse at the Royal Naval Hospital at Plymouth. It was whilst nursing at Lord Roborough's mansion Maristow House where sailors were taken to convalesce, to recover from surgery and illness, that she met her future husband John 'Jock' Campbell.

The road in the photograph leads to the bridge and the house behind them was destroyed in the floods of 1952. It used to house the Golden Guernsey Milk Bar, run by Mesdames Dashwood and Sanders; this was relocated further up in the town.

During one of the last summers at Hinham came the final summer visitor; Paddy Sampson daughter of Major Sampson the first visitor with his family and the Model T Ford. She lived as one of the family, and fittingly brought to a close, the long line of guests who had stayed with the Heywoods for their summer holidays.

John and Jean on the pavement at King's Corner, Dulverton, taken in 1943.

9

JOAN ELMA NICHOLSON

AS CHALK IS TO CHEESE, so Joan and her background was to Hector and his background. Her father was born in 1880, one of six sons to Frederick and Annie Nicholson, brewers in Maidenhead, Berkshire. They all went to public schools Charterhouse, Haileybury or Uppingham in her father, Geoffrey's case. Three of the sons Reg, Arch and Geoff held posts in the brewery. Prior to this Arch and Geoff went to the Institute of Brewing in Copenhagen, where they had to learn the language before they could master the course, to round off their brewing education. The brewery was an important part of life, having been founded in 1840 by Frederick's father William, who died in April 1916 aged 96, with all his teeth in his head.

Although Geoff came from a, wealthy, privileged background when it came to enlisting to fight in the Great War he did so as a private in order to start at the bottom. He felt any advancement of his rank should have to be earned by merit, not through his social position. He did eventually get a commission and became Lt. Nicholson. He lost his brother Laurie who was wounded at the First Battle of Ypres on 24th October 1914, and subsequently falling to gangrene in a London hospital; his mother Annie caught the train every day to London, to visit him until he died on November 2nd. Laurie was awarded a DSO. Another brother Ned was awarded an MC, and after the

Fred and Annie in their Victoria about to be driven off, with 'Bessie' the parlour maid on hand with the rug.

war went to manage his rubber plantations in Malaya. Success from these funded the purchase of substantial land near Corowa, Victoria, Australia, where he ran a vast sheep station. In the years after the last war he had a new Jaguar car shipped out every year from England, and on the only occasion that I ever met him, about 1954 he had come over to visit England with his Jag. He took several of us cousins on a trip, which proved to be hugely exciting as we did over 100 mph.

To give an idea of the scale of comfort, Frederick and Annie employed a total of fifteen people when they lived at The Old Vicarage at Shiplake in Berkshire. There was a house parlour maid, a cook, two assistant cooks, upstairs girls, cleaners, a groom, a chauffeur/mechanic, a handyman and two gardeners with a third as head gardener. When the occasion demanded people from the village were called in.

Joan's brother William, my Uncle Bill now aged 96 has just written his memories of the Old Vic some of which are reproduced here; they give a good feel of the gracious living that Joan and her siblings would have experienced when they went to stay, together with their parents for two, three weeks or even longer.

"A shopping outing to Reading was a well regulated event. Makins the chauffeur had his orders the previous day and spot on time the car would be outside the front door. The car was a Wolseley Limousine. Driver and one passenger in the front were glassed screened from the passengers in the back. A voice tube carried orders from the back to the front! The back seat would take three people. In addition there were two let down seats with back supports. The passengers faced forward.

A studio portrait of Annie.

Bessie would be in attendance with a rug over her arm. Loading was very stately and orderly. I hardly need say it was always a case of ladies first, so I was last. Grandpa didn't care for Reading shopping and went elsewhere.

The first shop in Reading was Heelas. The car stopped outside the front entrance where there was a commissionaire to open the car door and help the passengers out. The parade would then start. By this time there was a floor manager in attendance. Granny always had a black ebony stick with a silver top. Pointing with it and tapping on the floor produced immediate results. There never seemed to be any discussion about price. However the goods purchased would then be parcelled and taken to the front door. Granny invariably bought something to be put into 'the bottom drawer'. I learned later that a big bottom drawer in a chest of drawers was full of presents to be used as and when required.

Back home for lunch. It was necessary for Bessie to be at the front door awaiting Granny. The car was fitted with a specially loud horn just like a ship's fog horn. To get this horn to sound off properly Makins had to accelerate and then sound off. This was before passing through the main gate. Bessie would be on hand by the time the car had arrived. Dismounting and supervising the parcels to be taken in went off to routine standards!

Grandpa did his shopping in Henley. Wet or fine, hot or cold he invariably drove a pony and governess trap. He also took his collie dog. He had to be accompanied by a groom/horse holder. The pony of the day was Powder Monkey. Powder Monkey was a fast trotter with a mind of his own."

For many years they were in the habit of doing their own grand tour for eight weeks during the months of July, August or September in Italy, staying on the Italian Riviera, Naples, Rome or Lake Como. They used to take a ladies maid and, as in the case when their young sons Geoff and Laurie accompanied them in 1905, a governess. It is hard to imagine that there was anything to cause problems for Annie, but for some reason she secreted a bottle of whisky into her bedroom every night and consumed much of it. Shades of 'Whisky' John Heywood perhaps? According to Michael Nicholson, Frederick was a lovely old man with a white droopy moustache who would take young visitors to show them a picture of a desert scene with a man on a camel. The camel, always known as the 'ship of the desert', was the origin of the Nicholson brewery logo stating, 'Best in the Long Run.'

It would not go amiss at this point to write a little more of the brewery and William

Fred is on his hack 'Daniel'.

Nicholson. The brewery site is now the Nicholson Centre, a shopping complex; it covers the 400ft artesian well that supplied the brewery with its water. There is a Nicholson Way and a Nicholson House that houses the public library. At their peak in the 1900s Nicholsons possessed 150 tied pubs. William was a great cricketer and a member of the Maidenhead team that beat England in 1835. He was also a pillar of the local church and greatly thought of, so much so, that the stained glass windows from the East end of a church built in 1834 and pulled down in the 1970s, were saved and incorporated in a new chapel built in 1980; these windows commemorate the Nicholsons and the Cails. His second wife was Annie's sister Elizabeth, i.e. father and son were married to two sisters. This gave way to the curious family situation of her being known by Joan and her generation as 'Aunty Granny'. The Cails were very much involved as planners and builders of new Maidenhead during the construction boom of the late nineteenth century.

In 1904 the parsonage house at Shiplake was sold by the Church and bought by the Nicholsons, known thereafter in the family as The Old Vic. It was to be the last family home of Fred and Annie. It had achieved landmark status before that, as Tennyson courted the vicar's niece there, and had married her in Shiplake church in 1850; he composed 'In Memoriam' there too, in 1850. Thirdly he was appointed Poet Laureate in that year as well. In the days of black and white television the 'Forsyte Saga' was filmed there giving Joan's mother Elma, great excitement as she knew it well and watched avidly to see what, if anything, had been changed. Whilst on acting, I must include an amusing anecdote, and here I quote from Michael Nicholson's *The Long Straw* where he writes about his father Arch. *"One day Dad paid a visit to Bray church, known to him and his family when they were young. It so happened that there was a wedding on, so he strolled quietly round the side aisles and ran into a young curate. Putting his hand in his pocket he gave the curate five shillings, saying, 'Take this, your need is greater than mine.' Many years later Ian Carmichael, a famous character actor, was being interviewed on TV and when asked if he had any amusing happenings he said, "Once, when we were filming a wedding scene in Bray church and I was strolling round waiting for my cue, dressed as a priest, an elderly gent came up and pressed five shillings in my hand and said...!"*

One of the young men who came to stay in the 1880s and learn the skills and profession of brewing was a John Barnes who married Connie Ludlow. They had three daughters, the second being Elma who was later to marry Geoff; sadly Connie died in childbirth with the fourth, a boy who also perished. This left Jack a broken man and he died not long after. Two of the orphaned girls and a cousin were dispatched to a convent in Belgium for their education, where they had to succumb to very rigid discipline, and learn to speak French fluently. In later years Elma, my grandmother, was the epitome of kindness and tried to ensure that her children and grandchildren never had to experience the traumas and unhappiness that she had done.

'The Old Vic' at Shiplake.

Geoff and Elma were married from the Old Vic in 1910, in grand style; the whole way from house to church had a carpet laid out for them to walk on. A honeymoon in East Africa followed, with rides on elephants to add to the occasion. I am in possession of an elephant carved out of ebony with ivory tusks that they brought back as a souvenir.

Being a partner in the brewery did not mean that Geoffrey had to live by necessity, near to Maidenhead. During the war, when posted to Edinburgh, he took a house for all the family. After the war he moved back to Chantry House, Bray, near Maidenhead.

Geoff and Elma had six children, Joan my mother the eldest, then Kathleen (Kay), William (Bill), Marjory (Pip), Rosemary (Bunty) who died with complications of Spina Bifida at a young age and lastly John. The family had a comfortable life, winter sporting holidays at Davos, or St. Moritz in Switzerland. Here Joan learnt to ski and skate; she became proficient at both.

One of the exploits carried out by the men folk was to go down an ice run, probably the Cresta run on a four-man bobsled with steering wheel and spiked brake at the back. They gave it a name, 'Stormy Petrel' and interestingly had the logo on their sweaters

L-R: - Kay, Pip, Bill and Joan with the instructress or nanny.

The Stormy Petrel.

and Cossack type hats. Nothing seems to have changed since then in the wearing of logos. In this photograph there are two Nicholson brothers, Arch on the left of the picture and Geoff fourth from the left. They competed for the Manchester Bowl in 1908.

When the matter of educating the children came up, it was an easy choice for Bill, and later John to be sent to Uppingham to follow in their father's footsteps. The best girls school at the time was considered to be Benendon, near Cranbrook in Kent, so all three were sent there for the duration. They excelled at sport, particularly hockey and lacrosse. Pip was the brainy one, Kay went on to throw pots on her wheel in later life, whilst Joan carried on with her painting when she had any time or could afford the materials.

This is an example of Joan's work aged ten; it is a watercolour on light card that had the calendar for 1923 stuck on above her and Kathleen's names.

Opposite: Nicholson Brewery bottle labels.

Opposite, top: Joan on her pony at a meet of the Staghounds at Comers Cross,1929

Opposite, bottom: Joan on Brian Livingstone-Learmouth's 'Conjuror' this illustrates her good seat, a legacy of Horace Smith.

Joan spent time doing woodwork and I have the coffee table she made, which I cherish. At some time riding became a pastime and having moved from Chantry House, Bray, near Maidenhead to a house in Holyport, Joan was dispatched to the nearby riding school of Horace and Sybil Smith to be taught to ride properly. It must have been an excellent establishment, as Horace Smith was riding master to five sovereigns no less. From Holyport the family moved to Folkestone in Kent, presumably to be near Benenden for the girl's education.

Unhappily matters were not going well for Geoff as he was beginning to suffer the problems of depression. It is thought that the gene responsible came from William Nicholson's first wife, mother of Frederick, who in turn passed it on down to his son Philip who spent much of his life in and out of institutions, and also to Geoff. Whether the domineering of his forthright eldest brother Reg who was said to be the one who held sway in the board meetings was a contributory factor I am not sure but family word has it, that it was. Any rate Geoff decided to take a back seat and build a house in the West Country. Having experienced the delights of a holiday on Exmoor in the dream village of Withypool, where there was riding for the children, in 1927 he bought the land and instructed Sanders of South Molton to build 'Westerclose'. They took a year to build it with stone quarried from an adjacent field, whilst the family stayed at the house 'Bigmoor' in the village. Frequent use of binoculars followed the progress of the house. They moved in to their new home in 1928, together with the now widowed Frederick, who alas died that year and was interred in Shiplake churchyard. According to the late John Blackmore who was living in Withypool at the time, 'Westerclose' was one of the best-built places in the village. All the woodwork, i.e. floors, doors and staircase, the latter two items being of Austrian oak, was made by Shapland and Petter from Barnstaple. Geoff employed a staff of five, including a full time gardener, two maids and a daily help. He also employed a male nurse Paddy Moynham, a delightful and cheerful Irish man, to help look after him in the black dog days. Paddy, a single man, lived in at Westerclose. Geoff's good friend Dr. Barny McKinney from Dulverton did all he could to make Geoff's life bearable, but at one stage had to have him sectioned and he was sent away for a spell, to the St. Mary of Bethlehem Hospital (Bedlam) in London. Dr. McKinney told John Nicholson that it was the worst thing he had had to do in life. Sadly the only medication available was sedation, which helped for a while, but in the end he took his own life in 1935. Paddy married after the war and lived with his wife Gertie in Oliver's Cottage, in the village.

The brewery was eventually taken over by the Courage Brewery. Before this happened various beers were made as shown by the variety of labels, one especially to commemorate the Festival of Britain, and another one for the Queen's coronation.

As Joan and her sisters were not expected to work for their living but to marry well some day, and be looked after in the custom in which they were familiar, they spent their time on cookery courses, riding, sailing down on the Helford River, winter sporting and travel. Joan even played hockey for Mecklenburg State in Germany and when the occasion necessitated had to give the Nazi salute with a Heil Hitler. With the move to Withypool she inevitably fell under the spell of Exmoor and the Devon and Somerset Staghounds in particular.

Joan was a bit of a free spirit; her time keeping was not of the best, and it upset her father that she sometimes could not turn up for meals. She, like Hector would sometimes raid the larder of next day's food. For whatever reason, perhaps to emulate her father who went on a course at Seale-Hayne Agricultural College after the Great War, perhaps to be in tune with Hector and his farming if she was harbouring secret intentions of being his wife, she attended Somerset Farm Institute at Cannington near Bridgwater for the academic year 1932-33. I think the end result was a Certificate in Agriculture. She hunted madly for the season starting with autumn stag hunting in 1934. This was interspersed with hunting with the Blackmoor Vale and Sparkford Vale Harriers on Arthur Brake's young horses that she helped to bring on as hunters. She also rode for Brian Livingstone-Learmouth.

Joan as a young woman

Here is an entry for September 15th 1934 in her hunting log:-

Hacked some of A. Brake's young horses (3) in the morning. Good fun riding green stuff. One bay mare bucked like stink, I expected to buy a bit of ground but didn't. Brian bought a lot.

She was clearly an accomplished horsewoman.

Joan was quite a party lover as the entry for August 14th 1934 shows:-

Nicholson and Deighton Dance at Exford village hall. A very hectic beat up. Refreshments were eaten to the sound of the horn by Jim Greenwood. The dance went on till 3.AM when it ended with John Peel and Auld Lang Syne, after which Jimmy Connell gave a ukulele party till 4.AM. Summary a Damn good party.

After Geoffrey's death it became a little easier for Hector and Joan to see more of each other, so much so that he sometimes stayed the night at Westerclose when harbouring in the area. He would have been the epitome of a well-behaved young man in Elma's presence, courteous and helpful. No doubt the outbreak of war added urgency to their relationship as it did with countless others; people did not know what lay ahead so they lived for the moment. As their engagement became known, so Ernest Bawden would have said, "If you marry that woman you have got to leave Hinham Hector." Tommy Hancock the Master of the staghounds was very helpful when he was made aware of the situation. The Holnicote Estate of Richard Acland was looking for a sporting tenant for Cloutsham, a small hill farm on the edge of the moor just north of Dunkery Beacon. Tommy Hancock had words in the right places that had the desired effect, and Hector became tenant, moving in to start farming it after their marriage and short honeymoon.

From an historical perspective it is worth including what Hector told me about the previous tenant. He took over from Mrs. Dick Foster, a widow of ten years since 1930. Her husband Dick was out following hounds after they had met at Cloutsham, in torrential rain *"Mr. Foster in crossing the flooded Horner Water at Eastwater Foot was thrown from his horse into the raging Horner River. A search for his body was put into being, Stan Hooper of Allerford who was on the scene told them the only place where they would find his body was below Newbridge where a large tree had fallen across the river and his body would get caught up. The search party immediately went to this likely spot and straightaway saw a hand flapping where his body was caught up in the oak tree. Someone risked their life by going out on a branch of the tree and put a rope around Mr. Foster's wrist, pulling hard upstream they were able to release his body from the tree .The rumour was he was full of whisky at the time and therefore the cause of the accident."*

- 10 -
NEW HOPES AND EXPECTATIONS

HECTOR AND JOAN were married on Saturday 28th September 1940 at Hawkridge Church. Joan was given away by her brother Bill, and Hector's long time friend Jimmy Taplin from Wootton Courtenay was his best man. Elma, Joan's sister Kay, and her brother John were there. A photograph shows Hector's sister Dolly in the crowd. Hector is dressed in his harbouring attire, but did not take part in harbouring a stag for the meet at Hawkridge that day. Instead his friend Sydney Westcott of Hill Farm, Hawkridge deputised for him.

The newly married couple emerge from Hawkridge Church. The little girl on the left is Joan Pugsley, later to be Joan Davies from whom, together with her husband Aubrey, we bought Sanctuary.

He was back to harbouring duties on Wednesday night for Thursday, a truncated honeymoon of four nights away at Hartland Quay. The Devon and Somerset lent Joan a horse for the day so that they could hunt together from the meet on Winsford Hill. Hector shot the stag under Newland Wood above Withypool from the opposite side of the river using a 16 bore with a single fragmented lead ball. To quote Hector: "*A very fine stag with a beautiful head of brow, bay and tray and four one side and three the other. Harold found his antlers the previous spring on Whiterocks and John the year before in the lower meadows.*"

In the photograph L-R:
Jimmy Taplin, Hector and
Joan, Elma, John and Kay
Nicholson.

Hector and Joan at the
meet immediately after
their marriage.

I do believe that Hector thought that he could put all his past troubles behind him and make a new beginning in a new home with a new wife. Cloutsham was an idyllic place, with its Swiss style balcony with views onto Dunkery and Easter Hill. There were deep wooded combes on two sides, of scrub oak, beech, ash and birch, with the fast flowing moorland rivers, the Eastwater and Horner Water. Thomas Dyke Acland the eleventh baronet and his wife Mary had two rooms added to Cloutsham as a holiday retreat. To quote Anne Acland again: "*She (Mary) could no longer ride her active little pony 'The Cat' over the Holnicote hills, but visits to Cloutsham were always the best tonic, and she would conspire with the coachman to drive there ('Cloutsham the Cure') if Tom seemed depressed.*" The sporting artists Cecil Aldin and Lionel Edwards both stayed at Cloutsham. During the 1920s Cecil Aldin made it his headquarters when he came down with his dogs, horses and personal chattels for a month of autumn staghunting. In 1930 he had been advised on medical grounds to live on Majorca but as his health failed he had the urge to make one last visit to England to see Cloutsham again, to follow the familiar Exmoor tracks and visit all the places he was writing about in *Exmoor – The Riding Playground Of England*. He wanted to see from Cloutsham, the harvest moon arising over Hurlestone Point; alas he had a massive heart attack on ship and died in the London Clinic in January 1935. At the very time when he breathed his last, his white bull terrier 'Cracker' as if by some sixth canine sense, set up an inconsolable howl 1000 miles away.

Lionel Edwards on one occasion whilst staying held a white dinner plate above a candle flame that deposited a layer of soot. On this using a matchstick, he drew a stag's head, whatever became of it I wonder?

From my own personal point of view, it is worth recording that just after Hector left Cloutsham an ear, nose and throat surgeon of world renown from the Berkeley country in Gloucestershire, came to stay with his hunters. He was also a dedicated farmer who showed his Guernsey cows at all major shows. John Angell-James CBE was based at the Bristol Royal Infirmary and among his exploits he had pioneered a new route to the pituitary gland that lies in the centre of the head under the brain, going through the frontal sinus cavity beside the eye, instead of trepanning the skull. He removed a benign tumour growing on my pituitary in 1965. As he lived a mere couple of miles from my sister in the 1990s, a visit was arranged for me to see him again, by now over 90 years of age. Imagine the excitement of firstly seeing furniture made by the mouse man of Kilham in Yorkshire who always carves a mouse in his oak furniture, then more excitement to discover that his mother's maiden name was Ashwin, the same as my wife Connie's. It transpired they were related as distant cousins! He had a brave and illustrious brother Brig. Manley Angell James who fought in the Great War, was wounded three times, taken prisoner, and awarded a VC and an MC. If this was not enough he fought again in the Second World War and awarded a DSO in 1943, quite some brothers. Over the years there have been many fortunate people to visit and stay at Cloutsham; they still do to this day.

Wild life was in abundance to satisfy Hector's great desire to find or see different things in his new environment. He was in his element combining farming and work for the hunt, as in his mind he could do both activities well. He built up stock numbers of beef cattle and sheep, grew corn, root crops and made hay, putting it into ricks. These he thatched in the traditional manner with bracken, cut in the old Sweetworthy fields under Dunkery, and rushes cut from the Embercombe rush beds. I remember him telling me of the occasion when he should not have been out there as the artillery from Ley Hill and Webbers Post were in the middle of live firing onto the "Exmoor Ranges", i.e. the impact zone being either Acmead, Kittuck or Manor Allotment. He totally ignored the red warning flags and was impervious to the shells whizzing overhead, they did not worry him in the least; he was doing what he wanted or had to do. He took summer grazing out on the Forest near Simonsbath to eke out his small acreage; the animals would have been walked out.

Because of the competition for grass, cereals and root crops by the red deer, who knew no bounds, the War Agricultural Executive Committee or War Ag as they were called, via their pest control department let it be known that if the D&SSH did not drastically reduce deer numbers on Exmoor, then they would. The hunt committee clearly decided not to let an outside body do this but undertook to do the task themselves with Hector playing a key role, having an intimate knowledge of the whereabouts of the deer and a good working relationship with most of the Exmoor farmers. He kept a little expenses notebook from 19th December 1939 until 17th April 1943. Why it stopped when it did, no one knows, perhaps domestic difficulties, perhaps the difficulties of wartime. There were 136 meets to harbour for, 10 days setting snares, 50 days shooting deer and nine days putting up wire, repairing fences and putting up cord (cord soaked in 'Reynardine' which the deer find off putting). Finally there were 30 days on deer damage work, i.e. assessing the degree of damage done to a crop or field of grass, and advising the farmer on the best course of action. If a day and a half is reckoned to harbour for a meet, I consider Hector was away from Cloutsham for 25% of his time, at a minimum, on deer work.

In addition there was also time away spent on Home Guard duties; he was classed as being in a reserved occupation and therefore not called up to fight. Like everyone else Hector was issued with a uniform, .303 rifle and some rounds of ammunition. He did tell of the exercises he took part in such as getting from point A to point B without being spotted. This meant crawling through the heather or undergrowth and making himself invisible. He always made it successfully and was complimented for it, unlike Rob Williams from Horner or other neighbouring farmers who would be spotted to the shout of "Hey! You are dead!" I find it remarkable that in an authoritative book about the Home Guard in West Somerset there is no mention of his name in all the lists or official photos of serving men. Perhaps he had what he regarded as more pressing and important things to do than attending group photographs. I have his medals so I know for sure that he did serve with them.

One day Hector had a visit from a neighbouring farmer Charles Harding from Stoke Pero. They were stood outside the house looking at the foothill of Dunkery opposite when they espied a large autumn stag. "I bet you couldn't hit that stag from here," said Charles. Hector as always, loved a challenge to do something out of the ordinary, so forthwith went inside for his Lee-Enfield .303 rifle. He carefully took up position leaning on top of the yard wall and fired. To his horror the stag leapt forward a few yards and fell down dead. He was on the horns of a dilemma; this would provide a wonderful supply of meat and yet he had in his own mind committed a cardinal sin. He went over to the spot, dug a hole and buried the animal. He had by now, become used to living his life according to the law of Hector that did not always equate with that of most other people.

In the drive for greater food production in the face of dreadful losses of shipping to the U-boats on the North Atlantic convoys, farmers were encouraged to plough up ground to grow cereals and potatoes. Hector responded, as he had acquired the use of a Standard Fordson tractor from the War Ag lending pool of equipment. One day there was great consternation in the Harding household at Stoke Pero; John Harding came home with the news Hector had ploughed up one of their fields and had commandeered it. He had probably thought that this field was not being farmed and he could do with it so he took it over. Similarly, the traditional meet field of the Devon and Somerset Staghounds was one field over from the house; it went with the vale farm, Horner, to provide summer grazing to allow a field at Horner to grow a hay crop. The farmer, old Mr. Thomas, was a great Methodist, who certainly did not swear or drink, but how he coped with finding the Exmoor ponies he put in his field gone and Hector's sheep there instead was never recorded.

Hector mowing with Standard Fordson.

During the first week of January 1943 Hector managed to break his wrist trying to start the War Ag Fordson tractor. In the days before self-starters, engines had to be turned over by hand using a cranked starting handle. The trick was to engage the handle dogtooth so that one had to pull from the quarter position to the twelve o'clock, ensuring that the thumb was held in line with the fingers i.e. not wrapped around the starting handle. If the magneto had been set in retard so that it would deliver a spark after top dead centre you were safe, but woe betide if the setting was too far advanced. This would result in a spark being delivered before the pull up of the handle was complete resulting in a violent back swing enough to break bones of the unwary. What was Hector doing? I have hazy memories of being ushered into see him, in bed with his arm all in plaster. Clearly there was some ploughing to be done as he sent for his cousin Ken Bawden. Ken's brother Alan regaled me with the saga. It was a period of fiercely cold winter, with lots of ice and snow, the sort of weather that if bare skin touches metal it sticks to it instantly. Ken used a towing chain to drag the plough onto a flat, narrow trailer. This he hitched to the Fordson that was now on rubber wheels, the very same tractor that Ernest had taken away from Hector. The spade lugged wheels for land work were loaded beside the plough, as was a supply of tractor vaporizing fuel, oil and a small quantity of petrol. Ken wrapped in a thick black coat, beret, scarf and gloves set off at a sedate five miles per hour to cover the 22 miles to Cloutsham with Alan aged nine together with an evacuee walking along beside his brother for the first four or five miles, and waving him goodbye at Marsh Bridge. Ken stayed at Cloutsham for over a week ploughing for several farmers.

Hector by his very nature always seemed to be involved with something unusual. There is for example, the incident of shooting the cow. I have earlier alluded to his difficulties with sleeping, either catching off to sleep or not sleeping well. He had weaned a calf from its mother and as always happens they bawl for each other for at least two to three days. If in earshot of one another, it is obviously much worse. Hector was driven to distraction when he tried to sleep, so much so he got into a temper, took his twelve bore shot gun and shot the cow and killed it. What a waste of a life, part of his breeding herd, to add insult to injury the potentially perfectly good meat for humans was taken by Dick Marley's lorry to the staghound kennels. Walter Perry an Exford boy of about ten later to be huntsman of the staghounds, was riding in the lorry and verified it all to me.

The 1936 Morris 8 Tourer, as resurrected by me in 1964.

During the war, travel was very restricted in a motor vehicle, as petrol was severely rationed, although as a farmer he had a small allowance. When he left Hinham he had a bull nose Morris Cowley with a dickie seat but I don't think it lasted very long at Cloutsham before it was scrapped. The Nicholson sisters had a Morris Eight tourer that Pip had collected new from the factory in 1936. They shared it for four years but after Joan and Hector had got married, there appeared a need of it on the farm so it was commandeered. The front passenger seat was removed to facilitate carrying sacks of corn, feedstuffs or whatever, but more importantly any deer that had been shot. All four side screens made of celluloid had metal pins that dropped into holes in the door and in the body beside the rear seats. They were also thrown away, as Hector arm over the door, liked to be at one with the elements or in a good position to hail people and talk. When cold, Joan with me, or my sister Elizabeth (Beth) would huddle under rugs wearing scarves, gloves and hats with nowhere to go to escape the fierce conditions. He would think nothing of driving it over fields and on really rough tracks just as someone would drive a four-wheel drive vehicle today.

The honeymoon period of moving to Cloutsham for Joan soon went, to be replaced by a life of hard toil, which she had never experienced before. She had to be resourceful and use her ingenuity to produce meals on a very limited supply of food. Yes, there were rabbits aplenty, milk, cream and butter; Hector did grow vegetables in the garden, but she had to ride two miles to Horner, to get the bread which had been left with Mrs Harding at Horner Vale, for her to collect. There might be a little venison on occasions, but the bulk of that went to the War Ag Pest Control as part of the national food chain. Her social life was about nonexistent, which for such a gregarious fun loving person was hard to bear. There were summer visitors, paying guests, or PGs as she called them, to look forward to. There was Ben Herod who passed through most days of the week; he would call in for a drink of tea. Ben worked for Farmer Thomas at Horner and walked in from Exford, a 14-mile round trip. Part of the attraction was Maud, daughter of Farmer Thomas on whom he was struck. Passing through Cloutsham one day he saw Joan struggling to milk a cow on a broken stool. Typical of the man, he soon made a good solid one out of English Oak and gave it to her. It is now another cherished possession of mine. Ben was a character, his dark curly hair sprouting from under his cap and always a red neckerchief to fill the gap of a collarless shirt, a countryman down to his last breath, but also possessed of the love to poach. He had three enormous stag's heads that Hector presumed he had killed in Horner Woods. When he made a visit to West Luccombe Farm, near Porlock in Dick Marley's lorry to fetch a load of mangolds, a .22 rifle was seen in the cab by Hector; very soon afterwards Hector saw blood in the road near Cloutsham and he could see where the deer had been dragged out of the woods. Blackcocks used to leck at the top of Embercombe, and at Hawkcombe Head. Cyril Westcott, Hector's neighbour and friend at Wilmersham used to grow oats; after being cut with a binder, the sheaves were put into small ricks on the stubble, each miniature rick would be carried in during the winter as needed, and the sheaves thrown in whole for the cattle to eat. This suited the black game and grouse as they foraged on the oat stubble. Ben Herod shot many of the birds, as did Pat Baker from Porlock. Pat worked for the War Ag Pest Control and used to shoot them early in the mornings as the birds were drying or dusting themselves in the road, or foraging for grit. The illicit shooting and the demise of Cyril Westcott's method of feeding his cattle brought an end to the black game and severely reduced the grouse.

Hector was not above seeing justice done if there was a good case for it even if he was thought badly of, for instigating it. He was riding down Stone Down Lane to Exford one day, when he saw in a field that was part of Coombe Farm, many ewes lying under the gate in the draft "to cool their agony" as Hector related. The ewes had not been shorn or weaned, and were riddled with maggots in great swathes. He called in to Police Constable Edwards at Exford saying "Have you been to Coombe lately?" The next day he met the RSPCA inspector and the Police in Mill Lane in a police car. The inspector thanked Hector for his action. The upshot was that Farmer Fred Winter from Wellshead put the word out that Hector was the informant. The farmer at Coombe whose sheep were affected was 'Drunkin Bill' Williams; he was an uncle to Rob Williams who followed his father in law, Farmer Thomas, into Horner Farm. Rob's brother Wilfred who lived at Stone Farm, Exford chanced upon Hector riding to Exford and lunged at his horse grabbing the reins and waving a bill hook in his other hand saying "You bugger I'll kill ee!" Hector managed to cool him down and said that he wished his uncle no harm, but it was terrible to see the sheep eaten so badly with maggots. The War Ag, unsurprisingly, turned 'Drunkin Bill' out of Coombe, and took the farm over. They were empowered by law to ensure that farms were correctly farmed to maximise output for the duration of the war. Ben Herod was taken on as foreman to run it. The memory of Maud Thomas obviously faded in the face of the pretty Land Army girl posted to Coombe. Grace was soon to become Mrs. Ben Herod.

Hector continued to be kindly to boys that crossed his path. One family had been evacuated from Bristol to Wilmersham Farm; the father, George Young was a member of the Royal Society for the Protection of Birds. He was aware that Hector collected birds eggs and was at crossed swords with him over it; to his chagrin his son and daughter formed a bond with Hector and in his words "Ran wild with Hector". Another was Gerard Noel, the son of Commander Montague Wriothesley Noel RN who was killed in action when his ship H.M.S. *Torrent* hit a mine and sank on 6th April 1941. He had happy recollections of Hector.

"Yes, of course I have treasured boyhood memories of your father Hector.

"I came across him because my father, a Commander RN and captain of his ship, was killed in action in 1941; the prep school I was at, at Westgate-on-Sea was evacuated to Alfroxton Park on the Quantocks and before he died my dad asked my mum to bring my younger siblings to be near the school so that we would all be in the same part of England if it was invaded. Mum rented a wing of Crossacres Hotel (the old tythe barn) at Selworthy and there we stayed for a while. Bill Pugsley, a farm worker I think, and certainly special constable and everything else going, introduced me to his friend Hector who used to take me and my brother harbouring around Horner.

"On one occasion I can remember a line of American tanks on the left of the road going up from Webbers Post all firing westwards. We lay in the heather watching them for a while and saw a herd of deer come out above Sweetry (sic) completely undisturbed. Others later came much closer to us and the tanks. Your dad said we should not be there and must not be seen by the tanks which made it all the more interesting for me and my brother!

"I remember your Dad telling me that once he saw some GIs drive a herd of ponies past an army lorry parked in the narrow lane behind Cloutsham and one of them jumped onto the back of a passing pony. Your Dad said he saddled up and tried to follow but 'could not get anywhere near him'!"

Gerard went on to Trinity Hall, Cambridge where he read Rural Estate Management which gave him full membership of the RICS. He ended up as the agent for the National Trust at Stourhead, Wilts. He maintained an interest in horses and hunting all his life and has been an avid staghunter in his quiet gentlemanly way. In his youth he rode in point to points and hunter chases on many of the top tracks including Cheltenham and Aintree. Perhaps Hector fanned the flame that burnt in Gerard to give him his lifelong love of Exmoor.

A writer and archaeologist by the name of Tudor Edwards came to stay early on in the war and wrote a piece that appeared in a national country magazine called *Out of Doors* in 1951. It was also reproduced in the *Western Morning News* in the mid 1950s. The flowery prose would suggest someone with a first in English from Oxford or Cambridge, or at the very least a good grasp of English that enabled him to write several books. He wrote *Worcestershire and Warwickshire* in the Vision of England series, *The Face of Wales* and in 1951 was investigating historic buildings for the then Ministry of Town and Country Planning as well as working on a literary fantasy and a collection of essays. I think it encapsulates the way Hector was during this early period at Cloutsham, before the cracks in his marriage started to appear.

Whenever a meet of the staghounds was in the vicinity of Dulverton, Hector would ride over the day before from Cloutsham to do the harbouring. He would leave his horse at the Lion Hotel stables for the night under the care of an old chum Charlie Hoskins who ran the stables and spend the night at Kings Corner with his sister Dolly. He was very fond of, and always got on very well with Dolly; being his elder sister she understood him, and could to a certain extent, control him. They would have had so much in common and she knew how to feed him, what his likes and dislikes were, and they would share all the Hinham memories. Miss Biddy Abbot was now living full time at The Cottage, Dulverton, so Alec Chanter, her chauffeur was residing in her cottage on the bend approaching the bridge. Alec and Dolly had three children, Mary the eldest followed by Archie then Pat. Mervyn How a contemporary and friend of the boys, related to me as how Dolly would organise them all, including one or two others, on a trip up the Barle valley when hounds were meeting in the area and likely to run into the Barle. Sandwiches would be made, with lemonade to drink, and off they would go, along beside the river up through Burridge Wood to Northmoor

The Stag Harbourer

BY TUDOR EDWARDS

AT THE BEGINNING of the war I was his guest for a brief space at Cloutsham, in the heart of an immutable moorland trenched with combes brimming over with woods of alder, oak, birch and ash. The farmhouse is an old hunting lodge lost between the flanks of Dunkery Beacon and the low-lying Horner Valley, a substantial squat house of stone with a Tyrolean balcony overlooking Dunkery. It was a lonely house built for comfortable evenings of relaxation after arduous days, the walls hung with hunting trophies and with the startling head of the great Hawkridge stag, and the cavernous vault of the fireplace, through which one could peer at a blue fragment of Exmoor sky, was filled with the wood smoke from a pyramid of branches fast dissolving into flame and ash. It was in all respects a hospitable house, with a delightful suggestion of the past and a lingering of traditional customs.

My friends were yeomen farmers of a type which has held these Exmoor farms for many generations, among them families named in Blackmore's *Lorna Doone*—Ridd, Dallyn, Huxtable and others. There was here a marked dearth of organised transport, and one either took a horse or walked, for walking amid these soft warm acres is no great hardship, and the villages on the Atlantic side are not far away.

It is but a mere stroll to the hamlet of Stoke Pero, and one could not easily tire of this David Cox setting, the remote tiny grey church islanded in a wind-blown sea of bracken and heather where roam the heavily-woolled cream-coloured horned sheep, and where, about the church porch, used to lie a number of French engraved mortuary glasses, as dainty as tiny wine goblets.

In addition to farming his land, selling his heifers and acting as guide to the local Home Guard, my friend was the official stag-harbourer to the hunt. He was a striking figure, gaunt and swarthy as a gypsy, in corduroy breeches, an old hacking jacket and a battered Bermuda straw hat, and he invariably carried a sporting gun or a pair of binoculars slung over his shoulders. In the hunting season he led a lonely life, lonely, that is, by a townsman's standards. For three or four months of the year he lived in the wilderness, studying the deer at close range. He was a harbourer in the tradition of Fred Goss, who in the latter part of last century harboured some twelve hundred stags in twenty-eight seasons, but there was more hunting in those day — and more deer; the steady decrease of the herds has made harbouring infinitely more difficult. To spend a day with him on field work was a revelation and a peep into the world of a Richard Jefferies. He knew every animal, reptile and bird on Exmoor, every flower, plant and herb, every copse, brook and track—or so it seemed. Certainly he knew the habits of the deer and the places where they ate, drank, sunned themselves and "lay-up," and he could tell from the "slot" or footprint of a deer its sex, approximate age, size and weight. He had an eye which was uncanny, an instinct which was unerring.

Under his guidance one discovered the haunts of the Dipper (which he called the "water colley") in the Eastwater valley and the Sweetworthy woods, of the yellow-breasted Grey Wagtail on the Horner Water, and of rare butterflies and hawk moths about the Horner woods. He was as knowledgeable about flowers and would point out the little red-flowered Cranberry in the peat bogs and goyals of Dunkery, the blue-flowered Campanula of the lower slopes, and the balsam-secnted Mountain Fern of the area.

Your true harbourer is something of a recluse, a hermit, almost a mystic. He has the sensibility of a naturalist allied with the instincts of a poacher and a commando, but to say that he is responsible for the ultimate deaths of those animals for which he has some affection is to take the crudest view of this paradox. It may be that something of this has drawn the harbourer within himself. Though he cultivates his arable land, can thatch a haycock and ride to hounds and shoot a moving target at an impressive range with the rest of them he does not go the way of all men. He is often reticent to the point of appearing taciturn, and rightly so, since a chatterbox would make the worst possible harbourer.

Harbouring apart, the purlieus of Cloutsham provided (and yet do) an Arcadian adventure in which something new was always cropping up, and one could never know enough of the surrounding villages —Luccombe, with its tumbling stream and yellow-washed cob cottages and Italianate cypresses in the churchyard, Bossington, with its great walnut trees and its Christmas hydrangeas and chrysanthemums. Horner, with its packhorse bridge and patriarchal oak tree and the remains of a medieval chapel in a farmhouse pungent with the scent of hot yeast. Occasionally one rose at dawn to be picked up by a trapper's cart on its way to Simonsbath or Exford, and on a day's tramp one encountered the postman who walked some twenty miles each day and who, in winter, was always helping some farmer to dig the sheep out of the snow—when the farmers were not digging *him* out.

But the major delights of Cloutsham were the evenings before that fragrant cavernous fireplace, with dusk settling upon the untramelled dome of Dunkery and a mountainous Ruisdael sky slowly filling with rain, the moorland air billowing over the Tyrolean balcony into the open bedroom, bringing with it, perhaps, a startled clouded yellow butterfly drawn by the light in this moorland oasis.

38

Tudor Edwards' magazine article.

House. Here, care was taken not to be seen by the owner, Colonel Clayton, so the string of children walked half crouched under the wall in front of the big house. From here they were led to the top of Invention Wood near to a summerhouse built when the Wills family owned Northmoor. The summerhouse, with lead glazed windows and heather thatched roof, had in those days an unimpeded view right up the Barle to the bend beyond Hinham. Meals used to be brought up if members of the Wills family wanted to spend time there. Nearby was a line of tree stumps that were just right for the entourage to sit on and eat their sandwiches, all the time being urged to be quiet and keep a sharp look up river by Dolly. If they heard the hunting horn at all, they were on red alert, watching for a galloping figure coming down Hawkridge Ridge. It would always be Hector, if he went to the left the deer would be in the Danesbrook, if he came straight on down then watch the river for the stag. This was the signal to be off, as they would not want to miss the kill, which might take place at New Invention or further down at Marsh Bridge. Sometimes it might be further on still above the town.

Hector once confessed to me as how he was coming down Hawkridge Ridge in a hurry to get to the deer (perhaps he was carrying the gun on this occasion) when he saw his two lady Masters Mrs S.L. Hancock and Miss B.K. Abbot going slowly down in front of him, filling the track. With no deference to them being his lady Masters who had the absolute authority for the day, he shouts out, and when Hector shouted it was with great volume "Get out of the bloody way you mommets!" A mommet is dialect for scarecrow, Hector said they appeared all arms and legs to prompt that remark. In most cases it was a sackable offence, but the good ladies knew of Hector's eccentricity and said nothing in this instance. However on another occasion when he transgressed it was a little different, as the words of his nephew Ross Campbell tell: -

"As a teenager your father asked me to help him with a hunt memorabilia exhibition he was organising. This involved me staying the weekend at Meadow Cottage with your parents, and resulted in a kind gift from your father of a D&S stag's head. Your father wrote on the back 'to Ross Campbell, for his sportsmanship'. I still, of course, have the head which is inscribed 'August 28th 1943. Found Nethercott Brake taken under Hawkridge Rectory'. I remember Hector telling me that he harboured the stag and shot it, encountering, in the process, the wrath of Miss Abbot, the master, who announced 'Heywood, if you ever shoot another stag that isn't bayed up properly by the pack I will take the gun away from you'!!"

As Joan was aged 29 when they married, her thoughts must soon have turned to having children. When the time came for me to be born she went home to Westerclose, Withypool and was attended to by the much respected and charismatic Irishman Dr. Barney McKinney. Dr. McKinney lived in Dulverton and had his surgery at his home; he was as it happened, great friends with the Nicholson family. On the eleventh of February 1942, I, an eight-pound baby was born. Hector was not there and only visited Joan once. My very early recollections of him were of a loving father who always came to my bed to say goodnight with a kiss. I never had any bad vibes as far as I can recollect from him. Clearly Joan thought it most important for me to have God Parents as three were appointed; firstly her cousin John Nicholson from Manor Farm, Bucknell was one. The second was her friend Joan Cooper from sailing days on the Helford River, and thirdly 'Uncle George'. I will now write about this most talented and remarkable man, known to me as Uncle George.

Benjamin Garnet Lampard-Vachell was born in 1892 son of Frank Lampard of Bath. His mother was housekeeper to a very wealthy bachelor in South Wales, who had no children. He left everything to Benjamin Garnet as long as he assumed the additional surname Vachell by Deed Poll; this happened in 1913. He was educated at Pembroke College, Cambridge where he took the Mechanical Science Tripos, getting his BA (Hons) in 1914 and MA in 1919. I assume the delay in being awarded his MA reflects his involvement in the Great War. Not only was he academically gifted but also he was a sporting Corinthian, he gained a half blue for cricket, playing for Cambridge and became a hockey international from 1920-28 winning 26 caps. He was made a technical officer at the Air department of the Admiralty and Air Ministry in 1916 until 1919.In that year he became a barrister-at-law in the Middle Temple. After this he had a strong flirtation with politics and contested as a Conservative candidate, the Wednesbury Division of Staffordshire in 1924, Lincoln in 1929, and lastly the Barnstaple Division of Devon in 1935, all unsuccessfully. This in itself shows great courage, self-belief and determination. He married in 1932 and was by now living at Weare Gifford Hall, Great Torrington in North Devon where he had one daughter. He became a Justice of the Peace for Gt.Torrington in 1937, then High Sheriff for Devon 1944-45. The involvement on many committees to do with education followed, such as Chairman of the South West Regional Council for further education 1956-61, being a member of the National Advisory Council in Education for Industry and Commerce, and Chairman of the Advisory Committee on further education for Agriculture with the Ministry of Education 1959. Finally he was appointed Pro Chancellor of the University of Exeter 1955. He also produced three books; it would mean so much to find copies of them.

Firstly: - *Critical Investigation into the performance of Aeroplanes* 1919

Secondly: - *Heraldic Shields of Weare Gifford Hall* 1934

Thirdly: - *Wild Birds of Torrington and District* 1944.

Since writing this I have found a copy of *Wild Birds of Torrington and District*, now it is two to go.

It was ornithology, his main recreation that led him to cross paths with Hector. How they met is lost in the mists of time, but he did come to Cloutsham with his mistress, one Mary Bice. 'Bicey' as she was known as in the family, was an unmarried schoolteacher and sometime governess living in Exeter, having originated from Crediton. She was a kindly but serious person who brooked no nonsense yet she had a heart of gold to match her stocky robust physique. The huge coincidence is that, as I learnt in about the year 2000 when I first met Gerard Noel, after he had told me that he knew Hector, was that Bicey had been the governess of his wife Caroline. Clandestine times together often took Garnet and Bicey to Exmoor and sometimes they camped at Cloutsham in the field towards Cloutsham Ball. Joan became great friends with Bicey, a friendship that lasted until Bicey died. Hector would have had great respect for Garnet who was so unassuming and humble in his demeanour, yet so knowledgeable and at times excitable. They got on well together walking the moors looking for birds and their nests and I cannot recall any disparagement towards Garnet. They continued to make infrequent visits to Hector and Joan right through the 1950s. Bicey and Garnet were still together in 1964, living the double life. Garnet would live in digs during the week at Exeter, to save making the journey to and from Torrington, as his work was Exeter based. How convenient that Bicey provided the digs! When the time came for me to leave Seale-Hayne Agricultural College, near Newton Abbot, South Devon in 1964 Joan came down in a car to collect me, and all my baggage. We spent the night at Bicey's bungalow in Heavitree; as Garnet was also there I was able to witness the performance in getting him off for the day. After much checking over the net curtains onto the road, when the coast was clear " You can go now Dear, goodbye", and off to work he would go just like any other commuter; however he had to be careful as in those days if found out, it would have been the end of his public life. That morning in June 1964 was the last time I saw him. He died in 1965 so they would have had at least twenty-five years of happiness, of a sort, together.

In the early days at Cloutsham Hector acquired a black cocker spaniel, which he named Simba. I remember the dog well and with affection. Hector worshiped the animal and they were inseparable. One day when clearing a dung heap, with Simba running around on it Hector suddenly saw that his lower lip was heavily swollen; he had been bitten by an adder. He was immediately on the phone to Major Rankin his vet at Minehead. "Bring him down as quick as you can." Major Rankin gave him an injection and gave instructions for the wound to be regularly bathed with a strong solution of soda. When Simba had properly recovered there were two scabs showing

Simba.

where the adder had bitten him. Dung heaps are a perfect environment for adders, warm from the decomposing dung and of course moist. If Hector was stalking a deer to shoot it in the woods, or over the heather, Simba would mimic his movements and never gave the game away. One day when Simba could not go with Hector, instructions were given to Joan to keep the dog shut up. Somehow or another Simba got out and set off to find Hector; he went all the way to Dulverton to Dolly's house at Kings Corner. Not finding him there he turned around and went straight back to Cloutsham. The distance measured flat on the map is twelve miles from Cloutsham to Dulverton, then twelve miles back and allowing for falls and rises the total distance is probably nearer to thirty miles. How that little dog knew that it was worth trying at Kings Corner is amazing. Here is a page and a half from HP Hewett's book *The Fairest Hunting* as he gives a lovely account of Simba when he writes about a Deer Fence separating the Dunkery range of hills and the farmlands adjoining the hill.

"A part of the fence forms a big salient *[bulge, Captain Hewett had been a military man so would talk about a salient]* up on to the hill and crosses a deep combe with a stream, which comes through the fence. The land in this salient had mostly gone out of cultivation, but was ploughed up again during the last war, just before which the fence had fortunately been thoroughly renovated. However, if deer have been in the habit of ranging certain ground, they will take infinite pains to circumvent the best of fences. One day news came of a stag in the salient, and the harbourer rode over with his spaniel to try to put him out and make good where he got in. He entered at a gate where the stream runs under the fence, and while he was latching the gate the spaniel hit a line and went away without his seeing the deer. Held up by barbed wire, he had to proceed on foot, and met the dog returning. Ahead he could see the top strand of the fence broken by something jumping out, and on getting there he saw a five-point antler lying in the ditch. He got over and picked it up. On the raw butt end were maggots and maggots do not hatch out in five minutes. He went back and slotted the spaniel's deer, and the slot was that of a three-year-old stag. So there had been two stags inside. Anyway, both were out and the land had peace for a space.

"Then there was a report of another stag inside, and I rode over to look around. The fern was now well up, and there was little evidence to be found, but by a stroke of luck, as I was taking a last look across the valley, I saw in a fern bed the tops of antlers. The harbourer was fetched. He had excellent glasses, and at once

Sidney, Simba, Hector, Bruce and Joan at Cloutsham 1943.

said there were two stags there, one a three-atop, and of the other he could see only one horn, a two-atop. Though they had obviously settled for the day, both stags suddenly got up, and moved off uneasily. We had the wind, but presumably an under-tow from our side had carried our taint right across to them. The wind plays queer tricks in combes. The harbourer handed me his glasses. 'Well, I'm d— —d!' he said. 'The lower stag has rights (i.e., brow, bay and trey) and two on the off horn and his near horn is in my house.'

"He took his spaniel across to the line of the three-atop, while I watched to see what one-horn did. It was most amusing to watch with the glasses that great twelve-pointer fleeing before the little black spaniel, who went driving along, throwing his tongue and hunting admirably. The little spaniel had had quite a hunt by the time the stag had found a place in the fence where he could jump out, whereupon the dog came back. Meanwhile, one-horn had gone down to the stream, and lain down in a fern bed, so the spaniel was taken to him, but could make little progress. After a turn or two the stag made up his mind, and went straight up towards the place where he and the three-year-old had jumped out before. Suddenly, when about halfway there, he swung off at right angles. I have no doubt he suddenly remembered what had happened to him there before, for he made a bee line for the fence about a quarter of a mile lower down, and jumped out there. This time he left no mark on the fence."

From this extract it is obvious how Simba played a key role in Hector's life. He probably thought much more of the dog than his two children, who were after all little more than babies at the time. Again, everybody has gone on who might have been able to throw light on what happened to Simba. Apart from siring some pups, one of which went to Wallace Harding at Horner, and sadly did not last long as it died of fits, I don't know how Simba met his end. All I have is a very hazy thought that he was run over outside Cloutsham by a military vehicle; he was not around in 1946/7. Hector would have been devastated, as he really loved the dog and the dog him.

No doubt anecdotes and stories will continue to come to me, just as this one, on 25th October 2011, from Terry Groves. Terry, a native of Wootton Courtenay, is a life long staghunter. About 25 years ago he started taking a group of elderly men, near or over 80, out in a Landrover to follow the hunt during autumn staghunting, for a fortnight. This went on for over ten years. These old boys used to love to tell about the stories that they had heard, about the people or events from their youth. One that was often talked

Hector acting the goat at Cloutsham, with sheep's wool moustache and pipe. He is holding a freshly detached head of a stag whose horns are in velvet. The photograph shows that he did have sense of humour that would be seen on rare or infrequent occasions.

about is the following: Hector was living at Cloutsham and had harboured the stag for a meet at or near North Molton. At the meet he told the Master and staff that the stag had summered at Cloutsham and had only left two weeks before. He told them "You will have to pick your feet up as he'll go straight back to Cloutsham." The stag did just that and was killed at Eastwater Foot, half a mile below Cloutsham. Hector maintained that the slopes and combes around Dunkery Beacon were the largest deer nursery on Exmoor, and on innumerable occasions deer way out on the Exmoor Forest would always, if hunted, run back to the area they knew best, especially the Horner Valley.

1943 saw the death of Ernest Bawden following an accident on 7th September at Hinham whilst helping with the corn harvest, when he tripped and fell, only for the wheel of the loaded cart to run over his chest causing massive internal injuries. He died three days later on 10th September, in Minehead Hospital. This would have seriously rocked Hector, as he lost someone who he would have hero-worshipped when growing up and had great respect for as an adult. Yes, they were at odds, at times, and Ernest did deny Hector the opportunity to farm at Hinham, yet they were uncle and nephew hewn from the same tree. Whether loosing yet another close member of the family marked the crossing of the Rubicon for Hector is conjecture, but difficulties in his life, hereinafter seemed more prevalent.

- 11 -
THE BEGINNING OF THE END

JOAN DID HAVE FRIENDS to enliven her life a little. One being the land girl at neighbouring Wilmersham Farm, who became Felicity Hodder-Williams; she took up residence in Exford after the war. Another was Annie Maggs whose father farmed at Larcombe Farm, Exford. When Joan's second baby was due, it was arranged that Annie would come over and drive Joan into Minehead to the nursing home. The due time arrived when the first signs of labour were evident; Annie was called and started driving Joan to Minehead. They had crossed Cloutsham Ford and were going uphill on the narrow little road, when they met an army convoy. They had to reverse back down to the ford. The problem being that Annie could not for the life of her reverse a car, especially with a steep drop on one side of the road and nothing but a few trees or vegetation between the road and the drop. Nothing for it but Joan got out and manoeuvred her ungainly and uncomfortable self in to the driving seat, and reversed the several hundred yards to a passing place back the other side of Cloutsham Ford. After the convoy had passed she said, "Well now I am here I might as well drive all the way to the nursing home". Their daughter Elizabeth was born soon after.

Occasionally she would see Maud Harding, wife of Jack from Stoke Pero. They became friends and Joan was godmother to their son Richmond. On the rare occasions when someone was needed to look after the children, Daphne Harding from Horner Vale obliged and walked up through the woods and fields. She was the daughter of Richmond and Catherine Harding; Richmond one of the many brothers from Stoke Pero, did not make older age as the gargantuan effort of collecting stones from the Horner Water with which to build his house carried him away, leaving his wife a widow. Daphne later married Harold James 'Jim' Stephens from Luckyard Farm, Wheddon Cross; her elder sister Jessie had married another brother Jack Stephens. Both the brothers were first cousins of Hector.

The postman 'Postie Parsons' walking from Porlock was a fairly regular visitor, as was Ben Herod in the early days. Now and again her mother would come over from Withypool until she let 'Westerclose' and moved to London. Every year, the firm of Gales would bring a lorry load of beehives down from near Bristol for the heather honey. I am not exactly sure where they were located, but somewhere close to Cloutsham and the road. A keen amateur beekeeper, Stan Burchill used to be the main helper in this exercise during his time off from driving steam locomotives of the Great Western Railway. I think he stayed for the odd night at Cloutsham on these trips down with the bees. He retired to live in Porlock and became my mentor when I took up beekeeping. It was on one of my visits to him that he told me of his trips to Cloutsham. He was appalled at how Joan had to rush round Hector to get him away for his harbouring or other work for the hunt.

"She even had to clean and polish his boots, on top of all the other work she had to do," he said in his powerful Bristolian accent.

It must have been whilst we were at Cloutsham that Hector travelled up to the BBC studios at Bristol and from there made a broadcast about nature on Exmoor; this was broadcast on the West of England Home Service. I know that I was a very small boy and had been taken to Ernie and Mrs. Parsons who lived at the bungalow 'Hideaway' at Exford. Ernie was the stud groom to the DSSH. It was whilst they were minding me that the broadcast was made. I was spellbound listening to the voice of my father coming out of their wireless in their tiny living room, but can remember nothing of the content. A letter to the BBC archives in Bristol in 2009 never elicited a reply, so I am still unsure whether a recording of that broadcast exists.

Joan had obviously at first been excited with her new life at Cloutsham, but the continual difficulties of wartime with shortages of food, petrol etc., a child of two, and a new baby to look after, lack of companionship, no help for her, but expected to help Hector, started to raise the pressure. She had after all, copper coloured hair, this was a pointer to a fiery temper when roused, and she had certain views and beliefs that she was not afraid of expressing. You could say Hector had met his match. I can vividly remember one morning in the front yard, her throwing a bowl of porridge right into his face.

Sidney Westcott of Bossington related, that: -

"Hector called to see my father Cyril one day to say that 'Joan threw the baby's piss pot at my head'!"

When Hector was in his twilight years, he told me one day, of how he was in the middle of shearing a sheep in the barn at Cloutsham, when all of a sudden he felt an almighty whack up against his ear. Joan had crept up on him to deliver the blow unseen. He confessed he never knew why she had done it.

To add to her woes, her cousin Laurence Nicholson from Manor Farm, Bucknell, (son of her Uncle Arch) was killed on 24th March 1945. Laurie was a Captain in the 6th Airborne Ox & Bucks Light Infantry and was involved with the Pegasus Bridge operation on D-Day 1944. Unfortunately he was wounded in one of the gliders on landing and was repatriated the next day. When I was a toddler and running around, I remember him coming to Cloutsham to say goodbye to Joan; he seemed to fill the entire doorway. It was only a fleeting visit in passing, as his transport was waiting outside, but even I at that young age could feel the awful trepidation and sadness, perhaps it was the tears that flowed down Joan's cheeks after a big hug from Laurie. She was especially fond of him, as were all the Nicholson family. The operation in which he died was codenamed Varsity (the Rhine Crossing), which concerned the capture of Wesel and the surrounding country including the Wesel and Issel rivers. Overall it was the biggest air operation of the whole war and the last major Allied offensive in Europe. The RAF and the US Air Force flew in 1,572 planes and 1,105 gliders, whilst the 2nd Tactical AF provided escort and covered the operation with 900 fighters. At the same time the US established a screen of 1,253 aircraft east of the target. Unfortunately the smoke from the previous twenty-four hour Allied artillery bombardment, and mist, gave survival cover to the German artillery, so that when the smoke and mist disappeared, the incoming gliders were cannon fodder. It was a direct hit on Laurie's glider from an 88mm shell that killed all but three of the glider's occupants.

One day in 1945 Joan could take no more; she and Hector had an almighty row during which she put the proverbial pistol to his head. He must quit the hunt work and concentrate on the farm, or quit the farm and carry on with the hunt work. She claimed he never made any money from working for the hunt, which might not be exactly true as his expense account book and National Savings Certificate book revealed. Hector stormed off in a rage down to the Holnicote Estate Office, which by now was run by the National Trust as Sir Richard Acland had made a gift to the nation of his Holnicote Estate, and gave notice to quit Cloutsham. This revealed what was of greatest significance in his life. The Devon and Somerset Staghounds, having played such an important role in his life and given so much excitement and so many thrills, especially when that helped to alleviate the feeling the guilt over Freddy's death, was something that he could never let go. He went back a few days later to the office and begged them to let him stay, but they wouldn't rescind, he had to go.

His outgoing sale was held on October 19th 1945, conducted by James Phillips and Sons of Minehead and Bridgetown. The auctioneer's sale notebooks make sad reading when I can hear Hector proudly saying he went to Cloutsham with nothing and came away with £1000. Most of his beekeeping kit including seven hives went, all his sheep, all cattle bar two cows, a cart mare, an eleven year old bay horse, quiet to ride, all his machinery, sheep netting, hand tools, fowls house and surplus furniture. Five items of furniture were bought by someone with the name of Bice; it can only have been Bicey. There is no way of knowing exactly when Cloutsham was vacated or when the bulk or best of their furniture went into store with Burley's of Minehead, but the last two entries in the livestock movement book list nine pigs going from Cloutsham to Minehead Grading Market on January 21st 1946 and five pigs on February 12th going to Brandish Street, Allerford. Certainly Joan and Hector went their separate ways, with Joan and us children going first. My friend from childhood Michael Upstone from Porlock has written his recollections of Hector and I include a sentence here. *"My father knew Hector of course and related how during the war when he was on his special police duties in a vehicle and they called at Cloutsham farm and Hector was there looking very miserable with a small fire to keep him warm. Presumably this was when Joan was away with the children."* He had lost his farm, the idyllic Cloutsham, his wife and two young children had gone, with all his dreams for the future swept away; this must have been a soul destroying time for him, yet he was a very strong minded person and probably quickly adjusted to his new circumstances. He went to live in the Great War billet hut at Horner Vale that belonged to Mrs. Kate Harding. He kept the Morris Eight Tourer so was able to travel about and worked part time for the new tenant at Cloutsham, Mrs. Rosemary Young, as well as continuing his harbouring and other hunt duties. I am uncertain as to what he got up to during this time; I know he had a horse and was still looking after two cows that he owned. One of them, 'Buttons' was a bit special and had great sentimental value, so I will retell the story as related to me by John Heywood.

A calf arrived at Anstey Station in the early 1930s, from the dealer Cliff Edwards of Ashill in Devon. It had been constrained in a sack, the neck of which was tied round the neck of the calf, together with a label. It was a 'bit of a Shorthorn' and when young, knocked the shell off its horn on one side. She was called 'Greybird' which would give rise to the cry 'Greybird has gone' when she was about to calve as she always broke out and escaped to Whiterocks or Durhams to have her calf. These were areas of semi-moorland with much vegetation of gorse and rushes. She died before the Heywoods left Hinham, but Sidney took two of her red heifers to Cloutsham, one of which had the triplets and the other 'Buttons' followed us until about 1951.

Greybird's daughter with triplets; they have not been born long.

Sidney with Greybird's daughter's thriving triplets.

I think he lodged his two cows either with Mrs. Young or with his friend Harry Rawle of Court Place, Porlock; indeed it might have been anywhere where he could have parked them.

I do know that he lived in the billet hut from about Lady Day 1946 until November when Kate Harding's son Wallace came home from the army. As Kate Harding thought the world of Hector, she in all probability, cooked meals for him. She certainly knitted thick long white socks for him. In turn he worked hard for her in the big vegetable garden, and as Wallace recounts "He used to grow some wonderful peas, I always remember that; he was a hugely mixed up man and didn't get on with very many people". As the National Health Service was not up and running at this time, there was no help forthcoming for his sleep problem. One night a young tawny owl set up quite a racket with its continuous hooting from the top of a pollarded tree across the garden from Hector's hut. In typical fashion, straight from his bed in pyjamas he climbed the tree and wrung the neck of the owl. As I have never had a problem with sleep all my life, I find it difficult to see the other side, but quite clearly sleep deprivation must be most unpleasant. Poor man.

Apart from my personal memories, which mean going back to being a four-year-old boy, there is little documentary evidence of Joan's journeys during 1945/46. Whether during the brief time when her cousin Laurie called to say goodbye, she said she wanted out and he had said go to Bucknell, is a possibility. I do know that she was very fond of the Nicholsons at Manor Farm, Bucknell, having been taken there on visits over the years, and there was spare room in the large farmhouse. At any rate we arrived there during the late autumn or early winter of 1945 as I remember the bitter cold and having a fire lit in the bedroom fireplace. I was kept occupied by playing with my second cousin Richard from Banbury, roaming about on the farm, afternoon walks, or attending the village school for the summer term. At times trips away took place, visits to my godfather John Nicholson (Joan's cousin and father of Richard) at his farm at Drayton near Banbury; staying at West Wittering on the Sussex coast with a friend of Joan, and according to a postcard sent to me, we stayed at Exford with Pip, Joan's sister. I have no recollection of seeing Hector, having any letter or card from him, indeed his name was never mentioned in front of me as far as I can recall. One of the memories of the time was sitting for an eternity either on a suitcase in the corridor of a train, or in a compartment as the long, slow journeys were made. The boredom was not helped by seeming to be always hungry, scratchy and tired.

If it was not for the wisdom of the kind, compassionate, family-loving person of Joan's aunt Lilian, the wife of Arch Nicholson, I do not know what would have become of our lives. Her words of advice to Joan were that she should go back, attempt a reconciliation and to live with Hector for the sake of the children. Whether he had been imploring her to return is not known, but I am glad that she did as it gave me back my father.

- 12 -
FOUR YEARS OF STABILITY THEN CATACLYSM

THE NEW HOME for us to return to in the autumn of 1946, as a family, was the farm cottage attached to West Luccombe Farm, in the Porlock Vale, still on the Holnicote Estate and about two miles from Cloutsham. It did not matter to me that there was only one tap of cold running water at the back door, that there was no electricity, only Tilley lamps and candles for light, and that lavatorial matters were conducted via a chamber pot or the privy in the garden. It would not have worried Hector, but for Joan it was an unpleasant and unhappy price to pay, having been used to so much more civilised domestic arrangements; even Cloutsham had running water, both hot and cold, flush lavatories and a telephone. Water for our weekly dip in the tin bath was heated in the copper by a small wood fire underneath it. We did keep clean! Fortunately there were three bedrooms, one for Hector, another for Joan and one for Beth and myself. At least we were a family unit, and Hector probably could have felt a little pride at being head of the family. I consider that he felt his responsibilities now were to provide a roof over our heads and some form of heating. Apart from a supply of milk, he never appeared to contribute towards the cost of food, which became Joan's responsibility. He did help at Christmas, not by providing any presents but cutting holly and digging up a young fir tree, usually from the eastern side of Webber's Post, as our Christmas tree. This was replanted somewhere after Christmas so as not to waste it. His old Master, Miss Abbot, used to send him 100 Player's cigarettes in a tin box as a Christmas present, but because he had stopped smoking he had no use for them. Any normal person would have given them to their wife if they, like Joan, smoked, but no, he gave them away to somebody else. We never seemed to see much of him as he was always off somewhere. He had resigned from his harbouring finishing at the hunting changeover day of May 1st 1947. Without the facilities for keeping a horse or two, in summer and winter, a regular source of income and the backup of Joan, it was impossible for him to keep going. He had completed nine seasons and had helped to ensure that there were deer left on Exmoor to breed up and expand the herd from his estimate of 500 head of deer at the end of the war. In 2012 there were according to the deer count, in excess of 2800 head. He remained on the periphery of the Hunt, to become usefully involved when deer drives were organised. These were a means to cull numbers when deer were becoming a nuisance in certain locations and doing excessive damage to crops. During a deer drive, deer were flushed by the huntsman on a horse with a few hounds towards a line of guns. Hector's speciality was to create a funnel by impaling pieces of lavatory paper, probably the tough sort 'Bronco' or 'Izal', on vegetation at deer head height. He would position himself at the end of the funnel, unseen to the deer, and would hardly ever miss one. He would have a day following hounds in the car whenever it suited him.

Now in his early forties he was still very physically fit, not only from the farm work that he did, but also from walking miles on Exmoor either looking for, and at, deer, and in the pursuit of finding bird's nests. Whilst at the cottage he was, I believe, self-employed, yet committed to work for the farmer when he was needed. This sort of arrangement suited him by giving flexibility to his life, not being tied to regular hours and days; he remained self-employed until he could stop work and collect his state pension in 1970. When he retired from harbouring for the Devon and Somerset Staghounds he felt free to pursue with all the energy he could muster, the collecting of wild birds eggs. This became much more than just a hobby or gentle interest, more of a serious passion around which his life would revolve. It gave him entry to a brotherhood of collectors, many of whom became firm friends with him; although some he had no time for at all, they represented quite a cross section of the population. Those he had most respect and affection for and with whom he went on field forays will be written about in more detail later; however one of the first collectors and possibly the most pivotal was John Piers Dutton. Hector met him when he went as a student to the National Trust agent Col. Freddie Reeks at the Holnicote Estate Office, before or as part of his course at The Royal Agricultural College. As he lived in digs at West Luccombe Farm, Hector would have seen him frequently and been wised up, perhaps, as to whom he should contact for field trips. Hector had an unerring sense of giving people nicknames that always appeared to be so apt. For instance he gave John Dutton the name 'The Great Dumfunkum'. For years 'Dumfunkum' was in common parlance, never his real name.

Certainly whilst at West Luccombe, and reinforced with his farm sale monies, Hector made the first of four trips to Scotland from 17th May until 7th June 1949. I pieced together his movements from his collection data cards and on this expedition he went to Inverness and to South Uist in the Outer Hebrides; amongst the more interesting species of nests found were the corncrake and short-eared owl. I am not exactly sure of how he travelled. My sister Elizabeth says that he went with John Durrant in John's car with Algy Taylor from Bourton on the Water. I have eleven post cards that he sent to us from his four trips, always ending with love from Daddy-Doo, except on the one time when he sent one to Elizabeth and Joan and signed just HH. From the one addressed to me at West Luccombe in 1949 he says, "I haven't a timetable. Hope Mummy can meet me at Minehead Friday. First train from London," so maybe the first trip was by railway train. I remember that he told me that he had at one time been on a train pulled by the London Midland Scottish Railway locomotive in its maroon livery, the 'Duchess of Hamilton'. This locomotive was saved from the breaker's yard when Dr. Beeching made his savage cuts on the national railway system, being purchased by Sir Billy Butlin, and was for a time displayed outside Butlin's Holiday Camp at Minehead; it now resides at York in the National Railway Museum.

The National Health Service came into being in 1947 and I am certain that Hector was an early beneficiary, firstly with sleeping tablets, then an exploratory operation in a search for an ulcer. The sleeping tablets were 'Phenobarbitone', in other words barbiturates. He took these for years and suffered the side effects such as constipation that was countered with Sennacot, a laxative. Our local doctor was Dr. Tatlow from Porlock; he was also a practising surgeon at Minehead Hospital and persuaded Hector to undergo investigative surgery in the hopes of finding the cause of all his digestive upsets. He was looking for ulcers, and disappointingly found nothing, but did remove his appendix whilst he was in the vicinity. If the medicines of today had been available then he would have been prescribed Zantac or Lansoprazole, as I feel sure he suffered in common with many people an overproduction of gastric juices.

The farmer at West Luccombe Farm was Major Roger Sandford, to whom Hector gave the name 'Rat's muzzle' on account of his moustache and small dark eyes behind the wire-rimmed spectacles that he wore. Roger Sandford was from a well to do family, his mother was Lady St John of Bletso and they had an estate somewhere near Milverton or Wellington in East Devon. Lady St John was well known in Court circles as she prepared the rich young girls of the day for their coming out and presentation at Court. Sandford was a hunting man and together with his friend Leslie Scott, who farmed near Crediton, made forays on to Exmoor to hunt with the Devon and Somerset Staghounds during the 1930s. Sometime after leaving Eton, Sandford was made a 2nd Lieutenant in the Black Watch in 1932. By 1935 he was a full Lieutenant and finally Captain and Temporary Major in 1940. He served with the 14th Army in the Far East and several people have confirmed my thoughts that he took part in the 2nd Chindit Expedition in 1944 under Major-General Orde Wingate, operating in Burma behind the Japanese lines, fighting a guerrilla war with air drops into the jungle of all necessary supplies. After the war he wanted to go farming, and as Leslie Scott had become a tenant on the Holnicote Estate at East Lynch Farm, he asked Leslie to find him a farm. Accordingly he was given the tenancy of West Luccombe Farm in his absence. Until he returned home from the Far East, Leslie Scott kept an eye on the farm and had one of his men live in the house. The local farmers did not approve of this at all, as it was a lovely rich vale farm being let to an unknown quantity. It soon became apparent that Roger Sandford, the kind, upright gentleman who was always well mannered and doffed his cap to ladies, was no farmer. Joan Weaver née Richards from Sparkhayes Farm, Porlock described him 'Like a blind man farming' he was so unpredictable and erratic. An example would be the purchase of a pair of twelve bore shotguns especially made for him by a first class maker. In the days when hammer guns were being considered definitely inferior to the hammerless guns that everybody was buying, Sandford had to buy a pair of hammer guns costing thousands of pounds in those days. When asked why "I like to be different" was his reply.

He bought a lovely herd of Ayrshire cows to milk, but he couldn't make them pay. He had a flock of sheep and kept poultry. He even ended up keeping many of the poultry in the bedrooms of the farmhouse. The farm became infested with rats, but he struggled on. He was generous to a fault giving meets for the local hunt, the Minehead Harriers, entertaining local farmers to dinner with as much as they wanted to drink. He had an open top sports car and took Derek Dascombe, son of neighbouring farmer Claude, away to Wales on holiday, frightening Derek to death by his driving. Another example of his eccentricity was on the occasion when another neighbour's sheep got into one of his fields. Instead of just returning them, he took them up to West Luccombe and fastened them in a shed. A moonlit night followed and in the morning he got up and the sheep had gone. The neighbour, Cyril Robins from Lynch Farm, Bossington, went up demanding where his sheep had got to as he had heard that Sandford had moved them. This caused Sandford to get in a fluster of great embarrassment. Cyril Robins had of course moved them back to Lynch in the moonlight.

As an example of his thoughtfulness, when the electric generator broke down, during a snowstorm, on the off or hill farm, that went with West Luccombe, he immediately set off on foot, to repair it. This was an uphill trek of about three miles. Since small children were living there, it was important that heat and light were restored as soon as possible.

At some stage, Sandford acquired a housekeeper, a Mrs. Lewis with a son Colin. This woman by all accounts was very manipulative of Sandford and could get him to do anything and was the ruin of him. Derek Dascombe told me that after many years of sharing the same milk stand for their milk churns, they were suddenly without reason told not to use it. Derek was not even allowed to visit the house. Hector must have crossed Mrs. Lewis over some matter, for the next thing he knew was that his employment was terminated and he had to get out of the cottage by the end of the week. "That bloody Rat's Muzzle" or much worse would probably have been his response. In those days there was no recourse to arbitration or tenant's rights, it was out and you had to get out. Because this matter was so out of keeping with Roger Sandford's customary kindness and his trip in the snow to mend the generator because of little children, it had to have the hallmark of the dreaded housekeeper.

Roger Sandford struggled on until 1962 when he went into voluntary liquidation and quit the farm. The agent for the National Trust was an ex military man Colonel Freddie Reeks and was perhaps too sympathetic to another military man; at least he was not firm enough in stopping the rot. When a tenant left a farm in those days (and the practice remains the same today) it was customary for an auctioneer/valuer to carry out a tenant right valuation on the improvements that the tenant had made (or dilapidations), on the manurial residues in the ground or in any dung heap, state of the gates, fences and hedges, and buildings, as well of course the state of the farm house. A valuer would act for the landlord and at the end of proceedings a sum would be worked out what the landlord might owe the tenant or vice versa. In normal cases the process might not take but a whole day or two at the most. In Sandford's case it took five days for Jack Hosegood acting on behalf of the estate of Roger Sandford in bankruptcy, with Roly Ford assisting, and Clifford 'Spuddy' Phillips acting for the landlord with Tom Rook assisting, to sort the matter out. According to Jack Hosegood his book was nothing but pay, pay, pay and Clifford Phillips' was nothing but draw, draw, draw. In the words of Tom Rook when going around the farmhouse "God I must have a cigarette I can't stick this, dead fowls, dead rats," and then to me "You've never seen anything like it in your life." Derek Dascombe was one of those owed money by Sandford, who said to him "Don't make a claim, I will see you right." The one attribute that could never be denied Sandford was that he was a gentleman, who would never go back on his word. After three years Derek was paid the money owing to him. A new tenant was found for the farm and within a year it had nearly been turned around.

Now that we had had our marching orders it was important for the family to stay fairly local, as I had been attending St. Theresa's School (convent) in Minehead and was settled there. This was a girl's school with a small preparatory school for boys run by nuns with some outside teaching staff. On our return to Hector at West Luccombe, I had had a term at the local village school at Allerford. I would think that Joan was not happy with my progress so I was moved to the convent; her mother Elma would have seen to the paying of school fees, I seem to remember. In desperation, for a week is not a long time to move out and find somewhere to live, all the furniture was put back into store with Burley's in Minehead. Claude Dascombe at nearby Burrowhayes Farm was approached for the use of a caravan; he may well have volunteered it. As he had a campsite and several caravans he lent it on the proviso that he would have it back by the beginning of May ready for the tourist season. It was set up in Claude's orchard on the opposite side of the river to the cottage that we vacated. Bearing in mind that the time of the year was the beginning of October just added to the difficulties facing Joan. Hector elected to buy a new green ridgepole tent from Pauls of Martock, into which he put a single metal-framed bed, duckboard covered in old hessian cattle cake sacks, a small table and chair. Thus he slept throughout the whole winter, through rain, frost and snow. There was, adjacent to the caravan, a little hut with an Elsan lavatory in it. It amuses me to think now, of where it was emptied, and I have a strong suspicion that the contents went into the fast flowing Horner Water. A milk churn of water, for drinking, was kept at the door of the caravan, and I have memories of Joan's frantic efforts at keeping the mud at bay. Newspaper and hessian sacks were part of the front line defence; muddy boots were removed on the steps in a balancing act changing into slippers. The caravan was by today's standards very basic, a table with bench seats one side of the door, cooking arrangements by Calor gas in front of the door, with many overhead lockers, and then to the right were the sleeping quarters. These consisted of two small drop-down beds and a double under the window. The roof was a single skin of aluminium with no insulation so we became adept at getting to sleep, and sleeping for the duration of the night under the drumming of heavy rain. I have seen Hector's tent white with frost and at other times covered in many inches of snow, yet he was happy or so it seemed, as he never moaned about the situation. He always claimed he was snug in bed with a hot water bottle. To Joan's eternal credit she made the whole experience seem to me at least, like one big adventure or holiday in a caravan, as I have no unhappy or unpleasant memories of the duration. How she coped with washing our clothes or bed linen is a mystery. Perhaps she would have had the use of a friend's copper to boil the water etc., quite probably that of our recent neighbour old Mrs. Reeves who lived with a spinster daughter Anne. We were very friendly with them, and Hector with Mrs. Reeves' son Harold especially. Harold kept bees and Hector kept his two or three hives alongside those of Harold, behind his carpenter's shop at the side of his mother's cottage. Elizabeth had started school in the autumn term of 1949 at St. Theresa's so, upon reflection, Joan deserves even greater credit in getting two small children ready for school to walk the half-mile to catch the bus to Minehead for the whole of the winter and lent terms, from the confines of a caravan.

Whilst my sister and I were at school, Joan took part time work in Peter Leach's shop attached to his dairy and milk bottling plant in Porlock. To get to and fro the mile and a half or so, she rode a bicycle that just happened to be a gent's model with a crossbar to add to the difficulties. We were reasonably served by delivery vans from the butcher, baker and Upstone's special lorry supplying paraffin, Calor gas and all hardware requisites. However I have recollections of Joan struggling back loaded up with provisions in baskets and rucksack, but never Hector bringing them in the car. Peter Leach was a pre-war friend of Hector and they spent many a happy hour rabbiting with ferrets, or on the deer shoots organised by the DSSH, and following the staghounds in Peter's green Austin van. Peter was one of the many sons of Bill and Lucy Leach who farmed at Brandish Street Farm, Allerford on the Holnicote Estate.

Every autumn it was important for us to gather part of nature's bounty for consumption during the winter; by this I mean hazelnuts and walnuts. Joan made collecting bags with pull cords from the old cattle feed sacks for us to gather as many hazel nuts as we could, which was quite easy when the time was right, either from the ground having been shed naturally, or by climbing up the nut bushes and shaking the limbs or by picking them direct off the stalks. The grey squirrel was not yet widespread so there were always nuts to be gathered. Walnuts were a different story, these were knocked down by sticks thrown up, unless Hector was around when he would climb up with his amazing skill into the walnut tree and then out onto a branch; by jumping up and down a shower of ripe nuts departing their blackening skins, would descend for the eager people below. On one occasion in West Luccombe, I remember some Porlock lads being on the scene and scarce believing their eyes and good fortune. I quote my friend Michael Upstone again: -

"My father used to take the family out for a drive most Sundays [*He used to have the hardware shop in Porlock and therefore Sundays would be a family day having been tied to the shop all the rest of the time*] and I remember us coming back through Horner and seeing Hector up the walnut tree shaking the nuts down for people to collect underneath. We collected some ourselves because my father was very fond of nuts."

- 13 -

GILHAMS DAYS

HECTOR'S MADE HIS second trip to Scotland to look for bird's nests from10th April until 2nd May, this is confirmed by a postcard dated 22nd April 1950 sent to Beth and me. "Aviemore, Saturday. I am all right but tired we are going out today and hope to get one new one. The news of E is very disappointing will write from S.Uist."

The E refers to Golden Eagle, which perchance that very day of sending the card he found a nest near Inverness. I understand that although the nest was guarded by gamekeepers, Hector somehow or other used his skills of concealment and climbed up to the nest unobserved and took the eggs.

The postcard was sent to Gilhams, Porlock and confirms that we were living there. We had probably moved at the beginning of the month making a total of six months living in the caravan. Gilhams was a pair of farm cottages that were attached to Holt Ball Farm, still part of the Holnicote Estate, about two miles to the east of West Luccombe. The farmer was Norman Kennelly, a good friend of Hector, who gave Hector work on the farm when he was needed, as a means of at least paying the rent for the cottage. Although the facilities at Gilhams were non-existent, i.e. no electricity, so it was candles and Tilley lamps for light, no indoor sanitation but up the garden path to the privy and no water at the cottage, we coped. Water had to be pumped by hand from a well about 80 yards away and carried by bucket to the kitchen. This meant running the gauntlet of slopping the water with the consequent wet leg or worse still, socks and shoes for me at least. There was a black range to supply some heat and when there was coal to supplement the firewood, it would get hot enough to cook with. Hector always seemed to have a tight control on the fuel and we would be frequently told when he went to bed at 7.30 or 8.00pm "Don't put any more wood on that fire".

The cottage had three bedrooms, all small and pokey but he could have one to himself, I had one and Joan and Beth had the third. Downstairs was the main living room and a box room adjacent with a kitchen complete with a copper. Joan used to cook with a paraffin stove plus oven, and a primus stove. Even with these very basic tools she produced wonderful food and we never went really hungry. I remember the epic day in 1952 when Exmoor experienced the most severe cloudburst that caused the massive flooding on all the Rivers Barle, Exe and Lyn with some loss of life in Lynmouth. At the time we thought we had been badly affected by water pouring into the kitchen to a depth of five or six inches, until we heard the news. For all the time we were at West Luccombe we would have felt the full effects of rationing. When the war ended it did not mean the automatic end to rationing, far from it, meat and meat products were self-rationing as there was so little to go around. Bread was rationed from 1946-48, potatoes in 1947, petrol came off rationing 26th July 1950, sweets came off in February 1953 and sugar in September 1953. Clothes, soap, furniture and building materials had all been rationed. The early 1950s were a time of great austerity but somehow we survived, no doubt due to a plentiful supply of rabbit meat until 'Myxie' arrived and milk from our cow 'Buttons' that appeared on the scene from somewhere. A shed was constructed for her as a lean-to building in the orchard that went with Gilhams. This was put up by Harold Reeves from West Luccombe with Hector as builder's mate, using galvanised iron on the roof and off-cut slabbing from the sawmill as walling. I was taught here how to milk a cow and took great delight at squeezing the teat in the direction of my mouth. The calf lived in a section of the shed, to be let out to suck after we had milked enough for ourselves. Sadly I don't think Buttons lasted long as she had been sold by the time we came to move out in 1954. The only thing that really stands out was one time when I was very hungry and it was sometime before the next meal and I grizzled "Mum I'm hungry what can I have to eat?" She cut off a slice of bread, spread some margarine on it then sprinkled some granulated sugar on to that. We called them 'Mousies' and they were delicious in those times of hunger.

Whenever we were taken anywhere in the Morris Eight Tourer, which was not very often due to the scarcity of petrol and Hector having priority usage, we always coasted down the hills with the engine switched off to save fuel, then on nearing the bottom of the hill the clutch would be let out to fire up the engine and on we would go. The main outings seemed to be visits to his sister Dolly in Dulverton, or to go to the station so that we could catch a train. I see from the egg data cards that Hector made trips to Ringwood in Hampshire, Ollerton in Nottinghamshire, Ferndown and Portland in Dorset, and Chudleigh in Devon in spite of petrol rationing. He must have saved his coupons well beforehand to buy enough fuel.

For Hector and us children the four years that we spent at Gilhams were good and happy ones. He had the freedom to come and go as he pleased, with any work for Norman Kennelly not a chore but enjoyable in the company of his friend. Hector gave him the sobriquet 'The Flying Pencil' after a small horse of the same name, that Norman rode hunting, with the staghounds of course! Norman gave the recognition to Joan that she deserved, and always spoke kindly to her. The frequent bottles or cans of fresh milk which were sent down to her helped enormously especially when 'Buttons' was no longer on the scene

Tim Williams the psychotherapist from Hawkridge told me that Hector liked to give boys aged nine to ten an entrance into the adult world to compensate for the loss of Freddy and I was just about on that threshold as I was eight when we first moved to Gilhams. Father and son had some good times together. I went ferreting with him, feeding and handling the ferrets that he had; he showed me how to make rabbit snares to which I earlier alluded in chapter five. He gave me advice and encouragement on how to climb a tree, insisting that I always had one good foothold and one good handhold. I should never trust a limb that had any rot in it, never look down and keep well into the trunk of the tree unless the branches were plentiful and strong when I could go from branch to branch away from the trunk. We went on bird nesting forays on to the moors; Chetsford Water, Weir Water and Chalk Water were his favourites. We looked for ravens, buzzards, ring ouzels, dippers, merlin, as well as the ground nesting whinchat, stonechat and wheatears. He taught me to stop in a likely place and sit or lie still for five minutes, after when birds would start to show themselves, and we had to watch them carefully without sudden movement on our part. It was surprising what there was to see after those five minutes, everything came to life. We would see deer and he would show me the slots or hoof prints they made so that I could distinguish between a stag and a hind; he was in his way, trying to teach me of the things that were so familiar and that meant so much to him. In other words, how to use my eyes to see, not just to look at things.

He also had a sense of fun or perhaps the ridiculous as I can demonstrate with words from my friend Michael Upstone:

"Also I remember at Gilhams – lots of days over there with him in varying moods. When he was happy he was super – remember him bowling chin-chin-chinaman balls at cricket in the road outside the cottage laughing and acting the fool. But I saw him angry and moody and he gave Joan a bad time – not just arguing but being bloody minded over apparently nothing. He went on one of his Scotland trips and brought us both back some eggs – I had an artic skua single egg which I cherished. I sent off for egg blowing equipment around now and he approved it and showed me how to drill eggs etc."

Ironically, having at one time been praised by the RSPCA, he may well have been prosecuted for seemingly apparent cruelty to his horse 'Tom Tit'. At the end of the hunting season his friend Harry Rawle from Court Place Farm, Porlock, used to allow friends to graze their horses on Porlock Marshes for the summer. The grazing was good and the horses by the end of summer would have put back the lost condition of the past hunting season, going home sleek and fat. Harry Rawle had a man from the village called Gibbons to work for him to whom Hector must have been derogatory, or upset him in some way; to get his own back in a spiteful way, he reported Hector to the RSPCA. Sadly 'Tom Tit' had to go.

1951 saw Hector make his third foray to Scotland; he was away 26th May until 11th June, a shorter visit this time that was specifically to the islands of North and South Uist. On this trip he successfully found and collected the eggs of the following birds: -

Red Throated Diver	Oyster Catcher	Twite	Black Headed Gull
Dunlin	Rock Pipet	Lesser Redpoll	Rock Dove
Hen Harrier	Ring Plover	Arctic Skua	Hebredian Song Thrush

These represent quite a haul of the more unusual species.

Hector sitting in the front right of the boat in animated conversation with his friend Algy Taylor visiting an island.

During our time at Gilhams Hector acquired a hen house and some hens; I would consider he wanted to keep them to generate some relatively easy money. Two things stand out in my memory, both due to the kindness of Norman Kennelly. Firstly he allowed Hector to put the hen house on a field of barley stubble, so that the hens could forage and live well on the wasted barley ears of whole grain, weed seeds and any greenery. It was not always Hector who shut the hens up in the evening, more often than not whilst at home on school holidays, I was sent to do the job. This meant a walk through a large wood (Whitlands Moor) to get to the stubble field, I would collect any eggs that had been laid and walk my way the quarter of a mile or so home. Sometimes

I stopped and foraged for suitable sized pieces of timber for the copper fire, these I would stack up beside the path for Hector to haul away at some date. Secondly Norman allowed us to go gleaning. With the arrival of the first combine harvesters that had a header of a width of more than the gateways, gateposts had to be removed and in some cases the gateways themselves had to be widened to allow the machine to get into the field. Arthur Case from Withycombe, to the east of Dunster was one of the first to have a combine, a Massey-Harris 780 bagger model and he did all the harvesting of Norman's corn crops, although some would say that come finish there was as much weed seed coming off the combine as proper grain. When the grain had been harvested and the straw baled and removed we were at liberty to glean; this entailed using baskets and buckets to gather up the unthreshed ears of grain that had been cut but never made it into the machine. From the baskets, sacks were filled; these were as many as seven or eight to provide free food during the winter when there was not much else for the hens to eat. The sacks would have weighed about 56lbs or 25kgs, this represented quite a saving of scarce cash. The collected eggs were carefully wiped clean with a damp cloth, stacked onto trays and collected once a week along with any rabbits by Bill Ball for the Dulverton butcher Gordon Summers. Hector enjoyed the times when Bill Ball, balding, bespectacled, and wearing a white apron, who he knew from Hinham days, used to call as they would chatter away about Dulverton news and people.

It is difficult to get the timing right, but I would presume that it would have been the harvest before the arrival of Arthur Case's combine when the binder was used for the last time. In the field adjacent to Gilhams I was able to witness a spectacular happening. Norman's Allis-Chalmers model U tractor was pulling a trailer loaded with sheaves of corn being driven by a young George Burnell from Wootton Courtenay. It appeared to be driven at full throttle across the slope of the ground when all of a sudden there was a bang and the trailer had turned over onto its side; with good fortune the tractor stayed on all four wheels, the drawbar pin having sheared. George had not yet married and settled, he was in his wild phase. Although responsible when driving local people in his garage's hire car, he was seriously untamed and unrestrained on his 500cc Triumph Trophy motorcycle. This is well illustrated by the day Norman called into the garage at Wootton asking if he could be taken to Exford to meet a deadline, not knowing that he was about to be pillion passenger on the motorbike. George made it to Exford covering the eleven miles in eleven minutes and Norman made the deadline. That was quite some feat when considering the route, firstly a winding small lane of two miles to get onto the main road which itself has many bends and a climb of several hundred feet. In the words of George, "Norman Kennelly was a good passenger, leaning and moving his weight at the right moments. Norman thought it was the fastest that he had ever got to Exford." It would be interesting to know if that time has ever been equalled or beaten, I somehow doubt it as back then in the very early 1950s there would have been far fewer vehicles on the road, giving way to long clear stretches which is certainly not the case today.

Regarding our education, Hector would have had no say in the matter at all. He would have been happy for us to go to the local village school and then to the secondary modern in Minehead, but Joan had other ideas knowing of the great benefits of good education. Sending me away to a normal boarding or public school was a total impossibility, the only alternative was to write dozens of letters in the hope of finding a donating governor who was prepared to present me to Christ's Hospital and pay for my time at that school. Christ's Hospital, or the Bluecoat school, was founded in 1552 in the city of London by King Edward VI, the boy king, as an institution on the site of the old Grey Friars monastery for the poor children in the City giving them accommodation, food and an education. To this day it is still a school for poor under privileged children and those from disadvantaged circumstances, but it moved into new buildings on its own estate near Horsham in West Sussex in 1902. Joan was at last successful by using the good offices of Miss Biddy Abbot, Master of the Staghounds 1939-51. She was friendly with Lady Fortescue from Castle Hill, Filleigh, N. Devon whose brother was Viscount Allendale. He was a donating governor to Christ's Hospital and presented me to the school. I started out from Gilhams in September 1951 to become a new boy at that school. I said goodbye to my mother and grandmother who took me there, and became caught up in that vast, strange place. I missed my home, my father and mother, and cried into my pillow most nights for a week. Of course it would not have been a good idea to be seen or heard by the other boys as it would give the impression of being soft, although many others felt just the same. I feel that Hector was sad, as he had been deprived of the presence and company of his son whom he was trying to give an entrance into the adult world. He never once in the nine years I was at CH, came to visit me; however every week of every term for those nine years on a Monday morning there was always a letter for me from him, and latterly it came with the *West Somerset Free Press* which he sent on so that I could keep abreast with local news. I never even gave it a thought at the time, but I am sure he was doing his best to maintain good ties with me and in his way to say 'son, I love you'. We were allowed three visits from parents or family a term, from 12.15 pm after the last class on a Saturday until 6.00pm, or on a Sunday again 12.25pm until chapel in the evening at 6.00pm. Joan could usually manage one visit per term; her finances would not stretch to more. This is in stark contrast to the seemingly endless exeats, half terms, and other days off that children appear to have today.

For a number of years after my ninth birthday Hector would sometimes say, "I wish I could put stopping salts on you so that you would stay aged nine and not grow up." Whether he was allying me with Freddy or whether he thought that by Joan sending me away to school he had partly lost me and wanted to keep me at the age I was when I went away is unknown. Many parents might think that at the age of nine their sons are still children but are becoming interested in non childish things, can have sensible conversations and have not yet become awkward rebellious teenagers who answer back. Perhaps he made up for my absence when I came home from school, as I have good recollections of various occurrences, such as in the harvest field being told by him to get onto the seat of the little grey Fergie as Harry Ferguson's revolutionary new tractor was called. It was revolutionary as it was the first tractor to have hydraulic arms at the back on which implements were mounted. Once on the seat I was told to put my foot on the clutch, and put the gear lever into a gear and then let out the clutch slowly; when the cry of whoa went up I depressed the clutch pedal whilst the sheaves of corn were tossed up onto the trailer, from the nearby stooks, or stitches as they were known locally. On the command of 'forrard' or 'onwards', on I went to the next little group of stitches.

From a little diary I kept at the time, I note on 11th April 1953 Hector and I went down to the beach at Glenthorne. Glenthorne lies between Porlock Weir and Lynmouth, perched on its cliff face plateau, midway between top and bottom of the cliff and surrounded by scrub oak woodland. We had driven down the drive of the big house in the Morris Eight tourer, parked it, and then walked further on down to the beach. When here, we found somewhere to sit so that we could watch the cliff face. Soon after the magic five minutes we saw the peregrine falcon and located the whereabouts of its nest watching it going to and fro. Hector was delighted and from then on was in good humour. My diary reveals that on Wednesday 14thApril we went to get the peregrine's eggs. I remember that we, that is, Hector, my cousin Ian Stuart-Lyon and I, travelled in Peter Leach's green Austin A40; this was the delivery van for his milk round. We boys had to rough it in the back, sitting on a box or with our bottoms on the van wheel arches until the time came to get out in the last field before the scrub oak woods of the cliffs. It was a lovely warm spring day, the sun up and no threat of rain as Hector led the way with his climbing ropes worn across his shoulder, crossing his chest like bandoliers of ammunition. Soon we were through the fence and wending our way carefully between the trees, when all of a sudden a spring stag came flying along the path we were about to cross, it gave us all a bit of a start. How Hector knew the exact spot on the top of the cliffs to get to is mystery to me, but he announced,

"We are here" and started to sort out his ropes. These were especially strong, dark red and white cotton climbing ropes, the best of the day. He was dressed in his normal attire of shirt and tie, cord trousers and hacking jacket with a flat cap to round it off. One rope he tied around his waist and passed around a nearby tree, this one Peter Leach took charge of; the other also around a tree he held on to and we boys held it also. Keeping the ropes taut Hector backed to the edge of the cliff with a remark of something like " Don't ever let go, keep the rope tight but let it pay out slowly until you hear me shout, then pull like hell to get me up." Then he was gone and we did our best to do as bid. Later we were to learn that he had gone down about forty feet of the 100 to 150 feet cliff face. Anyway sure enough we heard a holler and started to heave away, soon Hector's head came into view, with the telltale bulges in the front of his cap, he had got them. In next door to no time he was on his knees and placing the eggs with great care into his special egg carrying boxes that had thick felt compartments, and a pad of thick felt on the bottom and top of the eggs. Then into his haversack with them and we were walking back to Peter Leach's van as though it was just an everyday occurrence. It was a relief to see him in a good frame of mind and happy for once. What was going through his mind no one will know but the looming legislation later in the year that made it illegal to take or own a wild bird's egg must have been a thought. Although Michael Upstone related as to how he saw Hector angry or moody at Gilhams I don't think, upon reflection, that I was too affected by it, perhaps I had built a subconscious wall to keep it out. He never once hit me during those days, or even offered to; a good rasping from his tongue was enough. In fact he never laid a finger on me all my life, but got close to it once when I was feeling my feet as a fifteen or sixteen year old and gave him a lot of verbal abuse and taunting. He tore after me throwing stones, clods of soil and anything he could lay hands on, and was gaining on me. If it was not for the prompt appearance of Joan who told us both to behave and positioned herself between us, I dread to think of the consequences.

At Gilhams our first neighbours next door were Tony and Queenie Hale with their son Richard with whom I often played, as we were close in age. Relations between Hector and Tony were permanently strained or so it seemed, I remember words flying one day and Hector hastily taking his jacket off, up with his fists and saying "Come on then you bugger". Tony Hale backed down and there was no fight, thank goodness. Hector could get well and truly fired up and looked very fierce.

Warner Robbins who used to farm at Selworthy Farm on the Holnicote Estate was particularly helpful to me as he knew Hector very well and for a long time, ever since 1940 when he came to Cloutsham. I consider that he had just about got the measure of Hector and had many an exciting time together with him. Warner provided some interesting stories and an accurate objective assessment of him. He told me of another peregrine incident, of which I was in total ignorance. Warner's conversation I reproduce now. "He went to Roadwater to the old Treborough slate quarries. The old peregrine dive-bombed him when he was on the rope; it started screeching which brought the locals out to see what was going on. Father up the rope, he had to abandon the exercise because of the folks about". He had two or three helpers, one of which was Gilbert Davey from King's Brompton who related to Tom Yandle sometime later, that he had never seen anything like Hector on the end of a rope scrawling down over a precipice. Warner again, "I've never met a chap that was so unpredictable, that's not quite the right word. He would change tack and direction in a flash. He was working for one aim-keen on conserving the deer. We went down Hallslake Wood on a deer shoot, when we had finished they said Hector's got several down. I had a Landover in those days so drove down. Hector had shot prickets, male deer the whole issue, not just hinds [*as they were expected to do*], yet his ingenuity was amazing, he had taken toilet rolls down and made a funnel and the blooming deer went to him, he had a real slaughter eight or ten deer."

Back in those days if a hunted deer from the cliffs went to sea, it was standard practice to go to Porlock Weir and get into Preston or Arthur Ley's boat and wait off shore. "One day Hector went out in the boat and didn't know or think what to do. The system was that a rope was thrown over the stag and you pulled him against the boat, Preston always had a humane killer, and it was bang and haul the deer aboard. Hector got excited that day out there, got hold of the humane killer, bang killed the deer which had not been secured with a rope, and it promptly sank. All was not well for a while after that. We stopped the boat trips as a result of shenanigans with the antis."

I have the head of the last stag shot from a boat, by Hector. Warner then went on to tell me of how that he had been taught by His Majesty's Government during his National Service to perform unarmed combat, which he put into practice with some anti hunting men. "I had the gun that day and was about to shoot a hind that stood in the edge of the water, when a couple of locals were getting a bit stroppy 'If you shoot that one we will throw you into the sea'. I shot the hind put the gun down, 'Come on then' – one finished up with a broken arm and the other a dislocated thumb. Thing was in those days you had all this training, the ole boy said don't ever hesitate as the one that does is the one that gets shot."

Warner's prowess is illustrated with an incident which took place in 1961, and using Warner's own words again.

"Hector was always a character, he had just had a way that was all his own, I always accepted him, but I could get exasperated. Like when he shifted out that stag, if he thought it was right he would do it, no two ways about it; I was just about in my prime then, I would have floored him if it hadn't been for Tom Rook. There was a beautiful autumn stag lying in the wood below Luccombe Mill, Bill Harding was harbouring at the time and said to me, 'You know thic stag, you go and harbour 'un '. I used to play second string to Bill Harding, so I slotted and harboured this stag in Whitlands Moor. Tom Rook arrived 'He's in the covert Tom'. We walked down across the field and who should come out of the covert but Hector. He said 'That's too good a stag to kill now', he had put it going. I was fairly fiery in those days; if Tommy hadn't been there Hector would have been flattened. I told Col. Murphy [the Master] what I thought, making a fool of Bill Harding and myself."

I am glad it never came to blows as I am sure Hector would have come off worse.

The wisdom of the old soldier who had been in the Intelligence Corps in the Army, and who had set up the German surrender signing on Lunenburg Heath for Montgomery in 1945, came into play. He contacted Hector and asked him to harbour the stag for the forthcoming meet; Hector was placed in a difficult position and could hardly say no to the Master, so he successfully harboured the stag. It was the day of Tom Yandle's wedding to Margaret Joyce attended by several hunting folk including Tom Rook. Tom recalls that as soon as he could escape he did, changed out of his suit into more suitable clothes in Barlynch Quarry and raced on to try to find hounds. Too late, they had killed the stag after a very short hunt, in Annicombe. This was the day that more or less finished Sidney Bazeley as huntsman. The drill was that when a stag had been killed it was taken to a local spot where there was room for all and sundry to park their vehicles and horses, to see the stag being paunched. The huntsman removes the bowels and entrails from the carcase, takes out the heart which is given to the person on whose land the deer was found, and also the kidneys and liver which is cut up and given to anyone keen to have it. (There is nothing like eating fresh liver fried for supper after a day's hunting.) The slots are carefully cut off and offered usually to visitors as a trophy to get mounted on a shield. When all this is finished, the people are asked to stand back, the huntsman blows his horn that is a signal for the pack to rush forth and feed on the paunch. That is their reward for all the hard work that they have done. If it was decided to carry on hunting to find another stag, the one that had been killed would be stuck and bled, then opened up at the end of the day. No huntsman would ever take hounds to find another stag after they had had the paunch that is until that day. The conversation went something like this:-

Col. Murphy "Aren't you going to get on and paunch the thing?"

Sidney Bazeley "Aren't you going on again sir?"

Col. Murphy "It doesn't make any difference whether you go on again or not, paunch the thing."

Sidney Bazeley "If we go on again you don't paunch it."

Col. Murphy "If I say paunch it, paunch it."

Old Murphy didn't understand it that he was in the wrong and it really upset Sidney Bazeley to the point that he resigned and left at the end of the season in May 1961.

Warner Robins again,

"Hector was everywhere, he was well known around the area on the naturalist side and feared by people who wanted to conserve the rare birds. He was remarkable at being able to conceal himself [hence getting the Golden Eagle's eggs]. I've watched him when he harboured that stag, he didn't know he was being watched, I never let on, when he came out of the house at Venniford in the dark, no lights. I was close enough to see him go. I thought 'I wonder what he was going to get up to' the only way you would have stopped him was physically he wouldn't take any notice of words. He went over and harboured that stag. He had such ability he could see a slot on a tarmac road, it takes a bit of doing, it just doesn't happen you have got to know what to look for. He did what he thought was right at the time and moment, it was just his way. He worked entirely on impulse, and the only things that really interested him was nature and egg collecting. He didn't mind how he did it, if he broke the law, he broke the law. It wasn't his law (Hector's Law), so it didn't matter. Since you rang up I've been thinking about it, I don't know how he would have got on today, he would have been locked up."

I would say in defence of Hector that he had a good quick brain and seemed instinctively to know what to do in any given circumstance. He was also very quick and good at judging people and summing them up, so I would disagree a little with Warner, it was not all on impulse that he acted.

Come 1952 he made what was to be his last trip to Scotland; he left on 4th May and returned on 12th June, a total of forty-three days away. He went to the far north, to the area around Inverness, and then to North and South Uist and Lewis. I think that the journey this time was made by car, as there is a record of him taking a clutch of peregrine eggs near Bala in North Wales on the 4th May. It is quite possible that he and his chums flew from the mainland to the Outer Hebrides, as I seem to remember the excitement of him reliving the flight in a Dakota aircraft. On this trip the species collected were as follows: -

Coot	Meadow Pipit	Arctic Skua	Arctic Tern
Sand Martin	Ptarmigan	Snipe	Sedge Warbler
Red Necked Phalarope	Redshank	Skylark	Hebredian Wren

He also brought home two eggs from a Canada goose's nest, which were incubated under a hen and for a number of years we kept them as pets. They were indistinguishable except for two little holes in their webfeet. They became known as 'Tear Web' and 'Holey Web'. Beth and I had a lot of fun on occasions, walking them up to the top of a hill and then chasing them down so that they could get up momentum and take off. After a couple of circuits and some honking, they would circle round and land. Hector also brought home the most delightful and loveable collie bitch pup from Solas near Stornaway on the Island of Lewis. Naturally we called it 'Solas'. I adored that little animal and it broke my heart when it died after a few weeks of having it; this would have been preventable had we but known. It died of fits brought on by a very high worm burden. The worm is a clever creature, for whilst it can lie in a dormant state in the host for years, the onset of pregnancy triggers it into life so that the worm larvae pass through the placenta into the foetuses. It must always be assumed that pups are automatically infected and wormed accordingly. We did not possess that knowledge and therefore did not worm poor 'Solas'.

Another very sad occasion was the death of Alfred Lenthall. He was the son of a Taunton publican at the 'Black Book' pub, born the year after Hector in 1906, and came to the stables at Exford as a stable lad aged 13. He progressed upwards and became whipper-in to Ernest Bawden in 1927; on Ernest's retirement he took the post of huntsman. Alfred and Hector had become firm friends from a long way back, so it was quite natural that Hector used to stay in his house at the kennels when he was harbouring in the vicinity. Alfie's son Michael thinks that his father started to go downhill in 1948/9 as the entries in his hunting diary were getting thinner and thinner. Alfie himself thought he caught TB from a hound that coughed right into his face, as the hound later died of it. He retired from hunting on May 1st 1951, and the last time he rode a horse was to parade the hounds at the Devon County Show when it was held at Chivenor; this was the first time the DSSH had paraded in front of Royalty.

Soon after this he went straight to the Quantock Sanatorium at Over Stowey. Hector was again faced with seeing someone he was close to, trying to fight the disease and slowly fading away. What thoughts of his sister Marjory must have run through his head? Hector visited Alfie as often as he could and twice took Mrs. Lenthall and her son Michael in the Morris Eight Tourer. He got quite excited on one visit as he saw a gold crested wren in the fir trees by the sanatorium with its nest. Alfie died on 15thAugust 1952 and was buried at Exford churchyard. The church was full and 72 wreaths were laid out on the ground, clearly a fitting tribute to a popular, respected and well loved man, just 46 years of age. Rex Hancock recalls that Hector was unable to control his emotion and wept openly.

Alfred Lenthall.

The sands of time were running out fast for Norman Kennelly and so was his money, I see from my little diary an entry for '25th March 1954, Lady Day, The Flying Pencil leaves Holt Ball Farm'. The incoming tenant Peter Ashford was the antithesis of Norman, a non-drinking, non-smoking, non-hunting clean living Chapel man. He soon made it clear to Hector that he did not require his services but needed the cottage for another worker. At least he had the decency to give us a month, this time, to get out. My diary recalls 23rd April 'Packed morn and afternoon, last night in dear Gilhams. 24th April Moved house to Meadow Cottage by Harold Prescott. Found c/5 Buzzard with Dad at Simonsbath.' Harold Prescott was the local haulier from Luccombe, with a little Morris Commercial flatbed lorry; it had dropsides and a canvas tilt cover. It was the prairie schooner of its day. The whole job didn't take long with our small amount of furniture and Meadow Cottage was only about one and a half miles away. I remember Joan had been over to clean it out beforehand taking myself and Beth to help. Upon opening the front door and walking in we were greeted by the damp and musty smell of the house, it was festooned with cobwebs and the distemper paint on the walls was flaking badly. The living room fireplace was littered with sticks and twigs that the jackdaws had brought for their nest but had fallen down the chimney.

I see that Hector's priority was going to find and collect the clutch of five buzzard's eggs rather than fussing about in the new home. It was not quite out of the frying pan into the fire, but nearly so. At least the privy was closer to the back door, which was a great consideration when it was pouring with rain; there was a cold-water tap inside the back door, feeding onto a small shallow sink beside the copper. This was a great boon on washdays as it was so easy to fill the copper with water; washdays were also bath nights as it saved lighting the copper fire again and made better use of the wood. We bathed in a galvanised 'Bungalow' bath; Hector always had the first dip, followed by myself with my sister and Joan to finish. Hot water was continually added to increase the volume of the murky and soapy contents. When it was time to empty the bath, water was bailed out by bucket or bowl until it could be dragged to the back door and upended onto the concrete outside and away to the stream.

Clearly my reference to dear Gilhams meant that we were leaving with some poignancy, as we had been so happy as a family in spite of all the hardships. Hector had undertaken the same arrangement of work with Leslie Scott of East Lynch of being self employed but available for work when required whilst we lived in one of the two cottages. Originally it had been one dwelling and over the course of time split in to two. A single woman Mrs. Loosemoor with her daughter Pat lived in the other half and she went up as a domestic help to the Scotts. Hector soon gave her the nickname of 'Tiddles'.

It was not long before he made the pronouncement that he was never going to move and live out of the sight of Dunkery Beacon.

- 14 -

NORMAN KENNELLY

NORMAN KENNELLY was one of the most colourful and charismatic characters and he deserves further mention, for his thoughtfulness, and kindness to us during our time at Gilhams.

His father, Maurice McDonnell Kennelly hailed from Lynmouth and went to sea in merchant shipping; he rose to be a captain as his name appears on the Captain's register at Lloyds for 1909. During the First World War he served in the RNVR and finished up being in charge of salvage and wrecks off the East Coast of Africa. He held the rank of Lieutenant and retired as Lt. Commander. Thereinafter he was always known as, and addressed as, Commander Kennelly, which was not strictly correct but no doubt easier off the tongue than Lt. Commander. He had two sisters who lived in Wheddon Cross and it was whilst staying with them that he visited the village shop and fell for the owner's daughter behind the counter. She was Millie Norman; they were married and had two children, a son who they christened Norman from her surname and a daughter Norah.

When Norman went to school at Blundell's his father and mother were living in Minehead, with his father listed as a Colonial Civil Servant. Norman was good at sport at Blundell's and played for the school in rugby matches '– and Kennelly were the best forwards' '– and Kennelly were good in the loose'. He also enjoyed boxing. He was born in 1914, went to Blundell's aged 13 and left ignominiously after four years aged 17. He was a great friend at school with Philip Weaver and I have the little tale from his widow Joan, née Richards, from Sparkhayes Farm, Porlock. As Norman and Phillip had developed a taste for beer, he slipped out of school one evening to go to a pub and bought some bottles. On his return tiptoeing past the study window of either his housemaster or headmaster, he tripped and fell. Crash tinkle tinkle the bottles smashed and he was caught red-handed. He was expelled, and in the words of the school archivist *"His name is conspicuously missing from the list of those who left in the summer of 1931, no doubt because of the manner in which he 'left'."*

After leaving school Norman worked for his uncle W.W. Norman at Gupworthy Farm, on the Brendon Hills; if ever the Staghounds came into the vicinity Norman was off, riding a carthorse just like Hector's grandfather James Bawden. In the words of Arthur Webber his brother in law, "Norman did things that nobody else could ever do". Douglas Lang who lived for many years in Wootton Courtenay and knew him well describes him as "not being a good farmer, but very sporting, a hellavah likeable chap, good company and a laugh a minute." To this I would add that he was a great favourite with the ladies and had countless liaisons. One of these was Di Holden, a keen horsewoman and point-to-point rider, who married Tony Collins from Porlock, and after he died in the first Comet aircraft that exploded over the Mediterranean, she married Dr. Martin Chappel from Minehead. The night on the hayrick mentioned in this dateless letter exemplifies this trait.

Dear Norah,
Congrats on passing the exam. How many credits? I fancy we haven't met for a deuce of a time, when are you coming up? On Monday. I reckon you've been having a pretty lively time, well old girl things haven't been exactly dull here, – four of us spent the night on a hay-rick, getting home just in time to start work –

but thereby hangs a tale. We've finished harvest and are now fern harvesting, it's about time you rolled up to lend a hand.

On Tuesday we had a day to hounds, Sydney & I went Sydney on Daisy & me on Smart.

We got in at the death at Horner amongst the first seven horses. Well it's about time to knock off now so cheerio for the present.

NMcD Kennelly

Norman's brother in law Arthur Webber told me that the four who spent the night on the hayrick were Norman plus A.N. Other and two girls. We had a good laugh about what they might have got up to. The Sydney he refers to is his chum Sydney Webber, the younger brother of Arthur and father of the twins Roger and Jenny (Richards), Richard, Susan (Atkins) and Angela.

The wedding of Sydney and Eileen Webber with Norman Kennelly at the back above the boy's head. This is the only photograph of Norman I could locate.

Sometime around 1938 Norman married Betty, the eldest daughter of Dudley Down from Wootton Courtenay. Soon after, they took up residence at Holt Ball Farm to begin farming, with amongst other things an Allis-Chalmers tractor given to them by his father as a wedding present. He had red hair and she also, with a temper to match her hair. According to Jack Hosegood, auctioneer and valuer, "I don't know what Norman said to provoke her but she picked up a lighted lantern and threw it at him, he ducked and it sailed out through the open window behind him. It pitched onto the lawn and exploded; damned lucky they didn't burn Holt Ball down."

Norman and Betty had one child, a son Dan, who was inevitably a red head. He was just a little older than me, but we often played together as children, at and around Holt Ball. He was not of his father's mould and after a variety of jobs including managing the prison farm at Dartmoor Prison and getting bashed over the head by escaping prisoners (I am not sure whether the 'axe man' Mad Mitchell was involved) he died at a relatively young age of aids. He was a likeable sensitive chap with a good sense of humour; he had been best man to Maurice Scott, the current Joint Master of the Devon and Somerset Staghounds, at his wedding. His mother married again and became Betty Long. We often used to see her on the roads exercising a hound pup as she lived quite close to us, at Oak Farm, Waddicombe, near Dulverton.

Hector's friendship with Norman probably began years before when Norman was hunting from Gupworthy, and he would have called to see him when harbouring in the area. Norman was a kindred spirit; they were both fearless and passionate about stag hunting and had great mutual respect for one another.

Norman was as tough as old boots, for example during one particularly cold spell with the snow piled up on both sides of the road he appeared in Wootton Courtenay driving his tractor and trailer in nothing more than slacks and a singlet vest. This strong constitution combined with a good physique stood him in great stead when embarking on boxing bouts or swimming in the sea after the hunted deer. The enthusiasm for boxing that was nurtured at Blundell's continued after he left school. Not only did he take on the guys in the boxing booths at Bampton Fair with frequent success but turned his attention to more serious fights. On one occasion a ring had been set up in the old Alphington cattle market at Exeter, in the days when it was a live market. Norman and an opponent had just started to fight when the police arrived. They stopped the fight to enquire as to whether they had a licence. They had not got one so had to pack it in. Dick Rawle, farmer from Highley near Parracombe, was his bucket and sponge man and well remembers this episode. Kennelly the pugilist moved up a grade and in so doing created history at the recently opened 'Moorland Hall' at Wheddon Cross in 1934. Now aged twenty and in his prime he had challenged George Catford, market gardener in the Avill Valley above Dunster, to a fifteen round contest. A professional ring was set up in the middle of the hall; there were seconds and a proper referee. There was also another fight scheduled to give folk a good evening of entertainment. The hall was packed solid with people and those who couldn't get in looked through the windows. The then secretary of the DSSH was Captain Wilton (1928-37) who lived locally at North Quarme; he had been a moving force and benefactor towards the construction of the hall, so it is not surprising to see him in a dinner jacket about to present the winner with a cheque or large note of money. The fight had been going well for Norman when a cut opened up above his eye and bled profusely. The referee stopped the fight in the ninth round and awarded victory to George Catford. This stung Norman as he felt he had the measure of Catford and wanted to carry on.

The four in the ring, L-R: Captain Wilton, Norman Kennelly, George Catford, the referee.

A return fight was arranged and took place in the Regal Ballroom in Minehead. Norman was able to convince everybody that he was the superior boxer and beat George Catford easily.

Norman was a good horseman. There was one well-known horse that he called 'Deer Slayer', it was a rough small animal barely thirteen hands three inches tall. You would want to call it a pony, but it was tough and long bodied, and only had two gears, walk and flat out gallop. To everyone this was called the 'Flying Pencil'. Norman had recently befriended Dick Hern, who together with Tony Collins had the responsibility of training horses and riders short-listed for the 1952 Helsinki Olympics at the Porlock Riding School. Eager to encourage the friendship Norman offered to mount Dick Hern for a day with the DSSH; so imagine if you will a very smart Dick Hern arriving at the meet in keen anticipation, to be shown this rough, small pony the 'Flying Pencil'. His immediate response was "I am not riding that thing" and turned on his heel. In spite of this incident Norman and Dick became great friends. Dick, together with Pat Wykeham-Fiennes with whom he was deeply in love, often-visited Holt Ball for many an hilarious evening. In the words of Tom Yandle from Riphay at one such evening at a party "They started betting on who was the best shot. Norman drew a target on the sitting room wall, inside the house, and they started shooting at it with a .22 rifle. After several shots Betty came in from the kitchen shouting and hollering as the plaster was coming off the kitchen wall and the bullets were flying around in the kitchen. This was in addition to the plaster coming off the sitting room wall." Dick moved on into training racehorses and reached the absolute pinnacle of that profession to train sixteen winners of British Classic races, including the Derby with Troy, Henbit and Nashwan. He also trained the brilliant Brigadier Gerard, described as 'The British horse of the Century'. To cap it all he had the honour to train for the Queen with great success.

On another occasion Norman and Dick were out hunting with the Staghounds, and during a good hunt Norman lost his bowler hat. Not wanting to get left behind and miss the best of the hunting, he did not go back to find it. Dick and some others thought that they would have some fun so unbeknown to Norman they put an advertisement in the *West Somerset Free Press*, something along the lines of 'Bowler hat wanted, condition and age immaterial, Norman Kennelly, Holt Ball Farm, Luccombe'. Later he was inundated which caused great amusement, "I don't understand it, people keep bringing me bowler hats and they arrive by every post."

Norman's sister Norah trained to be a nurse and from Norwich Hospital she went into Queen Alexander's Nursing Service to see action in Burma. She was part of a neuro-surgical unit just behind the front lines helping with head injuries. She was awarded the Burma Star, G.S. Medal and an A.R.R.C. Medal. It was a great honour for me to hold her Burma Star in my hand, the first I had ever seen in real life. It was thought by many that Norman ought to have been the one to be in Burma fighting the Japs as it would have appealed to his nature and he would have been very good at it. The nearest he got to the war was being a member of the Home Guard and going to arrest what he thought were some German parachutists only to find they were Americans!

His hunting exploits were legion, but here are four to give a good picture of what he could get up to. The first was during the mastership of Miss Biddy Abbot, before she retired in 1951. At the end of a good hunt the stag beat hounds and swam out to sea from Glenthorne Beach, one of the first to arrive behind the hunt staff and the Master, Miss Abbot, was Norman. Quick as a flash he was off his horse and said to Miss Abbot "Madam you had better look away". With that he took off all his clothes and plunged naked into the raging sea to swim out and drove the stag back to the beach where it was taken. Normally when a stag beat hounds to the sea if the boat was not out it was given best, and would swim back to beach itself and live for another day, but not on this occasion. Rosemary Pile from Brendon told of the time when the deer had gone to sea from Embelle Beach, which is up the coast towards Porlock Weir, and how she had to dismount to hold numerous horses whilst Norman gave a repeat performance. On another occasion the deer had got into Nutscale Reservoir. Espying a boat, Norman and his friend Dick Richards from Sparkhayes Farm, Porlock, thought the way forward was to launch it and drive the deer to the water's edge. In their haste they failed to notice a small hole in the boat that soon manifest itself when they were rowing towards the deer. "Take your bowler hat off Dick and bale the water out, faster," but to no avail the boat sunk beneath them and they had to swim for the shore. The final escapade also involved a deer again getting into Nutscale Reservoir, this time during the mastership of Mrs. Norah Cox, probably in 1953. Norman announced his intentions of removing all his clothes to swim after the deer and Mrs. Cox responded by moving the members of the field away to avoid embarrassment. She then went to the reservoir fence to observe what was going on. With the deer dispatched, she went around the field collecting handkerchiefs from people for Norman to dry himself. This was a fine and thoughtful gesture by Mrs. Cox.

Norman lived life to the full in every way possible and liked to have fun and a good laugh. During a dance in aid of the Staghounds in Porlock Village Hall, when naturally most if not all attending would have been pro hunting folk, an anti hunting woman made the mistake of entering the hall and creating a nuisance by making her feelings known. She was promptly picked up by Norman and others and laid down upon a carpet. The carpet was rolled up, carried to a corner and stood up; all that could be heard were muffled yelps. Somehow the police came on the scene and said, "We believe there is someone in that carpet." Hey Presto! She emerged flustered and angry but could not make any accusations, as it would have been her word against everybody else in the hall. At the Metropole Hotel in Minehead there was a similar occurrence, a local anti hunting man called Hemingway came in during a dance for one of the local hunts. Norman Kennelly, his friend Tom Cole, and one or two others picked him up, carried him outside and threw him over the sea wall into the water, the tide being well in. Shock horror, the man couldn't swim and was in danger of drowning, so off came Norman's clothes and he dived in to pull Hemingway out of the water. Tom Cole came to Holt Ball sometime in the mid to late 1940s to convalesce from polio and he and Norman were always up to nonsense. More is written of Tom Cole, in the appendix at the end, as he was another character whose story needs telling.

Tom Yandle from Riphay, Exebridge remembers being told of an occurrence, which illustrates the fearless behaviour of Norman. It was thus: after Dick Lloyd's wedding in 1953, a party which included Norman and the huntsman Sidney Bazeley, who told Tom of the story, repaired to the Jubilee Inn on the old Bampton to South Molton main road, for more drink. An argument took place about people being knocked out or hit on the head. Someone produced a 'bittle', this being dialect for beetle, a large wooden mallet for knocking in stakes. Norman Kennelly said "See if you can knock me down with that one." So somebody gave him a tap on the head, obviously not with the force to knock in a stake, after a while he went down on his knees. "Try again" he said. After another wallop it was noticed that blood was coming out of his ears, whereupon the party sobered up. It frightened Sidney Bazeley, but there never any problems resulting from the biff with the bittle that came to light.

The stormy marriage of Norman and Betty was not destined to last, but before it ended Jim Nancekivell son of Bob Nancekivell from Cloud Farm, Malmsmead, remembers how after a day's hunting they had been asked by Norman if they would like to call in at Holt Ball for a drink, to fortify them for the long hack back to Cloud. This must have been in the days of Betty, because, when in the living room Norman got some glasses and made for the open fireplace. Reaching up inside the chimney of the cavernous fireplace to a ledge, he produced a bottle of whisky and filled the glasses with the remark "If I don't keep it up there she will find it and there will be none left." Sometime in the late 1940s Norman and Betty got divorced, and he was soon married again, this time to Marjory Taplin or Marny as she was known, sister of Jimmy, Hector's best man. Marny's nephew David Barnes used to come to stay at Holt Ball and can remember Hector well as he was asked to climb up trees to some bird's nests for Hector.

This was another case of getting on well with a young boy. A daughter Clover was born in 1949 during the time that the clover crop was being cut. I have happy memories of Marny bringing lovely teas to the harvest field, of scones, thick cream and strawberry jam, sponge cake and hot sweet tea from a small urn. It was so unfortunate that Norman could not control his wanderlust, or be good enough a farmer, because in 1954 Marny left him and he had to hand in his notice to the National Trust to quit Holt Ball, as he had run out of money and his father could give him no more. Commander Kennelly just could not go on bailing him out, there had to be an end to it. Norman went off working for Clough Smith and Co of Wolverhampton, as charge hand to gangs of men erecting lighting in towns, and at other times on a trawler out of the West Coast of Scotland. He would make his way home, i.e. the Porlock Vale, spend his earnings then off again. It was on one such an occasion that I saw him for the last time; Connie and I had come home for the weekend at Meadow Cottage sometime about 1969/70, and were down at Porlock Weir visiting the Ship Inn having a quiet drink when in he walked. We had not seen each other for a long time but he recognised me, after a little while he said with an impish smile on his face "Yer I've got something to show 'ee, but we've got to go outside." We went out and he started in the direction of the gents, by now I was wondering what on earth it was that he wanted me to see, so with natural trepidation I followed him into the gents lavatory. Now Norman was a full-blown heterosexual, and this fact eased my mind as he proceeded to start taking his jacket and shirt off. His insistence that I follow him enabled my curiosity to be rewarded with a sight that I have never beheld before in my life. I would have been concerned if he had started to take down his trousers, but he did not, instead it was "What do you think of it? A lot of men have a naked woman on their chest, but nobody has this." What could I say; I was taken aback by the size and magnitude of the tattoo he had on  his chest. It reached from just below his neck to his navel and right across his barrel chest. It was the motif from the hunt button of the Devon and Somerset Staghounds, a stag's head with Prosperity to Stag Hunting around the periphery. I made some remark like "Wow that is magnificent Norman; I shall never forget this moment." I often wonder how many others were given a show, as it really was quite dramatic. He eulogised about the wonderful times he had with the D&S, and said kind things about Hector, and then we were gone. I never saw him again. He died of cancer of the throat in Bath Hospital in 1989 aged 75. His daughter Clover related that even in his last days he was trying to get off with, and flirting with, the nurses.

- 15 -

I SHALL NEVER LIVE OUT OF THE SIGHT OF DUNKERY

THE NEW HOME, in spite of all the domestic inadequacies, was soon to prove a reasonably happy one, prompting Hector to declare one day that he was never going to move out of the sight of Dunkery Beacon. There was a grand view of the hills, Robin How and Dunkery to the south, and further down the Vale we could see Ley Hill and Crawter. The climate of the Porlock Vale was more clement than out over on the moor, being in the rain shadow of the hills and having an annual rainfall of about 40 inches. Meadow Cottage was surrounded by quite a sizeable garden and about three quarters to one acre of orchard. Even though the surrounds to the place were very unkempt and run down Hector could see the potential of a good home that suited him, and set to work to tame the wilderness. He built a low wall in front of the house, cut the undergrowth back, and dug the garden. We had 'Tiddle's' share of it as well, as she was not capable of turning a spit with a spade. Flowers and shrubs were planted, together with the normal run of vegetables, so that within a year the place was transformed.

Hector's life settled into the rhythm of working for Leslie Scott at East Lynch Farm, occasional days hunting in the car and bird nesting in the spring and summer. He considered that he had discharged his obligations to the family by providing a house to live in, and what monies he earnt, were his to do with as he pleased. This fell far short of what was needed to feed, clothe and look after a family, i.e. the bare necessities, never mind little luxuries such as sweets, so the burden to provide the remainder fell upon Joan. It was around the spring of 1954 that she started working away from home finding what work that she was able to do. I see from my little diary that she went on the train as far as Taunton with me when I went back to school, to start her new job. She worked for Somerset County Council as a home help, which more often than not, unless it was very local, meant living in with the family she was helping.

Later on she didn't need the County to supply the work as word of mouth meant all sorts of people sought her services. She continued to go away to work in the term time from 1954 until about 1960. Beth, my sister was sent away to the convent school of St. Gildas from the age of nine until eleven as a border to allow Joan the freedom of leaving Meadow Cottage for her work. Beth then attended the convent school of St. Teresa in Minehead, a sister foundation to St. Gildas and it fell to Hector to get her ready to catch the bus in the morning, making sure that she was properly turned out. He even brushed and plaited her hair for her, and polished her shoes every day. During the school holidays Joan always made it her business to be at home for us. Hector did try his best for Beth by taking her out hunting or bird's nesting with him, but the price for her, was helping as far as she was able with cooking meals, washing and other housework. This is in stark contrast to most young teenagers of today.

As I went far away to Christ's Hospital in Sussex to school and then when home would go off to play with friends for the day, or when old enough, start taking an interest in girls, it meant my time with Hector became far less than in the years from nine to eleven. I think he felt that he had shown me the way into the adult world, but now my own interests came to the fore. Consequently I have great difficulty in recalling the detail of Hector's life and many of the main happenings, particularly as I write

Hector building the double stonewall to make a flowerbed.

about a time 40 to 50 years ago. However Hector did keep simple diaries recording his hours and where he worked, together with some highlights e.g. 'Taunton West Indies'. This would have meant that he went to the County Cricket Ground at Taunton to watch Somerset play the West Indies. To help me, I put most of the entries from 1957-1974 onto a spreadsheet; this gave the bones onto which I have tried to flesh out his life during this period.

Working for Leslie Scott at East Lynch was not easy as he was a hard taskmaster, expecting work to a high standard coupled with prompt timekeeping. His farming results were of the best, cattle and sheep always did well and looked right, cereal fields immaculate but his main forte was horses. He had made a great name for himself in the horse world, first as a point-to-point rider, then showing, and training racehorses for National Hunt racing. He always had a good stallion at stud for visiting mares. His name was known all over the country and used to say that when he was buying ewes at Hawick in the Borders, Ken Oliver the auctioneer would drop the hammer to the cry of 'Scott Minehead'. Hector had a quiet regard for L.G. Scott but was not afraid of him or would not be brow beaten by him. In the words of Derrick his son, "Suddenly he wouldn't turn up for work. Usually we thought he was off bird's egg collecting. He had a wonderful collection. It was quite amazing the stories he used to tell us about collecting them. What he knew about nature was nobody's business. He knew everything, quite amazing! I've never known anyone to know so much about nature, any animal, anything to do with nature." What Derrick did not know was that sometimes when Hector absented himself he was poorly. The diaries reveal that he was off work during 1957 for 50 days, probably the early days of depression that was to dog him for the rest of his life.

In the days when Meadow Cottage was a tied cottage to East Lynch, the track up from the main road was gated at each end, as it was part of the field. One day Leslie Scott penned a lot of sheep on and around the track to work on them, thereby creating one huge area covered in sheep dung. When Warner Robins from the neighbouring farm at Selworthy saw the mess, he said to L.G.S. "What the hell did you pen the sheep up down there for?"

"Oh just to stir the old bugger up," was the reply.

Lunch times were always a fraught time because Hector had an hour, and only an hour, off from work. He had to walk nearly a quarter of a mile down to the cottage, wash hands etc and want the meal to appear on cue. Joan's time keeping was not always perfect so that if the meal was not ready there were harsh words exchanged. Afterwards he would collapse into a chair or lie out on the floor until one of us would call out "Bill is going up". That was Bill Gunter who also worked at East Lynch and lived at Venniford. Hector would then pull himself together, boots on and he was away to climb nearly 200 feet over the quarter of a mile to the farm. For a man the wrong side of fifty this was not the easiest of times and it is quite understandable that he later chose to vary his work on different farms, people's gardens, cutting birch for the point to point jumps, beating for the Holnicote Shoot and helping to prepare Dunster Showground.

One major highlight, excuse the pun, was the arrival of electricity in 1955. In one way it was sad to see the end of the Tilley Lamp with its bright white light and attendant comforting hiss, but in so many other ways a great burden was lifted. Joan could have a vacuum cleaner and an electric iron to ease the hardship of the chores, but as far as lights were concerned it was 40 or 60 watt bulbs never 100 watts and we were fearful of the cry "Turn that bloody light out, stop wasting electricity" if we left the room, even for a few minutes.

Jack Hosegood remembered that when he was Master and Huntsman of the Minehead Harriers (1949/56) and riding home with hounds after a day's hunting Hector would often be at the road gate to Meadow Cottage and would like to have a report on the day's sport. Jack said that it was meat and drink to Hector, as he knew every path, combe, mound or stream and loved to see the hunt in his mind. It would have then been 'Goodnight' with still a fair hack back to kennels, which were on the outskirts of Minehead, now sadly built over with houses. To do such a thing today on the A39 you would need a convoy of protective flashing lights in front and behind the hounds. Plus ça change!

Here follows a piece that Joan wrote on May 2nd 1956 titled 'Looking for Merlin': she writes as seeing things from the eye of an artist, and it gives a feeling that their relationship at that time was fairly cordial.

'Looking for Merlin'

"Having packed the basket, put water into the old kettle and collected lighting paper and old coats Hector and I sallied forth in the rattle trap. Looking up at the hills the sea mist was blanketing up over the tops of some and it did not know whether to rain or shine, however it did neither but the afternoon and evening were pearly grey. At this time of the year the bracken is quite flattened out and the heather sticks of the larger plants appear silvery grey, likewise all dead wood is bleached by the frost and rain of the past winter up on the moors.

"We went up over by way of Luccombe where the cherry blossom is out and Webber's Post, Cloutsham to Lang Combe Head. Here we stopped the car and Hector got out. Coming up over we saw two lots of deer, about six in each party. Hector said that he had been told that there were a great number of deer on Dunkery, but most people have a way of multiplying by ten so he says when they come to seeing deer. Actually we could see one party quite clearly hinds mostly.

"Hector struck off down Lang Combe to make that good for Merlin. He worked his way down and round back up to the Wilmersham Plain and across into Nutscale. For two years he has not seen a merlin hereabouts, but had the good fortune to find the old crow's nest he was looking for with three eggs. Actually the one he was looking for lays a special red egg. She should lay another tomorrow or the next day to complete the clutch. Meanwhile I drove to the quarry on Chetsford Steep and left the car there. My job was to walk down Chetsford Water to Nutscale to meet Hector, keeping my eyes skinned for ring ouzel. I arrived long before he did naturally, as I wasted no time at all slipping round, and saw him a mile off on the skyline. So out came pencil and paper. I wish I had a paint box with me as I was enchanted by the colour of the green moss on the stones in the black water of the stream. I was well entertained by the really charming song of the wheatear, it's better than the nightingale. After we met up Hector put me to watch a piece of hillside for the ouzels whilst he went for the Smallcombe, they are desperately shy birds and wild. It is quite a thrill to see or hear one as a result. He had the luck, not me, to flush the pair but apparently they had not started building, although he thought he had found their site. So far very good going. We then decided that I should move the car three parts of the way up the hill in the Porlock direction and he would circle round right handed and come up over. My job this time was to make a fire and boil the Billy. Actually we arrived more or less simultaneously. It was grand in that ditch trow. Visibility was good and one had a lovely view back over Dunkery and all. The beech wood fire burned without a bit of trouble and smelt magnificently. Those fires go with such gusto that the kettle boils whilst one gets the eats ready. No time was wasted having swallowed tea, the fire was doused, a blitz pack into the car and away to go again. This time to Three Hedges Meet where Hector hopped out and went round the top of Weir Water whilst the car was taken by me to Colley Water, so had another hour or thereabouts to make another sketch of Porlock Common, Colley Water Bridge, Mill Hill and Brendon Common away out over in the distance.

"I can plainly remember when Colley Water was a mere water splash, the roads rough full of stones and potholes but now alas it's been glamorized with tar and drains. I did get cold this time, but time flew by and Hector had more good fortune to find two old crow's nests and saw the hen merlin squealing and making a fuss overhead. It does a body good to leave the Vale and get on top for pure air that smells of old heather mixed with sea salt, that is very good. Homeward time by now so we chug off by Hawkcombe Head and Porlock Hill. The larch had just come full out going down and the green was so bright it was quite dazzling. Blackthorn a good show too. The end of winter is a time unto itself on the moors; the colouring is all so soft – the old heather being dark brown to grey and the reeds a light gold with the sun or else yellow ochre. I did just get a glimpse of the young beech breaking out on the big hill, but it's slow. I counted five different types of moss but don't know their names, only sphagnum in the wet ground in Chetsford Combe.

"We returned back home at about seven o'clock and proceeded to make more tea!"

I was always fascinated to watch Hector blowing eggs: this always took place on the landing at Meadow Cottage with him sat in front of the window sill. He would drill a hole according to the size of the egg, then with a blow pipe in the shape of the letter J and gradually reduced in bore, he would blow the jet of air into the hole he had drilled; this would have the effect of forcing the yolk and egg white to be expelled from the egg. When all was out he would suck up a mouthful of clean water from the bowl in front and blow that into the egg through the hole. This had the effect of washing the egg out. The eggs would then be lain hole down on a towel to drain out. I was amazed at how gentle he could be with his great big farmer's hands and fingers when holding the tiniest of eggs such as the gold crest wren. When the eggs were thoroughly dry Hector would install them into his 'Hill' cabinets. These were made by cabinetmakers out of mahogany with the smallest drawers at the top gradually getting larger towards the bottom. Sheets of cotton wool were overlaid onto string mesh. Onto these the eggs were placed just as they would be found in a nest with the tapered point innermost, then a glass drawer top was placed into position to fit snug onto the drawer and by so doing kept the eggs in place.

Another piece of good fortune was to find a little cashbook belonging to Hector which detailed his expenses and receipts in an enterprise to make some money by keeping hens. It starts in May 1955 and runs for five years. He enclosed the orchard with a chicken wire fence to keep the hens in. How many there were I cannot remember, but he continued to sell the eggs to Gordon Summers, butcher in Dulverton. It would seem that for four of the five years he made a useful amount, before I guess the rise of the battery hen, which drove the price down.

In 1955 he made £49 10s 8d. During that year whilst at work he was earning 3/- (shillings) per hour. This equated to £6 for a 40-hour week.
In 1956 he made £109 14s 6d.
In 1957 he made £101 8s 6d.
By 1958 the amount had fallen to £58 14s 9d.
In 1959 it had become a paltry £20 1s 11d so that by 1960 as the hens were no longer a means of making any money, they were sold.

EGG COLLECTING AND THE R.S.P.B. RAID

AS HECTOR WAS really no longer an active hunting man, having no horse or the wherewithal to keep one, he was consulted less often and by fewer people, in other words sidelined from the affairs of the Devon and Somerset Staghounds, although occasionally involved in deer shoots. To compensate for this he threw himself into his bird's nesting and egg collecting, which inevitably meant that he came to know a wide circle of like-minded people. He would make trips or forays to different parts of the country and would reciprocate by entertaining other collectors on Exmoor. The collecting fraternity was composed of all sorts of people from peers of the realm such as Lord Rothschild, doctors, bank managers, butchers, retired and serving officers from the forces, clergymen, and schoolteachers down to more humble men. As many featured in Hector's life and were important to him, here are a few lines on some of them.

Walter Copp. Coppy as we used to call him was very local and Hector saw quite a lot of him. He was a tailor working from his council house home in Timberscombe. He made all the red hunt coats for the local hunts, as well as more mundane work, such as altering trousers for Hector or me. He was a modest, quiet, unassuming, churchgoing man who, in his roles of chorister, bell-ringer and primarily organist, gave over 70 years of service to the churches of Timberscombe and Wootton Courtenay. He was a talented musician, training as an organist at St. Mary's church in Taunton and in 1940 becoming an Associate of the London College of Music. He composed various arrangements for the organ; for example, writing new settings for the *Te Deum*. He was also known locally for his woodcarving; he helped to carve the screen and choir stalls in Wootton church. It is hard to imagine him ever having any more spare time but he was an avid cricket supporter and umpired for Timberscombe Cricket Club. Because he had such a good musical ear he was good at identifying birds by their song, as was Hector of course.

An entry in Walter Copp's diary for 4th March 1950 typically illustrates of his nesting activity: "Mr. Heywood picked me up with his car at 9-o-clock, went through Exford to Larkbarrow where found raven's nest without any eggs. Made for the moor, left car and walked about 2 miles over the commons by Doone Valley and down Badgworthy Water. Saw a nest that looked new, kicked the tree and the raven flew out, sitting tight for a raven. A fir tree about 40 or 50 feet high. Hector strapped on his irons and climbed up, found four large eggs, a good set though small in number."

Reverend Chris Pring. Coppy would have first met the Rev. Pring when he came to be vicar of Timberscombe in 1933, then Hector would have come to know him probably in the 1940s. I never met the man but by all accounts he was easy to get on with and quite a character, well educated, Clifton College and Oxford yet slightly eccentric. When as young curate in Yeovil, he bought his first car, he approached the garage owner for driving lessons. This was accomplished by jacking up the rear wheels of the car with Rev. Pring in the driving seat being shown how to work the controls. Having mastered the principles he set off home in his new car and not long after drove to the north of Scotland. When he taught Religious Instruction at the local school, he usually

Hector and Walter Copp out bird nesting, somewhere on Exmoor.

walked there, and examined the hedgerows en route. The schoolmistress knowing of this habit during the nesting season used to put back by an hour the start of the lesson. He got into trouble once at a funeral for having dirty shoes, as a result of doing a spot of nesting between funerals at the local crematorium! A quiet gentle man, Rev. Pring was the last of the old 'bird nesting clergy'. He got on well with Hector for I never heard the customary diatribe associated with those he disliked or thought little of. His name appears five times in the diaries.

John Durrant. I don't know how Hector met John who lived at Churchill in North Somerset. We all thought him a kindly gentleman, having been through the mill as either a bomber pilot or navigator during the war. What I can remember is that he had for then, a modern Morris Minor car and made the occasional visit to see Hector. He had been part of the trio, which included Algy Taylor and Hector that had made one of the birdie trips to Scotland, in the Morris Minor. From a personal view I was sad that he made so few appearances, as he was so likeable and got on well with Joan.

John Piers Dutton. I have already introduced this character from the period when we lived at West Luccombe, as 'Dumfunkum'. He had the good grace to accommodate Hector's idiosyncrasies and rudeness to make visits to Hector and Exmoor when he had time from his position as the agent on the Shane Estate in Country Antrim in Northern Ireland, then at Belvoir Castle and latterly the Milk Marketing Board. Before this in March 1953 Dutton drove from his home in Surrey and joined Hector and Walter Copp on a foray after raven. They parked near Simonsbath and walked about a mile over the moors before locating a raven's nest in a fir copse. Hector strapped on his irons and took a clutch of five. Dutton recalls Hector as "...a rough and ready climber but brave as a lion..." Back at the car they headed towards South Molton and at Twitchen they soon found another raven's nest in a large beech tree, Hector again climbing to take another C/5 (clutch of five). By now thick mist had descended on the high ground and they returned via Cloutsham with no further success. I think that the following comment was made by John Dutton, which is a good and fair summary of Hector at that time.

"Hector Heywood was a popular character in the field although by reputation occasionally difficult to work with. He compensated for this with boundless energy and stamina when working moorland species and, as one of his regular companions asserted... he always seemed to be able to make something memorable happen..."

Right up until nearly the end of his life he kept in touch, especially with Beth, who used to have both him and his wife Nancy to stay. After her death Beth would have him to stay to give relief to their daughter who was looking after him.

Hector looking into a raven's nest at Butterhill Plantation.

The Brasnetts. Gurney Brasnett was a butcher from Bournemouth, and had great knowledge on the natural history of the New Forest, and the heaths and cliffs of Dorset. This knowledge he liked to share with others, including Hector. Exactly when Hector and he met is unknown; it could have been in the 1940s as Hector's data cards show that he visited Dorset in 1947 and several times thereafter. They made several trips to Exmoor, always just day trips as the business did not allow more, but the two photos show Mrs Brasnett helping to make tea boiling the billy on a fire somewhere on the moor. They were kindly people and had Beth to stay on occasions; on one time taking her out for the day from St. Gildas School in Yeovil to rendezvous with Hector at the heronry at Curry Rival.

The Brasnetts bred pedigree Cairn terriers; this resulted in Hector acquiring a dog pup and a bitch pup in 1961, more about them later. He had clearly been harbouring a wish over the years to have a replacement for 'Fido' from Hinham days. It was on the day that Beth returned from staying with the Brasnetts that we were raided by the R.S.P.B.

Hector with Mr and Mrs Brasnet somewhere on Exmoor. Note the Morris Eight in the background with side screens removed.

Hector and Mrs Brasnett boiling the billy.

Bruce White. Bruce and Hilda White came from Tavistock on Dartmoor and made fairly frequent trips up for the day; some of these are noted in Hector's diaries. I couldn't take to Bruce as he seemed to me at that age, to have an air of superciliousness or smugness so I was always pleased to escape his company and consequently have few memories of his and Hector's bird nesting.

Jack Robson. Jack became great friends with Hector, and it was through him that Hector became acquainted with East Anglia, staying with Jack and his wife Greta, and being taken out to find Marsh Harriers, Little Ringed Plover, Crossbill, Black Tern, Black Tailed Godwit and hear the elusive Bittern booming at Walberswick, the last making an enormous impression on Hector. Jack was an interesting man, friendly and informative, having been a Captain in the Intelligence Corps in the Far East during the war and afterwards as a bank manager at Stowmarket. He had been a keen rugby player and was a good shot, particularly fond of rough shooting and wildfowling. He had his own duck punt as well. He made frequent visits to Hector, staying locally to go out for the day together. Hector was always keen on keeping abreast of all sport, reading the *Daily Telegraph* avidly; football the early day interest was superseded by rugger, perhaps fuelled by my school playing days to the extent that he went twice to Twickenham and once to Cardiff Arms Park. He clearly had a lot in common with Jack Robson, about whom he always spoke with warmth and affection, something he was sparing with to most people.

Algernon (Algy) Taylor. Algy was in on one of the trips to Scotland so could have been known to Hector by 1951. He was a bachelor living on his own at Bourton-on-the-Water, Gloucestershire, and did not drive, so more often than not he was driven down by a man called Ken Pickford. Again, as with Jack Robson, Hector always spoke with great affection for Algy. Beth stayed at Bourton-on-the-Water a time or two. The last mention of Algy in Hector's little diaries is 16th September 1966 'Saw Algy'. I have a feeling that he died not so long after. He had promised his collection of eggs to Hector should he die first, however Ken Pickford ("That shit" I can hear Hector saying) managed to change Algy's mind and got an undertaking that the collection should be left to him, rather than to Hector. The apparent reason for the change of heart was that much of Algy's collection had been acquired with Pickford, who had driven Algy around for so long. Needless to say great resentment was felt by Hector towards Pickford for the rest of his life. Hector would have had the last laugh, as the collection did not go to Pickford but to Gloucester Museum.

There were other collectors who were not in the bracket of friendship of the above, with the exception of one, **Surgeon-Captain Thomas Latimer (Peter) Cleave**. I think Peter Cleave only came to see Hector two or three times in the late 1950s or early '60s; I was introduced to him on one occasion. As Hector was taking so much medication he had a problem with constipation. This was meat and drink to the Surgeon-Captain who persuaded Hector that he should consume a good daily intake of bran. My vague recollections were that Hector said yes he would try it, and then when the good man had gone said something along the lines that he was "not going to eat that tasteless rabbit food muck". This was great shame as Peter Cleave was so far ahead of his time and much thought of as an important figure in the world of medicine. It is worthwhile to reproduce this article from the *Daily Telegraph* in 1979.

Gold medals for 'bran man' doctor by David Loshak

A retired doctor in the South of England, better known as the "bran man" has received two of the most distinguished medals in medicine for work that has highlighted the crucial importance of fibre in the diet.

Some of the country's most senior doctors and surgeons attended a luncheon this week at the Royal Naval Hospital, Haslar, Gosport, Hants, to present Surgeon-Capt. Peter Cleave, RN Retd, of Fareham with the Harben gold medal and the Gilbert Blane gold medal.

It is the final vindication of Dr. Cleave's life work which, for many years, was scoffed at by medical colleagues who regarded him as eccentric.

"No man has contributed more to highlighting the baleful consequences of eating today's processed foods," said Dr. Kenneth Vickery, chairman of the Royal Institute of Public Health and Hygiene, which has awarded the Harben medal to such greats as Lister, Pasteur and Fleming.

Unprocessed Bran

Telegram congratulations included those sent by the American Senator, Mr. George McGovern, for whom Dr. Cleave contributed to his select committee report on U.S. food policy in 1973.

Dr. Cleave, former director of medical research to the Navy was nicknamed the "bran man" for feeding sailors with unprocessed bran during the Second World War.

He shipped it aboard [*the battleship* George V] in sackfuls to give them, in his own words "bowel movements as smooth as the guns they fired". He claimed the bran compensated for lack of fresh fruit and cured their common complaint of constipation.

Although his theories were discounted for more than 40 years, they are now regarded as crucial in directly linking major heart and bowel disorders to the under consumption of fibre and over consumption of sugar.

Junk food

Dr. Cleave, now 72 explains his theories in his British and American bestselling book *The Saccharine Disease*.

He argues that we eat too much sugar in the form of white table sugar, white bread and general 'junk food,' coupled with the lack of natural roughage due to the over refining of food.

He says this is a major cause of obesity, diabetes, varicose veins, haemorrhoids, tooth decay, coronary thrombosis and other common related diseases.

Dr. Cleave says sugar consumption in Britain is eight times greater per head than it was 50 years ago. The remedy? Eat more fresh fruit and vegetables and cut out "the killer sugar" he says.

***

Today in 2012, thirty-four years later, nothing seems to have changed, just take a look at people in crowds anywhere and see the gross obesity, with so many overweight.

Although not a birdie man, **Harold Evetts** who lived at Parson's Hill, Halscombe at the top of Porlock Hill did not impress Hector, except for one thing. He was hugely interested in red deer and most wild life and he made a simple device that imitated the cry of a red deer calf. This was a piece of hazel stick slightly thicker than an average little finger, which was split lengthways into two halves. Some of the wood was whittled out across the middle of each, then a thick rubber band was placed long ways over one piece, finally both pieces of hazel were held together by whipping with string at each end. Hector tried it out in the vicinity of some hinds and calves and was astounded when a hind came really close to him.

Harold Evetts was, according to Joan Weaver, a poncey little man; he was full of his own importance, fussy, and dressed accordingly in stockings and breeches, a hacking jacket, trilby hat and a moustache to top it all off.

In 1954 legislation was passed by Parliament that made it illegal, to take wild bird's eggs, to buy, exchange or sell them and to even own them. I think it is permissible to own eggs that are older than 1954. The Royal Society for Protection of Birds must have been delighted and started to gather information on possible transgressors. Come 1957 unbeknown to him the net was closing in on Hector. The first intimation of trouble was a little whisper from the local village policeman of Porlock, PC Jack Treadaway that a search warrant was being issued to search Meadow Cottage that afternoon of 30th April. Frantic action stations resulted in the recently acquired three Hill cabinets and the Winsford-built cabinet being moved to the care of Joan's friend Mrs. Kay MacGregor at Blue Haze, Tivington. Other eggs were placed on top of the bees inside the active hives. Beth that midday had arrived from the Brasnetts at Bournemouth with a clutch of Garden Warbler's eggs. No time to lose, the tin was plunged to the bottom of the hen corn in a meal bin. I can remember the feeling of dread at the approach of PC Treadaway and two smug, confident men from the RSPB who wafted the search warrant at us. In they came to troop all over the cottage, looking into wardrobes, chest of drawers, under beds, in fact everywhere including the outbuildings and hen houses.

Jack Treadaway kept very official and did not even get near to giving the game away. When in the kitchen, Beth went to the larder and produced a tray of hen's eggs, and in all innocence said "Is this what you are looking for?" The two RSPB men tried their best to unsettle me, to get me to blurt out the wrong thing, but without success. They left after a while, confused, unsettled and mystified; the horse had obviously bolted! It took quite a while for the adrenalin to work its way out of us to allow us to settle back to normality.

Hector had a certain respect for Jack Treadaway, whether he saw a kindred free spirit in him I don't know. I do know that he referred to him, as a "bloody rogue" to me. Treadaway had at some time told Hector how to kill a deer with a rifle, by sighting onto the foreleg moving up to the wide place and pull. It was common knowledge in the Porlock area that Treadaway was a bit of a poacher. However, on one occasion he had carried out an act of public duty that earned Hector's admiration. Peter Leach, John Hepper, Hector and Beth were out Spring Staghunting by car when the deer went to sea down over from Worthy Manor at Porlock Weir. They were on the shingle beach when the remains of a human corpse were spotted; Hector stopped Beth and told her not to go further on. Treadaway was called for and removed the remains into a box; the headless, limbless torso was clad in a seaman's blue jersey and eventually after the inquest buried in Porlock Cemetery.

After about a month the cabinets came home. Mrs Lorna Robins brought her son Oliver up as Warner had been told of the episode, and they were shown the eggs on top of the bees. Hereinafter Hector and his birdie friends had to exercise care and caution in what they did, where they went and who they met. Gradually life as Hector knew it resumed. He had been invited to the Jourdain Society to a meeting in February of that year, as a guest; he took with him to exhibit an extremely handsome clutch of six Buzzard's eggs. They usually lay only three or four, sometimes five, but rarely six eggs. He joined the Society in 1961, but took no part in the Society's activities except attending the annual dinner once or twice.

Hector was not a book man; he only possessed about half a dozen that included: -

The Field Guide to Red Deer
Records of Staghunting on Exmoor
Fur Feather and Fin –"The Red Deer"
The Handbook of British Birds
Memories of a Stag Harbourer
The Romance of Nature – This was four books of bound copies of a periodical, for which Marjory had given Hector a subscription`

However, he took great delight to pull out a drawer from his Hill cabinet and sit of an evening either in an armchair or up to the table looking at his eggs. He would relive or go back in his mind's eye to the challenge of finding the bird's nest in whatever weather then perhaps a long walk or climb to get to it, then waiting for the hen bird to have laid her clutch before taking them. These were his books.

We all knew Hector to be moody and difficult, extremely difficult at times but then to bounce back into a better frame of mind to become lively and interesting. Michael Upstone was aware of his temperament whilst we were at Gilhams as I have written earlier, but I will now reproduce what he wrote of later times: -

"The move to Meadow Cottage and him working for the Scotts seemed to be associated with his increased bad moods, cursing at you and Beth and of course Joan who tried to act normally and keep the family stable. He must have shouted at me too and I was slightly afraid of him, but he seemed to like me and show me some respect compared with you and Beth. [*Hector's nephew Ross Campell states that he remembers being in awe of him because he had a commanding presence and a loud voice.*]

"I bought a pair of climbing irons from some mail order company and brought them over to Meadow Cottage one day. I was trying them out on one of the willow trees in the field near the side of the cottage and Hector came home, saw me and assumed I was using his irons but all he said was 'Take them off' whereas if it had been you he would have hit the roof.

"In good moods he used to pull our legs at this time about our attempts at courting: threatening to put the rubber ring [*used for castrating and removing lambs tails*] on us if we didn't behave. He called me Oswald Mosley in my black shirt and you were Garibaldi in a red one as we became fashion conscious!

"One day I found a nest in Collings's lower paddock – a lot of eggs and a curious blue colour which I knew was unusual so I cycled over to Meadow Cottage to tell him. You were all out but I knew where the key was and went in and left him a note on the table. He subsequently went to the nest and they were pheasant and a rare blue colour so he took them and was very grateful to me when I next saw him. It was his unpredictability that was the problem but it didn't really affect me except when I witnessed him balling you out."

It would seem from my observations of his little diaries that the RSPB raid had a seriously deleterious effect on his mental health causing his depression to become clinical. He had had a week off sick before the raid, then a week following the raid he was off sick for a month. He continued his bird nesting when he had recovered from his sickness, and had the good fortune to find several Cirl bunting nests. He had a visit from Algy Taylor and also went to Taunton to watch Somerset play the West Indies at cricket.

For the first three years at Meadow Cottage, there had existed an unsatisfactory situation as far as bedrooms were concerned. When we first moved in, there were only two bedrooms, Joan and Beth had one room and I had to sleep in with Hector. It wasn't long before I had my marching orders, he could not sleep with somebody else in the same room, even though I had been quiet as a mouse. I moved in with Joan and Beth, Joan having rigged up a sort of partition to give the very minimum of privacy. This did not worry me as at school I was one of 25 in a long dormitory and quite used to other people's sleep noises, grunting, groans, farts, snoring or sleep talking. The situation was made a lot more bearable by the departure of 'Tiddles' our next door neighbour, enabling the landlords of the farm and tied cottages, the National Trust, to restore Meadow Cottage to its original state as a single dwelling. This was accomplished by opening up two blocked up doorways downstairs and only one upstairs. They 'modernised' the cottage by installing an indoor bathroom and lavatory, but in their infinite wisdom they placed them downstairs next to the kitchen. It gave us all a lot more space much to everybody's relief, and gave us a greater sense of independence. Now with four bedrooms Joan could see that in the summertime, if some of us could move out to a tent or to the caravan that appeared on the scene, she could do bed and breakfasts to bring in some much needed cash.

It would appear that for the rest of the year Hector was fairly stable and had four days hunting and was in on a deer shoot at Hallslake, west of Brendon.

With the increase in size of Meadow Cottage and the 'modernising' it became possible to have Sidney, Hector's father to stay to give a break to Jean who looked after him. Jean bore the brunt of it as Sidney came to live with her and John Campbell when they got married after the war, living firstly in one of Hinham Cottages, then in a council house at Amory Road, Dulverton. What a saint, Jean was, to have coped with looking after a husband and father, as well as bringing up a family of two girls and a boy. She gave generously of her time to support the Red Cross and latterly became the school cook in the new school just down the road. Today she is fondly remembered by countless old pupils of Dulverton Middle School as a good cook who was very strict and brooked no nonsense.

Imagine her preparing Sunday lunch at home for the six of them and just about to eat when Hector would appear, unannounced, onto the scene expecting to have lunch with them. This would mean having to stretch the food to feed another mouth, with perhaps no second helpings as a result. This would also happen when he went to his elder sister Dolly for Sunday lunch. Because Dolly was used to his idiosyncrasies she was perhaps more accommodating. Sometimes Hector would announce to us that he was off to see his aunt Elizabeth or 'Kysie' as he called her. She was Ernest Bawden's widow and lived on her own at 'Hollytree Cottage' in Exford; he was especially fond of her as she was so like Sidney in her temperament and character.

We never found that having Sidney to stay was a problem. He was quiet and polite and certainly was never as demanding as his son, and Joan never seemed to mind having him to stay as it was always for a short period. I enjoyed hearing from him tales of the old days and was proud when he came to watch me play cricket for Wootton Courtenay against Roadwater. We have a photograph of the three generations, seated, each holding a different piece of wood and each wearing different headgear. Unfortunately it is not in very good focus.

Three generations of Heywoods.

This was around 1959-60; about the time my school friend John Snow came to stay in the summer holidays and played for Wootton also. He had, even back then, an electrifying effect on both teams with his ferocious fast bowling. We didn't know at the time of course, but he later played for Sussex and England.

It was with great sadness that I read Ross's notes about Hector, when he said "Our grandfather (Sidney Thomas Heywood), as you probably know, lived with us until his death and, sadly, I was too young to get to know him really well. I do remember that when my parents went away he would have a week's 'holiday' with either Dolly and Alec, or your parents. Although I was too young to understand I do remember him being unhappy staying at Meadow Cottage and can remember him crying about it, which as a pre-teen child was upsetting."

I could scarcely begin to hazard a guess as to why that should have been, and prefer to remember Sidney as the kindly old man that he was. His stoicism was unbelievable, thinking of the days in a darkened room having had the black powder cartridge explode in his face, or riding to Exeter and back from Hinham in a day, to visit a solicitor I understand, or to endure appendicitis until it was nearly fatal. He got on well with Joan, after all he would not have told her at length his recollections of Great Nurcott, and so his tears must have been something to do with Hector. His last visit to Meadow Cottage was during the very cold winter of 1962/3. He was staying with us when I celebrated my 21st birthday and he gave me a present of a hacksaw; needless to say I treasure it still. Hector never gave me one, in fact the only two presents he ever gave to me, in his life, were a Sturmy-Archer three speed for the first bicycle I had, and he handed over many years later the Westley-Richards 12 bore shotgun that he had been given by Jack Hill of Henspark. Even this was a liability as the Damascus barrels were badly pitted and I had to spend quite a bit of money to have the gun re-sleeved. Because of the atrocious conditions on the roads and our circumstances I had only one visitor, the then current girlfriend Jane Griffiths, but she did not stay long, so it was a quiet, modest evening in the company of Hector and Sidney until they went early to bed and I was left in the company of Joan and Beth. It does not bear contrasting with the average person's 21st birthday of today with the attendant mega presents and oceans of alcohol. C'est la vie.

In 1964 when October was nearly out we had the unhappy telegram from Dolly to say that Sidney had died. His funeral and burial in Hawkridge churchyard on 27th October was conducted in a manner that seemed to be so befitting of him. A simple service, no frills, a few tears, a quiet graveside and he was gone, to rest beside his wife whom he had not seen for thirty-one years.

As a point of interest I recall how the system of sending telegrams worked. If you wished to send a telegram you visited the nearest Post Office and filled in the appropriate form or had it filled in for you, keeping it to the very minimum, as each word cost money. You paid up and the message was relayed by telegraph to the nearest Post Office of the recipient. It was then taken by a messenger on a motorcycle and delivered to the door.

- 17 -

THE BLIGHT OF DEPRESSION

IN THE FOLLOWING year, 1958, it seems that Hector did some involuntary 'bull fighting'. At the end of May he was working with Nick Ayliffe, the groom for Leslie Scott, hoeing weeds in a root field beside the A39 Porlock to Minehead main road. They were quietly working away when the peace was interrupted by a solitary bullock jumping down from Headon Plantation into the field of roots. It made straight for them. Nick, not liking the look of the bullock that stopped, scraped and pawed the ground whilst fixing them with a stare, said, "I am off" and made straight for the hedge. Hector thought this very poor and declared "It's only a bullock, I am not afraid of it", and carried on hoeing. The next moment the bullock charged for him and tossed him right up in the air. Fortunately he was only badly shaken and bruised. Soon after this, two of the Webber boys (Colin was one of them) from Hindon Farm also jumped down into the field. It was one of their cattle and they had been following it for nearly a mile already, but they were in their prime for fitness and both members of the Minehead Barbarians Rugby Club, and had to carry on running as the bullock jumped the hedge and got onto the A39. Somehow it found its way down to Blackford Farm on the road to Luccombe, and somebody was able to get it into a cattle yard and make it secure. Nowadays, it would simply be a case of getting the farm vehicle, more often than not a Landrover, hitching up to the livestock trailer and going to collect the errant beast. The Webber boys had to walk back to Hindon, get a small bunch of cattle then walk them down the lanes, cross the A39, down more lanes to Blackford where the bullock was let into the group for the long walk back to Hindon. All in all it was a total of about nine miles. To cap it all, the farmer Jan Ridler made them clean up the dung and mess that the bullocks made, before they left.

1959 would seem to have been an 'annus horribilis' – one of several for Hector. He was off work sick for 134 days and only four days hunting are recorded in his diary. He did however become involved with the Holnicote Shoot as a beater in the autumn; this interest lasted up until 1971 when arthritis in his hips meant that he could no longer take part. As with everything that Hector found interesting, especially where there was an audience to whom he could play, he threw himself wholeheartedly into it. Again to quote Warner Robins: "When on a day's shoot he was so quick on the uptake as to what the pheasants were going to do and where people should be, it wasn't true." Warner got to know Hector well around this time, and got on with him as he realised how to deal with him: "When he went off the deep end you had to shut the system down till he came back again. If he decided to go home half way through a day's beating you didn't take offence at it. He was so wrapped up in nature that he reacted in the same way as nature does." Another anecdote that illustrated his ability and skills witnessed by Warner: - "I remember us in a field of kale walking in line, somebody shot a pheasant, it dropped into the kale and looked an absolute dead bird; the dogs couldn't pick it up. Hector said that it was a runner; no, they said it was a dead bird, the argument went on for a bit, and then Hector reiterated that it was a runner; that was the leaf he hit when he dropped and he isn't under it, so he is gone. He had picked out the one kale leaf in the field that the bird hit on the way down and remembered which one it was."

In 1958/9 Warner was clerk of the course at the annual point-to-point held at Holnicote for the Devon and Somerset Staghounds. One of his responsibilities was the acquisition of the birch bundles to renew or refurbish the jumps. It was not easy to find the labour to cut the birch trees down and to bundle up the branches into the requisite size but when Warner threw the idea to Hector he was met with a positive response. It was right up his street, as to quote Warner again, "He didn't like routine, seven to five wasn't in his book, and if he had a job he would go there when he felt like it. We didn't need the birch before April, so I would ask him in October, tell him where to go and leave it to him in the certain knowledge that come the end of April all the necessary bundles would be ready. Each bundle was perfect, they didn't need trimming all the bottoms were level. I had to be careful as he wouldn't recognise a boundary but go to where the best birch was growing."

Hector really enjoyed his time up in the woods cutting birch; in the early years everything was cut by axe and billhook and woe betide anyone who handled those tools with a casual attitude as he had spent hours getting a sharp edge with his whetstones. He was close to nature and would constantly be on the lookout for deer and other wildlife, especially when walking from his car to the birch cutting ground. In late March and early April if it was warm and sunny he would be on the lookout for adders sunning themselves after their winter's hibernation. He had an absolute aversion to snakes, a dead one was the only good one, and therefore it was not uncommon for him when he came home to say that he had killed an adder. During one Easter holiday from school I tried my hand at cutting the birch, and almost inevitably I was to see an adder curled up, so it too received the treatment. The colouring was quite a mottled green/brown, but the colour of the adder I killed within 200 feet of the cairn, on Dunkery Beacon was a decided grey colour to blend in with the lichens growing on the stones.

Towards the onset of arthritis in his hips he found the job harder, but by now had got the help of a chainsaw that made the work easier and quicker. His last work on birch cutting was in the December of 1971; his bad hips meant that he had to enlist the help of his neighbour Bill Gunter to get the work finished. He had had fourteen years birch cutting which reflects, I believe, his contentment in that work. A definite perquisite that went with the work was the trunks of the birch trees after the branches had been removed and used. These came home by courtesy of a neighbouring farmer's tractor and trailer to be cut up to supply winter fuel for the open hearth fire; this was vital as it was the only source of heat for the whole house. Electric fires were forbidden as they would use too much electricity and Calor gas heaters did not appear on the scene for many years.

When not suffering from the black dog days of depression, in other words when the pendulum had swung to the period of elation or creativity, Hector was not only bearable but unpredictable, you really did not know what exciting thing he was going to do next. Therefore there are a few incidents that must be recorded as they help to illustrate his capabilities and which set him apart from his fellow men. The first of these was related by Jim Nancekivel, son of Bob Nancekivel who farmed at Cloud Farm, Malmsmead, or Plover's Barrow as R.D. Blackmore called it, when he wrote *Lorna Doone*. Bob, a keen staghunter was a popular Master of the Devon & Somerset Staghounds from 1963 until 1974. One day towards the end of Hector's harbouring, after the end of the war, he had agreed to meet Bob at Larkbarrow en route to the meet. Bob would have been on the lookout for a suitable stag whilst riding up Badgeworthy Water from Cloud, in the company of Jim. It was a typically horrid Exmoor wet day, with rain being driven sideways by a strong cold wind and visibility reduced by mist. On approaching the Larkbarrow farmhouse, still standing even after receiving a few direct hits from the wartime artillery, there was no sign of Hector. "Where is Hector, I told him to meet me here punctually?" said Bob curtly. With that he looked up to see smoke coming out of a chimney, "I believe the old bugger is in there"; and so it was, Hector had got a roaring fire going in the fireplace and was drying himself in front of it. "It's too rough for me out there Bob". Hector must have been the last person to have a fire in any of the rooms at Larkbarrow as in the early 1950s it was deemed unsafe and the Fortescue Estate had it pulled down.

One day during Bob's mastership hounds were hunting an autumn stag on the land to the north of the Minehead to Porlock road, towards North Hill, when they threw up their heads and were checked by a lack of scent. It was a hot autumn day and they stopped on the edge of some ploughing; after casting around, they could do nothing, and the situation appeared hopeless. Hector walked across the ploughed ground and soon saw the slot of the stag; he then got down on hands and knees, and started throwing his tongue in imitation of a hound as he moved over the ground. Giving a great holler he got hounds going again much to everyone's amazement. "He was a proper case of it," said Jim.

The third incident told to me by Jim, happened in the Horner valley. The meet had been out over on the Forest and the hunted stag made for the Horner Water; Hector following the hunt by car had walked up from Horner in anticipation of meeting the stag coming down the water. Bob, whilst still Master and Jim were riding down the valley when they heard a holler, hurrying on they came across Hector and the stag. He had caught hold of it by its antlers and was lying across the animal in the water on a bit of 'a water slidey bit'. "I've got 'un for 'ee Bob, I've got 'un."

Warner Robins was able to give details of two examples of Hector's phenomenal tracking skill, equal, surely to the best anywhere in the world. The first of these occurred when hind hunting out at Haddon.

"The deer had run into Haddon above Bury, the river goes through a hedge down through the fields and comes out again at the bottom. I can't remember if it was under the reservoir. The hounds came running down the water and came to a wire deer fence that almost touched the water. The hounds went out around and on down but stopped, brought back they were cast around but could not find 'un. Hector said to Sidney Bazeley [*huntsman 1951-61*] "She's gone down the water."

Sid said, "She can't get through there." Words were bandied about, and then Hector said,

"Can't you see anything?"

Sid said, "What do you mean?"

Hector walked into the water to the bottom of the fence that was barbed wire, he caught hold of something and walked back out of the water holding it up and saying to Sid "Can't you see a deer's hair when it is there?" The hind had laid flat on her side to get through and was found two fields down and they caught her."

Col. Murphy retired from mastership in 1963 so this next event must have happened before then. It was during Spring Staghunting when the Colonel rang up Warner asking him to harbour for the meet at Wootton Courtenay, or perhaps it was Venniford, at any rate the area where they hoped to find and hunt a stag was Wootton Common and Grabbist. On his way out Warner thought he would call in at Meadow Cottage to see if Hector would like to come with him, and he did. They drove up the track above Headon Cross towards Wootton Common looking at the bank for signs of deer; they then stopped to get out, having a look where deer had crossed. Hector, leaning on his thumb stick studied the plethora of slots for quite some time. "I looked up and saw the deer; by that time I had got to know how to handle him, I had got way wise, prod'un in the right direction and he would go. You put a bit of bait under his nose especially if it was a problem, a nature problem and he would catch hold of it especially if you said it couldn't be done. He was just that sort of chap, he would try to do it, and he wouldn't be beat if it was nature. When he went up after the Golden Eagle eggs in Scotland they were guarding the nest but he got them. That job up on Grabbist, I saw these yer six spring stags, he stood looking at the track and said, 'I think its six spring stags.'

I said, 'No Hector I think it's only five', just out of devilment.

'I know its six,' said Hector and by now getting quite shirty about it.

'Yes Hector youm quite right, look up ahead.' There he was able to see the six stags. It was a hard forest track, we harboured them just as simple as that, anybody could see deer crossed there and yes I could see that they were spring stags, but to be able to work out six and no other number. If you look at the slots of a spring stag they don't vary very much when you come to study them. How does he do it? He could even see a slot on a tarmac road, and that takes a bit of doing."

Another example of Hector's extraordinary abilities was told by Tom Yandle. When Tom's father Ernest, one of the four legendary Yandle brothers of Tiverton Staghounds fame, was getting on in years he started to go blind. This would have been in the early 1950s as he died in 1956 aged 76. He liked nothing better than to reminisce about hunting and the old days with a knowledgeable person. The Yandle brothers had run the Tiverton Staghounds from 1919 until 1945, one was Master, two took it in turns to hunt hounds on alternate days and one was the whipper-in. Bear in mind that Ernest Yandle had carried the gun for the Tiverton Staghounds for over twenty years and had shot countless deer in all sorts of situations. Hector called in one day and spent a couple of hours with him.

"I've spent the last few days in the Bray Valley culling a few deer"

"How did you do that Hector?"

"I take my shotgun, I know the woods very well, and I just walk about quietly until I see a deer then shoot one or two. I got very close to a hind and calf that were stretching up grazing off ash, I shot both, and they didn't know I was there".

Ernest Yandle was astonished that this could happen and doubted it, he couldn't believe it, but Hector said that it was true, a matter of fact. The Hunt had asked him to cull the deer as they were doing a lot of damage to crops in the area. He shot double figures, 10-12 in two or three days.

The occasion of harbouring a stag by smell must have taken place around the same time as it was in the days when Hector used to go hunting with his friend Peter Leach from Porlock, in Peter's green Austin van, i.e. prior to the start of his little diaries which began in 1957, in which there is no mention of the day. The story was told by Tom Rook.

"They had met at Alderman's Barrow and it was foggy, Murphy was Master and didn't know what to do. We said, 'go back to the Parks' (the coastal woodland above Porlock Weir), although there were not many deer about there at that time.

He said, 'There is nothing in the Parks.'

We said, 'If you go back to the Parks we will find one.' Murphy said we will meet at Birchanger Bridge at such and such a time. I took your father dropped him off at the top of Porlock Hill where the quarry is. 'You walk through and I will pick you up down at the bottom Hector.' I made my way up the Toll road and heard him hollering like hell; I got down the road and said, 'What have you seen?'

'I haven't seen one but I can smell the bugger.'

'What do you mean you've smelt one, how do you know it's a stag?'

'Well it had a kind of pissy, staggy smell that only an autumn stag will have.'

Murphy was a man of his word, but by the time they were coming in over Whitstones the fog lifted; Dick Lloyd said 'It has cleared sir we can go out over.'

Murphy replied 'I told Tom Rook that I would meet him at Birchanger Bridge, and at Birchanger Bridge I'm going to meet him.'

They came in; hounds found the stag and killed it out at Luckwell Bridge."

Hector had remarkable skills and both stories just illustrate his capabilities as the master tracker in the knowledge of every creature or bird on Exmoor.

1960 was not much better than 1959 in so much as Hector was off work for fourteen weeks and went to see a psychiatrist called Bethell at Tone Vale Mental Hospital. During this year I saw the reference 'went to Quantocks with Minifie'. Ray Minifie was a dear person who was so long suffering of Hector's moods that he remained one of Hector's best friends until the end. My first recollection of Ray was at West Luccombe around 1948 when he arrived with his wife Ruth on the back of a powerful Triumph motor bike to go hunting with the Staghounds. He was a man with curious swollen top eyelids, looking as if he had been stung by bees, but nevertheless he always had a twinkle in those eyes and he wore a thin moustache. He ran his own pharmacy business from his chemist's shop in Weston-Super-Mare and because of this, days off were limited. As his business thrived so he could afford firstly to buy a motorcar then to buy better and faster ones. When coming for a day following the hounds he would call to collect Hector, who was given guest of honour position in the front seat to direct operations for the day. My memory fails me but no doubt knowing of Ray's kindness he would have provided food and drink for Hector as well. Come finish Ray could make the trip down from Bleadon, near Weston, down the A38, to Meadow Cottage in 44 minutes in his Wolseley car of the day.

1961 was better from the respect of only seven weeks off work. As Bill Harding the official Harbourer at the time was off sick the wise old war bird Colonel Murphy knew the best outcome, and asked Hector to be Harbourer for eight days in February and April.

Hector made several trips to North Wales in his quest to find a chough's nest, and took with him on two occasions, Reg Needs, his work mate from East Lynch. One of these took place on 19th April. Reg related how on one visit, they had located the chough's nest partway down the vertical face of an old slate quarry, and that the only course of action was to pass the climbing rope through a metal eye driven into the ground that they had espied some little way back from the edge. Between the two of them Hector was somehow lowered down until he could reach the nest, take the eggs and then make it back up to the top. I too, was persuaded to go with Hector to Bala in North Wales on another chough expedition on 18th April 1963. This time unsuccessful, giving me two memories, firstly walking alongside the dam of Lake Bala killing time before going to bed, in the same room as Hector at a ridiculously early hour, and secondly of exploring the abandoned slate quarries to find a chough's nest in a hopeless place to get to, half way up the quarry face. I also looked wistfully at an abandoned Standard Fordson tractor, worthless then but priceless today.

Early August of that year saw him starting work as one of the team setting up and making all preparations for Dunster Show. The show took place in the middle to late August and necessitated about two and a half to three weeks work. As with birch cutting Hector loved this work as it gave much needed variety to his life. He did it for ten years, his last in 1971.

1962 was another good year by the criteria that he was not off sick other than one week; he went beating for the Holnicote Shoot on 18 days and eight days hunting are listed. He mentions that Elizabeth went to Dartford; this was to start her two-year course of Physical Education at Dartford College. He even came with me when I started at Seale-Hayne Agricultural College a week later; he didn't offer to carry my luggage past the porter's lodge, and come to see my room, but changed to the driver's seat, said goodbye and drove my then motorcar, a post war 1946 Standard Eight Tourer, back home. In those austere days, first year students were not allowed any form of transport except a push bike, regardless of the fact that we were at least two miles away from Newton Abbot, the nearest civilisation.

The black dog was absent in 1963, he had 21 days beating, 16 days hunting, went to Cardiff Arms Park to see Wales play, and Twickenham to see England play France. Around this time Hector gave his sister Jean and nephew Ross Campbell a day out in his car hunting. I think it worth relating Ross's words as it helps to illustrate his uncle's character.

"In my late teens my mother and I met Hector at a meet and he announced 'Jump in with me'. The meet was out over the forest and resulted in the stag going to sea at Porlock Marshes. Your father knew where the stag was going to land and took us at breakneck speed down a long, steep, rough, stony track heading for the beach, I wish I could remember the exact location but it was obviously along the coast by Ivystone/Broomstreet somewhere. My mother and I were hanging on to the seats for grim death. The car seemed out of control. Up ahead a large bump in the track

Hector posing for the camera in front of a bird box he made, and used by blue tits. This is around the early 1960s whilst still fairly slim.

appeared. Too late to slow down the car was suddenly airborne and we landed several yards further down the track with a sickening bang from underneath the car. We eventually ground to a halt and leapt out to inspect the damage. There was a huge dent in the petrol tank but amazingly the car was still drivable and so on we went!!

"Another incident I remember as a passenger was along one of those twisty narrow roads by Heasley Mill when his wing mirror was completely ripped off by a tree. It didn't seem to bother him at all! He could be an impatient driver out hunting and obviously, like us all, wanted to be up with the stag, hounds or in at the kill."

It is significant that he spent less time working for Leslie Scott but more for Bill Partridge at Luccombe. Bill is a wonderful self effacing man, quiet and even humble in his way; he is a first cousin to Tom Rook 'The Lord Mayor of Exmoor', Tom's mother a Partridge married a Rook, as is so often joked about. He was understanding of people and Hector in particular, having had a difficult upbringing and fought with the Somerset Light Infantry in the last war. His efforts were recognised by promotion through the ranks to sergeant, taking part in the Normandy Landings on about D Day+6 and the subsequent fighting until he was wounded crossing the Seine, by a sniper's bullet. By now he had had field promotion to become an officer and had been awarded the Military Medal. It was always a relief for Hector when he set off for Luccombe as he enjoyed the work, the people, and his efforts and skills were appreciated. Hector rang the changes in his work by doing gardening for a few elderly people, thereby building a little clientele who needed his services over the next few years. He must have fallen out of favour with someone in the hierarchy of the D&SSH as for the next two years no mention is made of hunting.

It is possible, but I admit conjecture on my part, that a possible reason for the apparent absence of the black dog days was due to two small Cairn terriers, a dog and bitch. These had been acquired from the Brasnetts of Bournemouth as pups in 1961. We called them Fanny and Sabre, but to Hector these names were unacceptable especially as he took them beating on the Holnicote Shoot, so craftily he called them Pansy and Sailor. So similarly sounding were the names that the dogs would answer to either. They were happy, cheerful and plucky little animals that quickly won the hearts of us all, and would accompany us wherever we went. In the days of the Lambretta scooter which Joan had bought for her use, but needless to say was used by us all, it was not unknown for both or one of the terriers to travel small distances locally, sitting between our legs. Hector would seem to pour affection on to these dogs to the extent that it was not unknown for him to be seen lying on the carpet beside one of the dogs talking in the most endearing terms. Some could say that that was the manner in which he should have been behaving towards Joan.

After my leaving Seale-Hayne in 1964 with no National Diploma in Agriculture I signed onto the dole at Minehead labour exchange and continued to live at home. Now that the hens had gone and the orchard going wild I floated the idea that I would like to keep some pigs in it. Surprisingly Hector agreed, subject to two stipulations, firstly I had to have a double fence around the orchard, the second one electrified, and secondly the gilts had to have rings put in their noses. He had always kept a few pigs at Hinham and Cloutsham, so was I think, if not fond of them, quite liked them. No doubt he was curious to see what nonsense I was going to perpetrate as well. Anyway he had a hand in finding the stock, taking me to see his cousin Jack Heywood who managed a farm at Roadwater. Jack's daughter Cecily looked after the pigs there, so it was arranged that I should buy a well-grown Wessex Saddleback maiden gilt from them. Hector knew the farm manager Philip Snell from nearby Bratton Court, where Large Black pigs were kept, and two more maiden gilts were purchased to make a trio. They had to be named, so it was Sarah and the Pergies. Hector was hands on when it came to ringing the pigs. After being coaxed with food to the point that a noose could be slipped into their mouth and over their nose, a quick pull to get the rope tight and slung over a branch of an apple tree and the pigs were ours. The volume of squealing reached a climax as the rings were snapped closed through the top of their snouts,

"Never mind the noise, ignore it and concentrate on what you are doing," said Hector, as he made me apply three rings to each gilt. It certainly stopped the orchard from becoming a ploughed field or worse a mud bath, but did not stop the pigs from grazing the grass and when preparing to farrow, bringing copious mouthfuls into the farrowing hut to make a mound upon which to farrow. My funds were always low and could only stretch to tendering for a red ex Post Office mail van at Minehead. I was successful, and red quickly became blue via the paint brush, thus providing me with a maid of all work, well certainly one that would accommodate a gilt, and later sow to visit the boar belonging to Jack Leach at Brandish Street Farm, Allerford. All went well until one day Sarah became restless over the mile journey home and pushed aside the barrier separating her from the front of the van. All I could do to keep her still was to feed the slobbering chops a few inches from my ear, with peppermints whilst I drove as fast as the situation would allow homewards. The trouble was she didn't suck the mints but chomped them up in double quick time and soon wanted more.

When autumn arrived that year it brought with it a wonderful fall of acorns in huge carpets from several old oaks near Selworthy so Hector suggested that we go to harvest some, as pigs loved them. Armed with a yard brush and shovel we set off to gather them. In no time at all we had four sacks full. Those acorns gathered would be part treat and part saving on boughten food. Before giving any quantity to the pigs I offered an acorn to Sarah, this she sniffed and open her mouth a little, so I popped it in. Incredibly she didn't just chomp it up but carefully rolled it around her mouth then spat out the shell, and then she ate it slowly savouring it. Each pig always spat out the shells. Hector told me that acorns produce a hard white fat in pig meat which people like to see as opposed to the soft yellow fat that excess maize in the diet will produce.

Sadly the time came for the pigs to be sold as I had been successful in applying for a job with the National Institute in Dairying at Shinfield, Reading, so it was with a leaden heart that three sows and their litters of weaners were loaded onto a lorry bound for Taunton Market. I loved looking after them as they were so responsive to the human touch and gave me great confidence when years later I embarked upon a pig enterprise at Moor Farm with 120 sows with all progeny finished to bacon.

I am not exactly sure when our local G.P. Dr. Martin Chapel retired and a new state of the art youthful Dr. Keith Lister took over the practice, but it was around 1964. He would have been cognisant of Hector's medical problems and been up to speed on the most modern of drugs to help depression. He was a caring, kindly man with a lovely 'bedside manner' and was naturally able to give you great confidence in his diagnosis and treatment. It is perhaps to him that we must owe the years that were relatively free of the black dog, if not entirely, certainly he was a great help. When I talk of the black dog days it was nothing to see Hector sitting in a chair in the darkened sitting room, saying little, looking awful, and perhaps crying for hours at a time. If he was not sitting in a chair he would take himself to his bedroom and lie on the bed for an indeterminate time. Nothing we would do or say in trying to be sympathetic seemed to make any difference, "You don't know what it is like, it's bloody awful, and just leave me alone" would have been a typical response. From my own perspective I certainly owe Dr. Lister an enormous debt as he quickly diagnosed the problem that Dr. Chapel had virtually dismissed "Oh wait and see what you are like in six months time" or words to that effect. From my first consultation with Keith Lister and pouring out all my problems it was only a few weeks before I was in front of the biggest cheese in the South West in Endocrinology, at the Bristol Royal Infirmary. Another two weeks saw me as an inpatient at the BRI, then surgery under the knife of Mr. Angel-James, of whom I wrote in chapter ten, at the Bristol General Hospital, with final reassessment at the BRI, and home again after five weeks of hospital; no longer with a life threatening tumour (fortunately benign) under my brain.

The rhythm of Hector's life continued on through the 1960s not varying an awful lot from year to year until 16th November 1965 when he received notice to quit his job and to leave Meadow Cottage from Leslie Scott. I find it in incredible that this should have happened three times to the man; fortunately times had changed from the days of 'Ratsmuzzle' and tenants had more protection. A quick visit to John Thorne, solicitor of Thorne and Thorne, Minehead, gave Hector reassurance and confidence to face the ensuing court case that took place in September 1966 which Leslie Scott lost and had to pay all costs. It is interesting to see from the diary entries that it did not have any repercussions on Hector's health, and it cut the tie and therefore onerous position of having to work for the Scotts, even though rent had to be paid to them until the National Trust gave Hector an independent tenancy in September 1967. Curiously neither party seemed to bear a grudge against the other for Hector resumed working at East Lynch, this time for Derek Scott as his father had retired to Minehead. The difference being that Hector was asked to work, the compunction having been removed. Leslie Scott needed help to sort out the garden of his new home and asked Hector if he would like to do it; Hector also built a new front roadside wall in local old red sandstone, a feature that is still to see. Every time I pass it I mentally salute him.

His active egg collecting days were beginning to slow down, and because he had got what he wanted, his thoughts turned to preventing others from taking the eggs of some of the moorland species. This led to him climbing the mountain ash or thorn tree in one of the combes running into Nutscale Combe where a merlin had laid its clutch in an old crow's nest, and marking with an indelible pencil, on each egg the lettering RSPB. Thus the eggs were worthless to a collector, and should have hatched out. I read in the local paper in 2008 that a man had been observed in the same vicinity climbing up a tree and taking a clutch of merlin's eggs. A National Park Warden, Richard Eales, had watched him for some time; after this when passing through Exford the police were ready and stopped to search and arrest him. Would Hector have fallen into the same trap I wonder? I somehow doubt it.

- 18 -
THE STRUGGLES OF JOAN

AT THIS POINT I wish to write of how Joan, or Saint Joan as she could have been, fared with her life. Although she shared an existence with Hector she had to make a life for herself as it was not in her nature to wallow in self pity, and a divorce was out of the question. There was simply no money to exist on; nowhere to live, so was it a case of 'better the devil she knew than the one she did not?'

Because my mother was always an optimist who tried without fail to see the best in a person or situation, she could cope with anything she faced, especially after living with Hector. She had a musical ear and loved listening to classical music; she appreciated the arts and loved to paint, she was a good dressmaker who could sew a fine seam with her hand cranked Singer sewing machine, she could knit, she was a fine cook and could produce a tasty nourishing meal on next to nothing. She was well read and used the library service extensively as she was never in a position to afford to buy books. She had a tremendous sense of humour, was fun loving and fun to be with, she was kind and completely selfless. She was the complete antithesis of Hector, but having been brought up in an age when you made the best of a bad job, and divorce was not easy, as it created a whole new set of problems, she stuck it out with him. In the first instance it was to provide a home for us children and latterly to do enough that was required to make a home for them both, but both leading separate lives. Apart from a desultory peck on the cheek, I never witnessed any endearment, hugs or love between them in my whole life. However she was a wonderful mother to us children.

Joan working at Putham Farm.

Her first jobs away from home were in 1954 as I have already written about. At some point she was dispatched to a family living at Stawell, near Bridgwater to, using her words 'hold the fort' whilst the mother was having a baby. These people were Rob and Sheila Graham, fruit farmers and went on to be friends of Joan and the family ever since. Sheila was a Scot brought up near Pitlochry who missed the Highlands and had met Rob whilst nursing; Joan encouraged her to visit Exmoor that gave a taste of home. Their daughter Celia was Beth's bridesmaid and to this day keeps her horse with Beth and shares it with her. We are friends too, of the sons, Charles still at Stawell and Alistair working for the World Wildlife Fund as a consultant, living in Tasmania.

One local place she stayed at was Putham Farm, Wheddon Cross. This was owned by M.C. Houlder of Houlder Brothers Shipping Line, who was joint Master of the D&SSH 1948-51. His chauffeur Tom Sparkes, lived in the house; she 'held the fort' whilst his wife was having a baby. I stayed for a night there too.

For several years Joan worked in the run up to Christmas, sorting and delivering mail at Mount Pleasant, London. Once she befriended a New Zealand woman doing the same work, Laine Morrell had nowhere to go for Christmas so Joan invited her home to Meadow Cottage. Hector as can be imagined, was not enamoured with this arrangement and only just remained civil over the festive period, not that there was much in the way of festivities. To make matters worse she was a vegetarian and used a dowsing pendulum to make sure her food was 'safe'.

One year found her at Gratton, a hill farm near Brayford on the western side of Exmoor where she held the fort whilst a daughter was born to Major and Mrs. Greenwood. This was a sister for David who is now known to the indigenous population of Exmoor as 'Greengrass'.

Joan's cousin Michael Nicholson was particularly helpful and gave Joan work on countless occasions, when his four daughters were born, when they went away on holidays or when an event called for another pair of hands. She used to help a distant relation of Michael's called Rina Kennard who lived at Wonham House, Bampton; I am not sure in what capacity she helped but she did organise her 70th birthday party and made her birthday cake. To quote from Michael's book: "*Rina Kennard was an eccentric relation who was enormous fun, and rich, too. On one occasion she went into a shop in Bampton, Devon, to have her skirt altered. Promptly she took it off, wrapped the car rug round her, and spent the rest of the day in the town shopping. – The family spent several summers in Biarritz, and on one occasion my mother and Rina went on horseback into the Pyrenees, staying at inns. In order to make it more respectable and protective, Rina wore a wedding ring!*"

To Tom Yandle Rina appeared to be a large powerful lady. She was a very keen supporter of the Tiverton Staghounds and rode; her other passion was fishing and she had a considerable amount of salmon fishing, from Exebridge to Chain Bridge, a distance on the River Exe of three miles. An example of her behaviour or character occurred when she gave a Mary Doddington whose family farmed at Highleigh, permission to have a day's fishing. Mary Doddington was, to quote Tom, "a proper old poacher." After the day's fishing she went up to thank Rina for it, she was invited into the house for a cup of tea, "Have you caught anything?"

"Yes one salmon."

"Well you can keep that one," said Rina and being the wise old bird that she was, went outside and opened the boot of Mary Doddington's car to see three salmon lying there. When she returned to the house she said to Mary "I am having that one, you are not having any as I found three in your car."

On another occasion she invited Tom's two maiden aunts for tea. Upon discovering that there was no milk in the house for the tea, she got a jug and went out to the field where she milked some from a mare that was running with its foal. She brought it in and they had their tea as if it was just an everyday occurrence.

Rina's first husband was Admiral Kennard by whom she had three children, and when he died she married his cousin Jack Kennard from Guiting Power in Gloucestershire. I can remember Joan visiting them there to work; I would want to say as a house sitter whilst they went away.

Joan went down to Cornwall to help look after a Miss Lethbridge; she went over to Langley House, Wiveliscombe to help look after an elderly Col. Capper to give his wife a break.

Exactly how Joan became involved with Mrs. Wilhelmina Stirling I cannot say. Joan had an aunt and cousins living in London and her friend Sheila Piggott who used to live in Withypool had a flat in London as well, any of these could have directed her to Mrs. Stirling. Or indeed it could have been via an advertisement in the magazine *The Lady*. Joan used to work for Mrs. Stirling at Old Battersea House for two to three weeks when her cook/housekeeper was on holiday. She would fill that role but also drive Mrs. Stirling if she wished to go anywhere. They had a lot in common and got on very well, Joan would pick a large bunch of primroses in the spring, wrap them in moss put them into a plastic container and send them to her, as she loved flowers. She announced one day that she was going to make Joan a beneficiary of her will; this would have meant the world to Joan and could have eased her difficult financial predicament. After Mrs. Stirling died in 1996 just short of a hundred, Joan had a letter from her solicitors to say that she had been left some money; later she had another letter from them to say that the money had gone to another Joan Heywood. A bitter blow, as in all probability the solicitors had made the simple mistake of getting the wrong Joan Heywood, but nevertheless quite extraordinary that there should be two of that name, if indeed there were; dirty work at the crossroads? This did not sour Joan's memories or thoughts about a most remarkable woman. I reproduce a piece that I located on the internet about her. Beth has two of the books that she wrote, both inscribed to Joan.

Old Battersea House (1961)

Mrs Wilhelmina Stirling lives in Old Battersea House in Wandsworth, which she has transformed into a museum of Pre-Raphaelite art so extensive that a tour typically takes five hours. Her manservant Mr Peters shows a tour party round, illuminating the darker corners with a portable lamp.

Mrs Stirling is happy to answer questions from the tour party. Asked if the place is haunted, she says a friend of hers was convinced that the chairs were all occupied by ghosts, one wearing a rapier that might imperil anyone who sat down on it. Mrs Stirling has never seen a ghost herself, but she sleeps in a bed formerly owned by the notorious Lord Rochester, and she was once woke up by a loud sneeze.

The collection stems from her love of paintings and her late husband Colonel Stirling's passion for furniture and old china. The collection fills the entire house, and focuses on the later Pre-Raphaelite period. She has a highly personal relationship with most of the works: either she knew the artist or was present at the time of its creation. She shows a painting of the Archangel Ithuriel, and says that the real-life toad who modelled for an allegorical image of the devil was actually very pleasant company and frequently paid them visits.

The main link between Mrs Stirling and the Pre-Raphaelite movement is that her sister was the prolific painter Evelyn De Morgan, who produced hundreds if not thousands of canvases. Her husband, William De Morgan, was an inventor, ceramicist and friend of the great Victorian designer William Morris. He devoted much of his time and money to rediscovering the lost art of lustre glaze on pottery, though he finally achieved success late in life in a different field entirely: as an accidental best-selling writer.

Mrs Stirling reminisces about her sister's painting, which started when she was a small child. She had to paste putty around the cracks of her nursery door so that the smell wouldn't escape, as she had been banned from painting, and later resorted to smuggling water in a doll's teacup. Both Evelyn and William De Morgan cared little for what happened to their work: the act of its creation was satisfaction enough.

The Pre-Raphaelites weren't just idealistic aesthetes: their work spanned sculpture, furniture, architecture, design, fabrics, painting and pottery. Much of it was a reaction against the industrialisation of England, and their work is full of images of menace and treachery.

Mrs Stirling is confident that their ideals will return, as she detests modern art and thinks that people will yearn for the return of beauty. She cites the surprise success of a sale of an Edward Burne-Jones painting as evidence that the tide is turning. But she doesn't obsessively dwell on the past: she has published 36 books, and has finished another, 'Ghosts Vivisected'. Even at 96, she remains as tireless as her Pre-Raphaelite forebears.

Throughout all the years Joan tried to keep up her artistic interests, whether at flower arranging at the Minehead Flower Arranging Guild in the company of her friend Virginia Hawkins or attending classes under the locally well-known painter and teacher, Malcolm Ferguson RWA, in Minehead. An example of how she managed, was to take a lift as pillion on the back of Ted Prescott's high powered motor bike with her painting gear, every week, to get to Fergie's classes. Ted was the son of Harold from Luccombe with the Morris Commercial lorry that moved us to Meadow Cottage in 1953, and he lived in Allerford. Because she was such a caring and thoughtful person, she pocketed the biscuits at the coffee interval instead of eating them, to give them to Beth as a treat when she got home.

She painted with and got to know quite well, the retired Matron from Minehead Hospital, Margaret Genge.

I end this chapter with the words of Michael Upstone: "The more I think about it, the more saintly becomes Joan for putting up with things, sorting out finances and making sure that you and Beth got a good education and prospects in life."

- 19 -
ON THE SLIDE

1969 WAS NOT A good year for Hector, with no hunting but he did venture to stay with me in North Bedfordshire in the farm cottage that I rented in the village of Yielden whilst working for the then Ministry of Agriculture Fisheries and Food. I am in doubt as to his motivation for coming to visit me; on the one hand he could have been fulfilling a fatherly role and taking an interest in his son, but now that I know the extent of his medical problems I consider that the underlying reasons would be to experience, see and think about something different, to give him the much needed relief from the Freddie guilt and now his depression.

On the sixth of February he had a black out, saw Dr. Lister and was seven weeks off work.

One day in September of that year he had slowed to a stop on the main A39 road, indicating to turn right into our track and waiting for a gap in the traffic to do so, when 'wham' a car drove into the back of his ex GPO engineers van. If it had not been for the wire mesh behind the driver's seat he would have suffered even more whiplash than he did; it is quite possible that he could have had a broken neck. An ambulance was called for, and Hector was taken to hospital for a check over: fortunately apart from shock and bruising there was no serious damage to him, but the van was a right off. He suffered the ignominy of receiving a bill for the ambulance's services which was promptly thrown onto the fire! Finances were never his strong point, as the frequent final demands to pay the electricity bill with threats of being disconnected bear testament to, and we thought were the triggering mechanism for a bout of depression.

Many years before, somewhere in the same vicinity, Hector was bringing up the rear of a flock of sheep being moved on the main road when an impatient motorist drove so close to him that he felt the bumper push the back of his leg. With that, he turned round and brought his stick 'thwack' across the bonnet of the car and accompanied it with "Get back you impatient bugger!" I would have loved to have been there to witness the reaction of the driver.

His total amount of work had come down to twenty six and a half weeks, every year the total had been getting less, and now aged 64 he was eagerly anticipating drawing a weekly state pension, and not having to work at all if he did not have to.

As people get older and have therefore more of life to look back on, a frequently heard remark would be 'It was never like that in my day'. Two letters and one to the *West Somerset Free Press* are worth recording here but do have huge overtones of nostalgia. All three are from Richard Stapledon: -

1962, Dear Hector, Praise where praise is due! How very nice of you to write and bother to copy out your diary account of the hunt; I did enjoy it. Even though 25 years ago, it still remains as fresh as ever in my mind. We may bore the modern folk with our references to the good old days, but they will never know the fun of hunting with Sidney Tucker and Ernest, as well as the Yandle Brothers. Or even, may I add the exploits of one Hector Heywood!! Best wishes Richard Stapledon

1968, Hector. The memory of those golden years will never fade. When Ernest was at his peak and the thrilling note of his horn came floating down the Danesbrook in answer to a glorious holler from Hinham – glad we were we lived! Richard Stapledon

Knowledge of Stags on Exmoor

Sir, - I have known Hector Heywood for more years than he or I dare to count. Any letter written by him in your columns (the last, stag's heads) is invariably of interest, because he is the best-informed naturalist of our time in North Devon. Like his illustrious uncle, the late Ernest Bawden, he knew most of the stags in the country by their "Christian names", and by their voices he can paint a picture upon the canvas of his mind in the autumn mists, just what kind of a stag it is. His mother, on the other hand, used to regard hinds as her special prerogative. On hunting days she would sit on Brewer's Castle in the Barle valley, apparently engrossed with the sock she was knitting; but no hind could escape her eagle eye.

One incident bearing closely upon what I have written, will always linger in my mind. Some years ago the Tiverton Staghounds met by invitation at Five Cross Ways; Ernest had helped with the harbouring that morning. "Sir", he said to me at the meet, "the stag is lying in the ferns at the top end of Longstone Combe with four hinds, but he is a stranger and a foreigner. I don't recognise his voice nor do I know him." How right he was, because hounds eventually came up with their deer in the River Bray at Wallover Barton.

Dick Stapledon was five years older than Hector; he was born to a sea captain and his mother was a daughter of a shipbuilder in Appledore. To quote Tom Yandle "Dick Stapledon was a shipper from Liverpool and retired when he was 25 to come to live on Exmoor, to be a country gent. He thought he would live off his stocks and shares but the slump came and he was worth nothing, because he now had no money. He said he was going to start up his own prep school, which he did. He taught Latin, and he was an Oxford Blue. He ran it; it was called Kestrels. He ran it quite successfully for some years." He gave the name Kestrels to Knapp House, East Anstey, Devon, which has since reverted back to Knapp. He had a son Norwood Stapledon who married Tom Yandle's cousin Cherry Yandle, who had been groom and second horse girl to the Staghounds when Norah Cox was Master. Together they farmed Putham, at Wheddon Cross, which the Houlders had owned. Norwood got killed when a Standard Fordson tractor ran away whilst cutting bracken on the very steep cleeve below the farm and Cherry died of cancer, leaving a daughter Tina, who was raised by Tom and his wife Margaret.

1970 was another difficult year for Hector with depression as he had two spells of a month each of no work, giving a total of weeks worked in the year down to seventeen. He also had to come to terms with my marriage to Constance (Connie) Ashwin of Londesborough, York; if you live the life according to Hector and don't wish to do something, you don't. He had no intention of coming to our wedding but his illness gave him a good excuse not to, as is revealed in a letter to me:-

"Dear Bruce,

Just a line to wish you all the best for Saturday. I am sure you will go through with it alright, shall be thinking of you about 11.30, if all is well then, I shall be hunting with Bee Ho [Bill in dialect] at Alderman's Barrow. I have not been very well lately, terribly depressed, a good job I didn't decide to go to Yorkshire.

When I cut the grass around the bees a couple of days ago there was a strong smell of heather honey so perhaps you can have a look at them when you collect the tent. [Camping honeymoon I couldn't afford hotels] I hope you will stay for a night when you come. I was harvesting with Derrick yesterday but rain stopped us today.

Love from Dad."

Amazingly he came to Yielden to stay twice that year, firstly whilst I was still single and then in December when we married.

1971 saw his total work time as eight weeks. The arthritis in his hips was really getting him down, and he was given painkillers and steroids. It was a vicious circle; because he was less active he could not combat the increase in weight that the steroids brought, which in turn exacerbated his condition.

However the fact that I left my job with MAFF and we bought a 50 acre farm 'Shuteley' near High Bickington, N.Devon, must have given him fresh things to think about. Indeed he seemed to have a new lease of life as he would drive over for the day, two or three times a month, to help in whatever way he could. This was mainly in an instructive role, "do it like this, not like that". We hung the odd gate or two, did some stone ditching, went through the flock together sorting out problems, and he even drove a tractor turning hay. We frequently travelled over to Meadow Cottage for Sunday lunch that was a bonus particularly after Victoria (1971) and Oliver (1972) were born. It is ironic to think that we no longer seemed to fall out with one another; previously he would, at the slightest opportunity denigrate, castigate or swear at me. Many years before for instance, when he was not using the entire garden at Meadow Cottage, I tried my hand at growing vegetables. I considered the soil starved of nutrients, so organized a trailer load of dung for it. Wrath automatically followed; for he feared an untidy mess and perhaps that my results might have outshone his. I had to endure snide remarks about a 'kiddies rap'. A rap is a dialect word for an area; a 'rap of ground' would mean an area of land. However I had the pleasure of growing bigger and healthier vegetables than his, and that stopped the tirade. I like to think of the times when he helped in 1971/2 gave him pleasure and respite from his difficulties for there was much, much worse to come for him.

The call finally came for Hector to go to Winford Orthopaedic Hospital, near Bristol, to have his first hip replacement operation. He was in good hands as the surgeon was a Mr. Michael O'Driscoll FRCS who had trained under the father and pioneer of the operation Professor John Charnley; the operation although considered fairly new in those days had been launched in 1962. It consisted of a stainless steel stem inside the femur and head located into a polymer socket cemented with PMMA onto the pelvis. This last product, a transparent thermoplastic had been developed years before as an alternative to glass. It was known as Plexiglas and one of its many uses was the glazing in aircraft cockpits and gun turrets. All went well except that Hector, during the first night after the op, managed to climb out over the restraining cot sides of the bed. Perhaps, still partially under the influence of the anaesthetic, he might have been dreaming of trying to climb up after a raven's nest. The heat wave at that time, with Hector's bed in the direct sunlight, caused a few problems; these were overcome by his insistence that a sheet be hung up covering the large window. The one of thirst was helped by a fellow patient who befriended Hector; he got his wife to bring in orange juice and other drinks as they ran a village shop at Pensford, Bristol. Bert Coles and Hector became good friends and kept in touch for a long time. Elizabeth and I brought him home on 4th August back to Meadow Cottage, but within ten days he was an inpatient at Tone Vale Psychiatric Hospital. He was in for just over three weeks and this could have been the time when he had electro-convulsive therapy, otherwise known as electric shock treatment. Exactly what swung him into depression is unknown. It could have been post hospital trauma, and it could have been the gloomy prospect of life in the slow lane and not being able to resume doing all the things he loved. The most likely cause was how he was going to face up to and come to terms with the forthcoming marriage of Elizabeth, for she had been an uncomplaining companion and helper in so many ways since she was a teenager. His involuntary calling her Jean must reflect a transposing in his mind, of his daughter into the former role of his sister, i.e. a gofer or dogsbody; however they did bear quite a similarity in looks to each other so it is understandable, more importantly father and daughter got on well together. I am sure that in his mind he was going to lose her.

On the 30th September I had to deputise for him in giving the hand of Beth in marriage to Tony England in Selworthy Church, and afterwards at Porlock Village Hall. He couldn't face it so resorted to the only known comforter to his mind, a day following the DSSH. The enormous irony was just as the happy couple had departed in their motorcar and many people were still in the road, Hector appeared in his car from the direction of Porlock Hill. Remarks were exchanged as he slowed to a stop and it seemed that he had had a good day, and then he was gone.

People are either meticulous in keeping a diary or they are not. I fall into the latter category and therefore, sad to say the early enthusiastic entries into the farm diary ceased, to be replaced by a resume at the yearend. Consequently I have very little knowledge of Hector's happenings for 1973, except from his diary that reveals he worked for only about four and a half weeks, in the whole year. The Cairn terrier bitch Fanny who had become diabetic, died, and Sabre her companion died five months later. This would have caused sadness to both Joan and Hector, but they were not replaced.

Connie and I were starting to feel that the relatively small size of Shuteley was thwarting our farming ambitions, in spite of regularly buying grass keep to enlarge our activities, so that when we learned that the tenant of a 278 acre farm on Connie's father's estate was retiring, we wrote to her parents requesting that they consider us as possible replacements. They were delighted for such a thing to happen, so with rather a leaden heart considering we would no longer be 20 but 300 miles from Joan and Hector, we put Shuteley on the market with Price, Ogden and Stubbs of Barnstaple as we considered Ken Stubbs a good man. We sold it well and moved lock, stock and barrel to Moor Farm, Londesborough, near York in February 1974.

The mention of the word barrel, reminds me that Hector gave me during our last year in North Devon, his two shotguns. This proved to be a costly gift. One having belonged to Ernest Bawden had completely knackered, pitted barrels and was a hammer gun and therefore redundant. The other a Westley Richards hammerless gun had worn out Damascus barrels, so feeling flush with the potential sale monies from Shuteley I elected to have the gun sleeved, i.e. new barrels are attached to the stubs of the originals to make it safe and useable. If my memory is correct it cost about £500. It had been given to Hector by the sporting gentleman Jack Hill from Henspark, who had given Sidney the mare 'Stella', way back in the 1920s. Jack Hill married a Philby, sister to Col.O. Philby from Wotton Courtenay, who was father of the sisters Ann and Eve (now Carter and Webber). Col. Philby was first cousin to the infamous spy Kim Philby who was a high ranking member of British Intelligence who worked for 30 years as a spy for, and later defected to the Soviet Union. He was rumbled in 1963 as a member of the spy ring known as the Cambridge Five along with Donald Maclean, Guy Burgess, Anthony Blunt and John Cairncross. He was believed to be the most successful in providing classified information to the Soviets. He had an OBE but was stripped of it in 1965, only to be given the Order of the Red Banner, one of the highest honours of the Soviet Union.

I think Hector was rather chuffed that we had gone to a larger farm with more prospects, for he wasted no time before coming up to stay. We moved on the 4th of February and had to live temporarily in Connie's parent's house until the farmhouse became available. They had taken a long holiday so we had the big house to ourselves; Hector could experience at first hand our early excitements of Moor Farm, and what gracious living must have been like in a big house. By big house I mean just that, the grander half is Londesborough Hall and let out, Connie's parents lived in the other half, Londesborough Park.

With the move to the far end of the country, as it seemed, we thought that it would be reassuring to take with us some Devon heifers to start a small herd, shades of our cow from the far off days called 'Buttons' no doubt. As it turned out, Hector was chief procurement man, and we visited the Bawdens at Newlands, Exford. It was a delight for him to be visiting his distant cousins to do business, and after inspecting the stock and striking a deal with Ken and Allen, we took tea with their sister Mary in the farmhouse. It was on to the Richards of Surridge Farm, Skilgate, where four more heifers were purchased. At some time we called to see one of Hector's old chums from far off days, Jack Turner of Highercombe House, Dulverton. We were shown his stock, and again took tea but the buddies spent all the time talking of hunting, deer and the good old days. The legacy of that visit was a gift to me from Jack of a little book he had published, of his poetry, *Random Rhymes*.

Hector made several visits to stay and where he could, would do some work such as tractor driving to work ground down for seedbeds, turning hay or applying marking fluid to the ewes as I finished shearing them. He seemed to get on with the people who worked for us, or that we were involved with, and enjoyed reminiscing with me when I would spend a little time with him after he had gone to bed. It was during these times when he went back over the years that I found most interesting. On a couple of occasions I took scribbled notes, but in common with many people I never asked enough or spent enough time talking about the past. If he made a derogatory comment such as he did when I had purchased a five-year-old crib biting, wind sucking, thoroughbred for knacker's money "What on earth did you buy a bloody thing like that for?" I felt less inclined to sit and talk.

Here is one of the stories told. "Some years later another incident occurred at Tarr Steps that was that a stag had been drowned at Hind's Pit. As there was no means of getting at him in the flooded Barle, some of the field galloped ahead, unhung a gate near Tarr Steps and held it ready on the bridge until the stag's body appeared coming down stream. When they saw where the body was likely to pass under the Steps, they jammed the gate down and caught the stag's body; it was probably from North Molton." Whilst talking to Dick Lloyd to gather information on Hector, I mentioned this tale and he was able to put more detail into it as he was out that day. "I was 16 at the time, the meet was at Sandyway and the weather was wet and foggy. We stayed at Longstone Wells for hours and hours as the stag had been harboured at the top of Waterworks Combe. It cleared a bit at 2.00pm so the pack was put straight on. My pony swam the Barle at Horsen Ford, and the stag was shot under Bradley by Ralph Slocomb who was home on leave. I said 'that's all very fine but how are we going to get it out?' Somebody said 'the silly boy doesn't know what he is talking about'. I took off with a handful of others, it was wartime, no cars, and we galloped down to Tarr Steps. We caught the stag and in getting hold of it we let go of the gate that disappeared down the river. The trouble was it was a brand new gate. The hunt advertised in the lost and found section of the *Free Press*, it hadn't gone far and was found hung up at the bottom of Hardway, to be put back where it came from. It was a fine stag and its head hangs in Old Court Hall, home of the Poltimores."

I see from my scribbled notes that he related as to how he had himself seen all the happenings that Fred Goss, the harbourer before Ned Lang, his predecessor, had written about in his book *Memories of a Stag Harbourer*, published in 1931, with the exception of a ferret bolting a fox. He had twice seen a buzzard carrying an adder. The first when harbouring during the war, was on Winsford Hill as the buzzard flew from Draydon Knap in the direction of Contest he could see the sun glinting on the adder that had been gripped behind the head. The second time, he saw from his car a buzzard behaving in a peculiar way, flapping its wings and half running. He saw that it was chasing an adder. Eventually it stopped and took off with the adder swinging in the air; it was flying downhill and flapping its wings hard to keep up. This happened on the brake on the right coming up from Barbrook Mill. On the third occasion he saw a half eaten adder in a buzzard's nest with young, in Farley Water.

So it was a complete and horrible surprise when Joan phoned on 2nd July 1976 with the news that he had tried to commit suicide. At around 5.30 am she had heard him going downstairs and had a premonition that all was not well; it was a little while before she could get down to the bathroom to be greeted by the horrific sight of blood everywhere, with Hector sitting on the lavatory, asking how long it would take to die. He had cut his throat. Prompt and authoritative action by Joan saved the day, and he recovered in hospital. I have a strong feeling that it was her that pushed Hector into giving me the shotguns, as she was always fearful of what might happen, having lost her father in tragic and similar circumstance.

To add to Joan's woes her mother Elma died the next year, following a stroke, from which at first, she seemed to make a recovery, but another one finished her. Joan used to like to come to stay on her own, without Hector and so it was in July 1978 that she made what transpired to be her last visit. She had been pulled down by the stresses of coping with Hector and had high blood pressure. She made the sad mistake of presuming that the doctors had over prescribed medication for her and only took half the dosage. When I kissed her goodnight at the bottom of the stairs, she made a flattering comment, which I shrugged off with a little embarrassment, "You have been a wonderful son". These words she said again after she had had a stroke at around six o'clock the next morning. The children had awoken early and had got into her bed; we were awakened by Victoria saying, "Come quickly something is not right with Grandma." Whilst waiting for the ambulance she was quite distressed as she did not want to go to York Hospital, so it was no surprise that when the ambulance crew collected her, her agitated state produced another stroke from which she never recovered. Hector was mortified, but he pulled himself together enough to visit the sexton at Selworthy, Ivy Cann, to book a double plot.

Joan's funeral was memorable to me on two accounts; firstly although I had insisted on the hearse leave Londesborough really early to make the 300-mile journey, as it was a bank holiday weekend, the traffic was appalling. The service was due to start at 2.00pm, imagine if you will our consternation when 2.00pm came and went, with no coffin to be seen from Meadow Cottage, as we were to follow it on to Selworthy. At about 2.05pm it hove into sight coming down Venniford Steep on the A39. We were a bit late. More minor trauma, the coffin bearers went to take hold of the handles on the side of the coffin (I've a nice piece of oak or you could have some elm had been the conversation in his joiners shop) and started to lift, "Nay lads, they are only fer orniments, they'll pull off, carry 'er oondane'arth", in his broad East Yorkshire dialect; later when John Layton the traditional village carpenter cum builder cum undertaker stepped forward to organise lowering the coffin into the grave, there were no webbing straps or ropes. He didn't seem too perturbed, a slight misunderstanding of local practices, having come from far away; a miscellany of ropes were found in Mr. Barnes's 'motor hearse', but knots in the rope prevented a slick pull from under the coffin when down in the grave. Nothing for it but John Layton got a piece of 'four by two' timber and proceeded to lever the coffin about until the offending rope was released. Talk about a comedy show, my thoughts then were of the Irish comedian Dave Allen. They always say that when a staghunter is laid to rest deer will come to pay their respects; sure enough as we left the churchyard four autumn stags that had come out of Great Wood stood just the one field away watching proceedings. We mourners retired to Meadow Cottage to do as Joan had bidden us, and drank to her memory with 'Johnnie Walker' scotch. We had lost a wonderful mother and grandmother, who had done so much for us all, at great sacrifice to herself, she was totally selfless. She had gone far too soon, as she was just five days short of her 67th birthday, with so much to live for. She had often warned me "that when I am pushing up the daisies you'll have problems with your father."

Usually if one hip is arthritic, it is not long before the other one is affected, and so it was with Hector. Connie's father was a consultant radiologist at York Hospital, so it was through his good offices that a private consultation was arranged at the Purey Cust in York to fast track Hector towards another hip replacement. The Purey Cust was a nursing home that became part of the Nuffield Hospital group. Dr. Ashwin's colleague and friend, Mr. Edgar Price performed a successful operation on 31st October of that year. Alas three days later he had a coronary clot, together with a manic turn, to be followed by pneumonia on 5th November, this necessitated being transferred to the intensive care unit at York District Hospital. His strong constitution carried him through and he eventually returned to Meadow Cottage.

The next year 1979 saw him come up for a follow up visit to the Purey Cust, and another visit in June to stay with us at Moor Farm. Remembering 'Dumbfukum's' words "He always seemed to be able to make something memorable happen..." they were never more apt. As he was walking across the concrete yard and took a step up onto the wide concrete path he stumbled and fell across the edge of the path. The full impact was taken on the middle of his femur, judging by the outbreak of yelps of pain I knew something serious had happened. And so it was, he had not only broken his femur but also it later transpired that the metal shaft of the replaced joint had sheared in two. It was back to York District Hospital for another replacement, only on this occasion the embedded shaft proved to be a bit tricky to remove. The new shaft went down the femur as far as it was possible; for the break to heal and allow all to settle down Hector was in traction for six weeks and finally discharged after seven weeks in hospital. We tried to help by visiting as often as our busy farming life allowed; I distinctly recall in the early days, of his brain being confused to the extent that he related as to how he had talked to Peter Leach on the floor below, through a hole in the floor, and could I get some cigarettes for Peter. He also complained of the cobwebs across the harness room window at Hinham and would I remove them. It was very curious to be confronted by a jumbled, confused Hector and of course unsettling for us both, as he was adamant that he was talking sense. In spite of the fact that their patient had come from 300 miles away, the doctors were very good at following up his progress with two later consultations a month apart.

With his main prop gone Hector found coping on his own very difficult, so that in the end a home help or perhaps by now they are now called carers, was arranged to call in most days. Beth partially filling the role of Joan was always popping down from Almondsbury, to where they had now moved, to take Hector out, either for a run onto the moors, for a day following hounds, to do his washing, change the bedding, and clean the house or stock up the food supply. Local people were very kind and understanding such as David and Win Dyer from neighbouring Tivington Farm, unasked they would go across to see if all was well. It was around this time that he took to the bottle to deaden the distress. I know that Beth and I came down to stay for two nights on one occasion, we took him out hunting in the car which he seemed to enjoy, then when at home it was a slug or two of whisky. The only tape recording that I have of him is a conversation we had that evening and I read out the *West Somerset Free Press* to him. He declared in a delightful old-fashioned turn of phrase "I'm drunk as a handcart" and spoke in rather a slower, slightly slurred voice. His days at Meadow Cottage were numbered. Rather fittingly on my last trip out with him on Exmoor he directed that we go to Poulthouse Combe on Molland Moor, as it was May time and merlins would be nesting. Whilst he sat in the car watching, I went off as I had been bid, to hit the trunks of thorn trees with a stick that had a crow's nest in them, to see if a merlin would fly off, but there was nothing.

During a stay with us at Moor Farm in 1980 that coincided with his 75th birthday he became a bit morose and sad, or perhaps it was a touch of narcissism, for he asked me to write down in my diary details of his funeral service, of how he would like it to be. I reproduce here my scribblings:-

"The funeral service is to be at Selworthy Church and I am to be buried in a grave next to your Dear Mother, next door to Mrs. Davis. My bearers to be all personal friends, Fred Clatworthy from Westwater, Robert Clatworthy from Upcott, Maurice Scott from Brendon Hill and Ross Campbell from Dulverton.

The hymns to be   1) There is a green hill far away
                      2) Fight the good fight
                      3) Abide with me
No flowers by request.
I want two hunt staff wearing pink coats to lead the cortege, when the vicar has finished his prayers Denis Boyles [*huntsman*] to blow gone away."

On the one hand it was good to get those matters settled but on the other I felt that he was having an awful cheek to think about having hunt staff in scarlet, particularly as I would be the one to have to request it and didn't really know how the Masters would feel about it, especially as I thought it was way over the top.

- 20 -
THE TWIGHLIGHT YEARS

AFTER ELMA NICHOLSON died Joan was able to have the agreed share of her mother's estate; this was a modest sum of capital. Because of the time taken for the granting of probate, it was some months before the monies arrived. The only benefit Joan had, was the thought that she would be financially sound and would not have to worry any more, sadly that was all, for she died within months. Very sensibly and most fortuitously she made a will, allowing Hector to have the interest and use of the capital during his lifetime, on his death it was to be shared between Beth and me. There was much consternation as this sudden exposure to a little wealth was giving Hector all sorts of funny ideas, and it would have been so easy for him to have given it all away. Two letters I have, substantiate this, one dated 28.6.83 from Norah Harding, Master of the DSSH, which said "Thank you very much for the generous cheque for the 'Fighting Fund'. It was good of you to send this and will be much appreciated." The second was from Sir Robin Dunn dated 21.4.85 " I am writing in my capacity as President of the Appeal for the D&S Fighting Fund, to thank you for your generosity in subscribing as you did at the meet at Hawkridge. It really was a magnificent gesture, and much appreciated by all your old friends on Exmoor." I don't know what sums were involved, but by this time as he was living with Beth, he could save his pension, so perhaps it was that money he gave away. John Thorne the solicitor of Thorne and Thorne, Minehead had the right solution. We could purchase a property thereby locking up the capital but because Hector could live or stay there, he was in law, having the use and benefit of the capital and the property might increase in value for us too.

Thus armed with the green light we went ahead on 30th September 1981, and bought the dormer bungalow in Wootton Courtenay by the name of Red Cleeve, a good name but Hector wanted to change it to Hunter's Lodge. He did not get his way this time. We relinquished the tenancy of Meadow Cottage then hired a self-drive small lorry to move the contents of the house and two sheds three ways, some to Red Cleeve, some to Almondsbury and the remainder up to Moor Farm. It was quite a wrench to sever the ties with the house we had known for 21 years, and to leave the Porlock Vale permanently.

Hector had a long stay trying to live on his own at Red Cleeve but caught pneumonia and had to go to hospital. Clearly he could not cope on his own any more, so now lived with Elizabeth for most of the time, but came up to stay with us for several weeks at a time, to give her and Tony a break. To make his life a little more interesting and easier, we converted our sitting room into a bedroom for him and had John Layton knock a hole in the east wall of the room so that Hector could see the comings and goings of people, animals, dogs and tractors at the entrance to the yards, as he lay in bed, and not feeling locked away. As he became less mobile he bought an electric scooter, this would at least give him some mobility, for he enjoyed driving up and down our tarmac farm road that was over a quarter of a mile long. We did our best to make his stays comfortable and interesting to delay the time when he might have had to go to a home. Before harvest Ollie and I took him, sitting on his scooter in the transport box attached to a tractor, up and down the tramlines in the wheat and barley crops so that he could see at firsthand what they were like. Ollie drove the tractor.

Michael Upstone and his wife Marion came to stay at Moor Farm whilst Hector was there and wrote this remark: "The last time I saw him was when Marion and I came to

Myself, Hector and Ollie about to set off to inspect the crops; Ollie did the driving.

So typical of Hector, not wanting to look at the camera; a very serious expression and pose.

Moor Farm and he was in a very high bed downstairs feeling sorry for himself, drinking Scotch and not wanting to say anything."

In 1984 whilst Hector was staying with us, we had our first ever visit to Moor Farm, of my American second cousins the sisters Lorene Townsend and Doris Mayfield. They were the grandchildren of Fred Heywood who immigrated to the USA in 1897. Doris took this, one of the last photographs of Hector.

Yet somehow he could not come to terms with the fact that he could no longer be centre stage or do exciting things as he used to; I feel sure that as a result, whilst staying at Almondsbury, he had three more attempts at suicide. Fortunately the lily pond was only six inches deep, but he did slash his wrists and on the occasion of cutting his throat again, Beth and Tony had had enough. He went to Barrow Gurney Mental Institution and when well enough to move, he went to Boyd House, Minehead as a resident. Boyd House had been in its heydey a good class hotel. It was converted to an old folk's home, but today is part of Eastleigh Care Homes, whose owners it must be said, are keen riders and followers of the D&SSH. Even then he had little respites, as Beth brought him up to Moor Farm for four nights in September 1988. She would drive down and take him out hunting. I visited him there once, and was pleased for him to know that the wife of Ruben Bowden who had farmed at Withypool, and knew him, was there to share the daily round. Rex Hancock made it his business to visit him, but on the very last occasion was greeted with the words "Go away Rex I am watching the Rugby." Most incredibly he tried again to commit suicide by drinking cleaning fluid, the reward for which was to have his stomach pumped out.

His sister Dolly died on 9th January 1988, Beth and I went to her funeral in Dulverton, and afterwards at Bridge View for tea and drinks. It was difficult to gauge the effect on him, if there was indeed one at all.

Whilst I was bedding up some calves at Moor Farm on the morning of 27th October, one of our men Nigel Donkin brought the news "Bruce I am sorry but I have bad news for you, your father died this morning, I took the call in the office, as there was no one in the house." He had had a heart attack and was aged 83. It was phone calls all round to organise his funeral at Selworthy. This was complicated for us by the fact that one elderly worker had left the day before as I had made him redundant (not a nice thing to have to do, because the man was such a kindly understanding stockman, even if, to quote Hector "He talks too much") and a tractor driver left the day after of his own volition.

The service at Selworthy was as Hector had planned, except that the bearers of his coffin were Peter Leach, John Hepper, Robert Clatworthy and Fred Clatworthy. The Masters of the D&SSH came up trumps and sent two second horse boys, and two hunt staff in scarlet, and Denis Boyles did blow him away as the coffin was lowered into the grave. His dear friend and cousin from way back, Percy Bawden and his other cousin Alan Bawden were there, together with Ken and his brother, Alan Bawden, from Newlands. There were no mishaps this time round, and no deer watching either.

When I talked to John Hepper whilst gathering information for this book, he said to me "Your father played a dirty trick on me, wanting me to be a bearer. I had broken my collar bone three weeks before and had to carry the coffin and it was not a light weight, on that shoulder, down all those steps and downhill all the way to the grave." It was he who related also, than when Hector learnt that his Brother John's wife Doris had given birth to twins, came out with the remark "He must have fired both barrels to wance (once)."

AFTERTHOUGHTS

IT IS ONLY AFTER WRITING this book that I feel as though I can say that I have got to know my father a little better, especially as to why and how he behaved, so much of which must be laid at his brother Fred's sad and untimely death. Hector was a troubled soul ever since then and showed remarkably selfish behaviour, even narcissistic as has been suggested by the psychotherapist Tim Williams. He was so talented and at one with nature that if he so chose, I feel sure that he could have achieved much more than he did. He was able to enthral the Porlock Young Farmers Club talking about his eggs and hunting, as he was with the Pony Club in the days of Lady Pilcher from Lynch, Bossington, who was the then District Commissioner. He even took the members of the Pony Club on mounted rides. Christopher Binnie from Wootton Courtenay recalls that he had one or two most instructive and interesting rides from Horner or West Luccombe up the combes onto the moor to end up near Nutscale Reservoir. He would show them deer, birds, and wild flowers, and tell them the names of every track or combe.

His knowledge of Exmoor was extraordinary; he knew every farm and farmer, the name of every hill, ridge, combe, track, lane, stream and river. He could have capitalised on it.

Perhaps he thought that by marrying Joan there might have been some money coming their way. The only money that did trickle through was an annual dress allowance of about £200 that each of the three sisters received from their father.

He was a difficult person to love, Joan must have loved him once, and Beth and I did in our way. He showed affection sometimes, especially when we were younger, more pliant and naive; when entering teenage years it became more difficult as we had minds of our own. But on the whole he was a difficult man to live with as he was, at times, so aggressive, hectoring and overbearing unless at the time we were being disciples of 'the law according to Hector', in which case he would be interesting, lively, and almost fun to be with. As with all families we had to take the brunt of frustration, the nearest and dearest always do. He had a limited sense of humour, being serious and earnest in so much of what he did.

I sometimes wonder to what extent his sister Dolly was involved with Fred's demise, and how it affected her and what secret she took to the grave, for she suffered from depression too. She also went to Tone Vale for electroconvulsive therapy and had her black dog days.

In some ways I feel that the then psychiatrists failed in their treatment of Hector and possibly Dolly and treated the symptoms and not the cause. Ann Carter, then Philby, following a horrendous point-to-point racing fall, suffered depression and she too went to Tone Vale around the same time as Hector. She had ECT and can vouch to me that no one, at any time, tried to ascertain what was causing her depression. I can only hope that psychiatry has made the giant strides that other branches of medicine have done.

I am proud to carry the name Heywood when I consider all those who have gone before; I am proud of Hector for all of his achievements, but not for some aspects of his behaviour. My cousin Ian Stuart-Lyon's comment is quite valid when I told him that I had never received any Christmas or birthday present in my whole life from Dad. "Ah yes but he did give you something more precious than anything, the best present of all."

"What's that?" said I.

"The ability to observe and see things in nature."

I like to think that through his efforts during the war in controlling deer numbers he was sympathetic and mindful for the wellbeing and future of the herd. He was able to assert authoritatively that at the end of the war the total number was around 500 on Exmoor. Today by comparison, their numbers are in the region of 2800.

Although we are mere specks over the course of time on this earth, as long as there are Heywoods I hope that the name of Hector might just be talked about and remembered in the family, just as nowadays I imagine Sidney and Hector walking in the road outside of this house taking animals to or fro Anstey Auction.

Sanctuary Farm 2012

ACKNOWLEDGEMENTS

I have used some small printed content from:-

Anne Acland:	*A Devon Family the Story of the Aclands*
A.C.Cole and W.M.Trobe:	*The Egg Collectors of Great Britain and Ireland*
Richard Stapledon:	*EXMOOR Elegance & Rhythm*
Michael Nicholson:	*The Long Straw*
Paddy King-Fretts:	*Staghunter*
H.P. Hewett:	*The Fairest Hunting*
H.J. Marshall	*Exmoor Sporting & Otherwise*
Mike Hawthorne:	*Challenge Me the Race*
David Hodges:	*The Le Mans 24-Hour Race*

Without the kind help from many people, some of whom are no longer with us, I would have struggled severely to write this book. To them all I offer my heartfelt thanks for their patience and recollections.

In alphabetical order they are as follows: -

Nick Ayliffe
Pauline Balder
Alan Bawden
Ken Bawden
Percy Bawden
Christopher Binnie
John Blackmore
George Burnell
Jean Campbell
Ross Campbell
Margaret Chorley
Derek Dascombe
Clover Down
Sir Robin Dunn
Elizabeth England
Terry Groves
Molly Groves
Rex Hancock
Colin Hancox
Wallace Harding
John Hepper
John Heywood
Henry Horseman
Jack Hosegood
Mervyn How
Douglas Lang

Michael Lenthall
Dick Lloyd
Doris Mayfield
Jim Nancekivell
Reg Needs
Gerard Noel
Bill Partridge
Walter Perry
Rosemary Pile
Dick Rawle
Admiral Steve Ritchie
Tom Rook
Derek Scott
Kathy Stevens
Clifford Stone
Ian Stuart-Lyon
Jill Taplin
Lorene Townsend
Michael Upstone
Joan Weaver
Arthur Webber
Roger Webber
Sidney Westcott
Tim Williams
Tom Yandle

My gratitude goes to Connie and Victoria for their help in so many ways, proof reading, suggestions, encouragement and forbearance.

HEYWOOD FAMILY TREE

John, batchelor of Witheridge

William
b. 23.6.1795 Oakford
d. 1865 Nurcott

William
b. 1820 Clayhanger

William
b. 1845 Winsford

John
b. 1848 Winsford
d. 1911 Nurcott

m. Mary Norman
b. 1849 Winsford

George William
b.1870 Winsford
(Kemps)
3 children

Frederick John
b. 1871 Kemps Emigrated to USA
4 children

Herbert Henry
b. 1873 Kemps
3 children

Harris Edwin
b. 1874 Kemps
5 children

Sidney Thomas
b. 1876 Kemps

m. Elizabeth Bawden

(Ernestine)Dolly
1901 - 1988

m. Alec Chanter

Frederick
1903 - 1912

Hector
1905 - 1988

m Joan Nicholson
1911 - 1978

Marjorie
1907 - 1935

Mary
m. Paddy Kennedy

Archie
m. Kathleen Puttock

Pat
m. Ann Goldsworthy

Bruce
m. Connie Ashwin

Elizabeth
m. Tony England

Debra

Mark

Grant

Neil

Victoria
m. Dennis Blackmore

Oliver
m. Sarah Gordon

Thomas
m. Georgina Spicer

Louise

Jolyon

George

Harry

William

Tabitha

m. Elizabeth Norrish

m. Mary Ann
  b. 1798 Clayhanger
  d. 1876 Bridgewater

Mary	Elizabeth	Jane	John	Anna
b. 1825	b.1830 d.1837	b. 1832	b. 1834 Oakford	b. 1836 Oakford

Mary Ann	Thomas	Elizabeth	Robert
b. 1851 d 1898	b. 1854	b. 1856	b. 1865

Elizabeth Anne	Laurence Edward	Maurice Eugene	Frances Jane	Mary Norman
b. 1878 Staddon	b. 1881 Nurcott Emigrated to USA m. Annie Stephens	b. 1882 Nurcott 2 children	b. 1885 Nurcott m Dick Stephens 9 children	b. 1873 Nurcott m. Joe Bawden No children
m. Ernest Bawden	5 children			

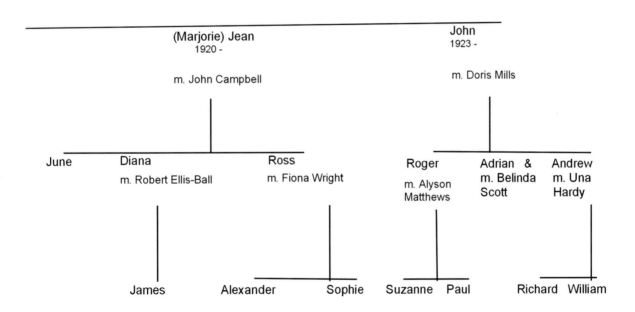

(Marjorie) Jean
1920 -

m. John Campbell

John
1923 -

m. Doris Mills

June   Diana   Ross
        m. Robert Ellis-Ball   m. Fiona Wright

Roger   Adrian &   Andrew
m. Alyson   m. Belinda   m. Una
Matthews   Scott   Hardy

James   Alexander   Sophie   Suzanne   Paul   Richard   William

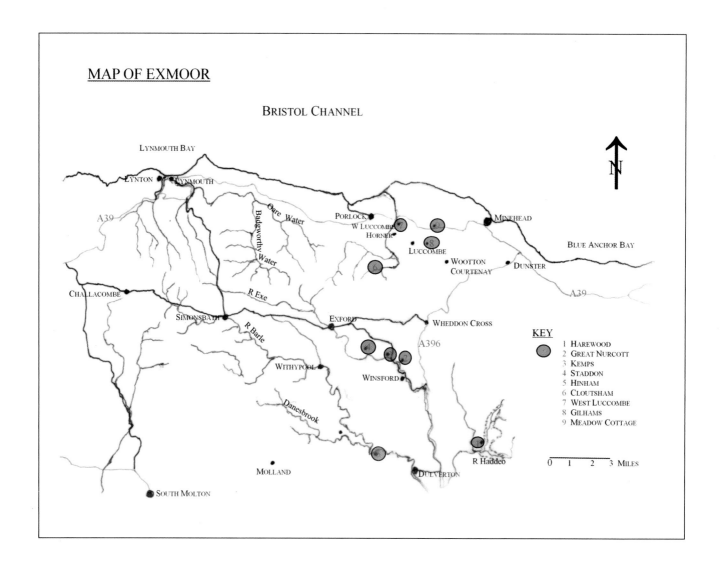

APPENDIX (A)

Tom Cole

THOMAS LIONEL HOWARD COLE was born 11th June 1922 at Llandaff, near Cardiff in South Wales, to English parents. His father was E.K. Cole an early electrical engineer who made a vast fortune manufacturing wirelesses, early television sets, and interception radar for the RAF, Fleet Air Arm and Navy. He also had a plastics factory to make the Bakelite cases for the television, wireless sets, telephone handsets, lavatory seats, picnic plates and cups, lemon squeezers, in fact just about anything you could think of in plastic or Bakelite. The names of TV sets such as Bush, Ferranti and Ekco in the 1950s and '60s were household names, and it is not hard to see that Ekco was derived from E.K. Cole.

Since Tom Cole suffered from polio, and for years was confined to a wheel chair, it is doubtful that he took part in the war. He first came to Holt Ball as part of his recuperation and thereinafter made frequent visits to the farm in the 1940s and early 1950s in between his motor racing. Was it the years of frustration confined to a wheel chair that led to his love of the absolute opposite, speed? He was a visitor to Gilhams once or twice and since he rode out hunting with Norman Kennelly following the Staghounds, Hector used to take him out to show him the deer and other wildlife. Hector saw him often at Holt Ball. It may just have been a little tame for Tom Cole as he lived life in the fast lane, riding his horse out hunting just as he would race a car according to Joan Weaver. She saw him going flat out straight into a bog opposite Cloutsham Farm, and fly through the air onto a soft landing. In addition to Norman, Tom Cole was a good friend with Roger Sandford and the pair of them would drive around West Luccombe and Holt Ball Farms shooting rabbits from the vehicle with a service revolver, harum-scarum indeed.

Apart from a Humber Super Snipe motorcar that he used for general motoring, he had in the late 1940s a Jaguar model SS100. This he drove at a furious pace around the by-roads in the Porlock Vale and surrounding area. Molly Groves or Blunt as she was, when as a girl growing up in Porlock, would cycle over to Luccombe to visit her brother Peter. If she heard the exhaust note of the Jaguar she was off her bike in a flash, jumping up into the hedge dragging her bike up with her. This was the only action for survival as he roared past at a high speed. Norman Williams from Horner Farm recalled as to how Tom Cole would love to attack the hump back bridge over the Horner Water at West Luccombe, from the direction of Horner, at a high speed so that he would get the Jaguar airborne. Norman said that at one time Tom Cole's body was up level with the steering wheel and his face in a grimace when in mid air. He possessed a speedboat that he brought down to Porlock Weir that he took out from time to time. Molly Groves recalls seeing it being driven nearly vertically through the water and remarked to me "It was almost as if he had a death wish." Warner Robins used to hear it banging through the waves when he was up at Selworthy Farm, at least two miles away.

Since George Burnell when aged about seventeen or eighteen was also enthusiastic about speed and quite a good mechanic, Tom Cole took him to Ireland as his official mechanic for one race meeting. This was in 1948 to Tallaght on the outskirts of Dublin. Racing for the Leinster Trophy started in 1934 in Bray, Co Wicklow then moved in the second year to a new road circuit at Tallaght. Racing had been suspended for the war and restarted in 1948. Nothing of note was achieved with the Jaguar SS100, except that it was quite an experience for George. What made an impact on him was the quantity of fruit, especially the tins of peaches, which were in abundance in complete contrast to life at home.

Whether it was for his health, but Tom Cole spent a lot of time in the United States, especially California and with the help of the enormous wealth of his father it was easy to commute to England by air. He raced a J2 Allard with great success at the Bridgehampton and Watkins Glen tracks in the USA.

Tom Cole was a very competent racing driver, often competing against and beating the great names of that period, I summarize some of his races and quote from the late Mike Hawthorn's autobiography *Challenge Me the Race*, in italics, as appropriate.

In 1950 Le Mans 24 hour race he was third in a J2 Allard powered by a Cadillac engine driven by Cole and Sidney Allard. At 2.00am it lost all gears except top and had to complete the race in one gear.

Tom Cole's J2 Allard.

1951 Le Mans the J2 Allard retired.

1952 he drove a 4.1 Ferrari with Pagnibon and retired.

The next big event was the Leinster Trophy, another handicap event on the Wicklow circuit—and a very fast Chrysler-engined Allard with Tom Cole at the wheel. Tom Cole was the winner of the sports category and I came second.

The next reference is at the Grand Prix at Syracuse in Italy 1953 which opened the European racing season with Tom Cole qualifying 6th on the grid. *We began to overtake the slower cars and as I went into a fast left-hand turn at the bottom of a hill I saw smoke, thick, black, oily and ominous, belching up into the sky. Tom Cole, the hard-trying American driver, had lost control in his brand- new Cooper-Bristol, slid into the outer wall and split the fuel tank. He got out without a scratch, but the car immediately went up in flames. As I came round the corner I found the road partly blocked by the blazing car and, in front of me, taking most of the remaining space was Tornaco, the Belgian independent Ferrari driver, braking hard. I moved out to pass him on the outside, but as I did so he too moved out. I tried to cut back to the inside but my car began to slide and in a fraction of a second I was skating through the flames from the burning Cooper, to finish by crashing backwards into the wall. I got somewhat knocked about by the impact, but I managed to scramble out of the cockpit to find the back end of my own car was alight. Oil in the undertray had begun to burn and was working up a fine fire right under the fuel tank. The only thing I could think of was the fact that I must somehow get the fire out and get back into the race, so I grabbed a handful of earth, threw it on to the flames, blew frantically and the fire went out,—— I was by then absolutely desperate and frantic with frustration, but suddenly two people arrived – I think Tom Cole was one; they gave me a push, the engine fired and I was away.*

After this came the famous Mille Miglia. *Tom Cole on another privately owned Ferrari was fourth and Reg Parnell was fift*

The Daily Express Internati[...] owed this when
he finished second to J.M. Haw[...] final we had the
*sports car race over 17 laps. In the [...] re Ferraris were
opposed by three works entered XK[...] Rolt——Tom
Cole came into second place and the [...] Collins beat all
the Jaguars to take third and fourth p[...]*

May 31st. This day saw him com[...] shed 7th on
a Cooper T23 Bristol beating such p[...] ari.

June 14th. The Le Mans 24-hour ra[...] fastest lap
to Fangio whilst driving his privatel[...] Vignale
Barchetta. His co-driver was Luigi Ch[...] s. In the
sixteenth hour of the race just as the ea[...] killed
when his Ferrari left the road, impacting[...] road,
at Maison Blanche. He drove in the the[...] was
thrown from the car onto the road and die[...]ds *In
addition, Tom Cole was sharing the wheel of h[...]rina
and I went into Le Mans for a night's sleep ar[...]day
morning it was to learn the sad news that Tom Co[...]om
was a popular and courageous driver who dro[...]n
wondering whether his will to win was not forcing[...]e
done. Now he had made a fatal mistake on the one [...]*

To recall Molly Groves' words "It was almo[...]
seem that she had prescience, and not in the least[...]
been killed.

In the summer of 2009 Connie and I had a hol[...]
our way from Brittany down to the Perigord regi[...]
enough to make a detour to Le Mans, which we [...]
memorial. After much searching and a visit to the Sar[...]
racing we failed in our quest. Upon searching the inte[...]
gall to discover that he was buried on the edge of [...]
Cemetery about half a mile from where we had been s[...]

APPENDIX (B)

THIS IS THE STORY OF my father Hector, but by necessity, as I hold great store by family history, I have started it with the first mention that I could find of a Heywood in 1745. There have been long searches and good work done by my American relations the sisters Lorene Townsend and Doris Mayfield without which my task would have been a lot harder.

On reflection, I feel that whatever latent interest I had in history was hugely stimulated and cultivated by the History Master at my school, Christ's Hospital, when I was en route to 'A level' History in 1959. T.P. Law made me think, research, challenge and question: these things have stayed with me all my life. Tim Law, whose real name was Thomas Pakenham Law, was unconventional for the time, yet commanded great respect and affection. He could be cycling with no hands on the drop handles of his bike, across the quadrangle when I, hundreds of feet away would be greeted by a booming "Hello Farmer, How is your essay coming along on Napoleon?" or some such similar subject. My soubriquet "Farmer" was given to me after getting a beta double plus for an essay on the Agricultural Revolution, where I obviously made known my knowledge of "Turnip" Townsend and the four course system. Tim Law to us boys was very humane and considerate as was demonstrated one very hot summer morning when we had a double history lesson and beginning to swelter in the form room. Bear in mind the fact that we were wearing the uniform that is peculiar to Christ's Hospital, i.e. long blue coat, knee breeches, and long yellow stockings which was fine for cooler weather but not in the hot.

"Right chaps I think it a good idea if we all move out to the grass on Big Side to continue the lesson in a more comfortable environment." So we sat in a rough semi circle on the grass of Big Side under the shade of the lime trees assailed by the smells of freshly mown grass of the playing fields and lime blossom, with the sounds of the bees working the lime flowers above us. Occasionally another sound, that of an electric train on the London to Brighton line rattling and clattering along, would puncture the flow of history and challenging questions thrown at us. To enliven proceedings when we began to flag, he would crack a joke. One limerick has stayed with me from those far off staid days when we, eager older boys, might not have seen a girl to speak to, for the whole term.

'There once was a girl from Australia
Who went to a dance as a dahlia
The petals revealed
What they should have concealed
So the dance as a dance
Was a failure.'

As he was such an exceptional man, I would like to write a little more of him. He turned to teaching after war service as a Naval officer, based on a destroyer H.M.S. *Tuscan* in the Mediterranean. The Navy must have been in his blood as he came from a family of sailors, his cousin becoming a well-known admiral. Before coming to Christ's Hospital he was on the staff at Gordonstoun, and then on leaving CH he became head of an independent school in Bude, Cornwall. From 1972 to 1978 he was headmaster of Hemel Hempstead School, guiding it through the difficult transition from grammar school to comprehensive. It was here that he is recalled, according to the Hertfordshire press as 'quite a character and very much larger than life' who believed in people as individuals and not part of a target setting exercise. His son remembers him 'as *a great encourager, supporter and listener, someone who gave wise advice because he was a deep thinker who founded his thinking in a principle of being sensitive to the person. He was incredibly generous of himself, quite unconventional, mischievous and fun with an almost childlike quality of taking delight in things. Throughout his life there was a principle of serving others without seeking reward.'* This perhaps initiated by having a handicapped sister.

I should therefore acknowledge here my debt to him that I set about writing this book, a book about our family and in particular Hector, for the family. If others read and find it of interest then so be it.